DREAM A BETTER DREAM

DREAM A BETTER DREAM

Change Your Mind to Save the World

MARINA SHAKOUR HABER

First Printing, October 2017

ISBN 978-0-9994947-0-7 Print
ISBN 978-0-9994947-1-4 eBook

Interior & Cover Design: Author Support
Editing: Heidi Grauel

Published by:
DreamWorks Publishing, Inc.
3920 North Flagler Dr., # 301
West Palm Beach, FL 33407

Email: info@dreamabetterdreamnow.com
Website: www.dreamabetterdreamnow.com

To the Dreamer and to the World

"Every great dream begins with a dreamer. Always remember, you have within you the strength, the patience, and the passion to reach for the stars to change the world."

HARRIET TUBMAN

Contents

Preface

I have been thinking about writing this book for many years, until I finally decided to just go for it. However, I did want to get an affirmation from the Universe after all—a kind of "insurance"— that I should proceed with this project. So, in the summer of 2016, I sent out a mental request to my spirit guides for a sign telling me to move forward. I asked for a white bird to sit on my car as the sign to go ahead. I live in Florida and my car is usually parked outside during the day and, believe me, birds sit on cars all the time. After the request, I didn't see any birds in the parking lot anymore. So, I made a small adjustment, and asked for any color bird and added the guardrails on my terrace as an additional location. Still nothing.

As I was writing my last few pages, I sat inside to avoid the intense Floridian heat and humidity of June. I had started at 5 AM and was watching the sunrise while I was typing away. Lo and behold, as it was getting lighter, a dove flew over and sat down on the railing right in front of me. She was looking at me and we really did have eye-to-eye contact. I thought, *how odd for a bird to be sitting there so still and staring at me*. Frankly, I had forgotten all about my request. Then it dawned on me—this was my sign and it was a dove, no less.

The bird stayed there for about 10 minutes and then flew off. Later in the afternoon, I sat outside and the dove returned. It kept me company while typing the last few sentences. I am taking that as a divine blessing. When I told my daughter about the dove, she reminded me of a bird that had flown into my bedroom through the terrace door and hidden on my side of the bed. When I went to sleep, I heard this rustling, and some strange noises with electrostatic light coming from my pillow. Of course, I immediately blamed my husband for adding a new snoring sound to his existing repertoire until I felt the bird's wings on my neck. Both the bird and I were quite startled. Frankly, I jumped out of bed screaming, "There's a bird in my bed!!" Well, after I calmed down, I grabbed a flashlight, opened the terrace door, and out flew the little bird. I consider that a sign and blessing for my book as well.

Indeed, I have been blessed as I have received so much heavenly guidance in writing this book. Therefore, I thank God first and foremost for His love, compassion, generosity, and strength throughout my life. I am deeply grateful for His support and encouragement with this project. Likewise, I am profoundly appreciative for all the help and messages I have received from my angels and spirit guides throughout this process, and throughout my life.

I would like to thank Michael Reccia and The Band of Light for their work on bringing forth spiritual information from the Spirit Joseph to our world. After reading the entire collection of *The Joseph Communications*, I must say that they are truly informative—actually, out of this world. As are the series of books by Sanaya Roman who has been channeling the spirit Orin, whose mission is to assist their readers to reach within and connect with their Divine spark to help them grow in joy and abundance. I recommend these books, from both authors, to all who are seeking greater knowledge and wisdom to help bring about change to our planet.

I also must thank Heidi Grauel for her tireless efforts, incredible insights, and keen mind in editing my manuscript. As Heidi improved upon the content, Jerry Dorris created a fabulous book cover design that truly tells the story. Furthermore, I would like to express my gratitude for all the help I have received from Steve Harrison and the Quantum Leap coaches, specifically Martha Bullen, Geoffrey Berwind, Judy Cohen, and Brian Edmondson, for their support in bringing this project to fruition.

I would also like to thank my husband Lenny for his love and support, through all our ups and downs. My deepest love and gratitude to my daughter Celine and my son Darius for your support and encouragement! I don't think I could have done it without your uplifting words when I was down, or your steady nudging me on to follow my dreams. I am deeply grateful to my friend and sister-in-law, Moira, for being my advocate and morale booster. Also, my three brothers Robert, John, and Richard, who are my rocks—always have been and will be forever. My deep thanks to my sisters-in-law Elise and Karen, my nieces Jackie, Arielle, Larissa, Rebecca, and Isabella, as well as my step-daughter Melissa. I am deeply appreciative of my friendship with Parvin, Karen, Jessica, and my cousin Irene which span decades and continents—I know you've got my back at all times—thank you. And last, not least, to my beloved parents, Hassan and Corry, thank you for all you have done for me—you have sacrificed so much that can never be repaid. Thank you for giving us the best anybody can ever expect parents to give their children: love, respect, attention, and a deep desire for them to become the best they can be. You have taught us by example to give and do more for others. I am forever grateful and am still striving to make you proud.

Love you forever,
Marina Shakour Haber
October 2017

Introduction

Ask not what the World can do for you,
Ask what you can do for the World.

Based on JOHN F. KENNEDY'S
Inaugural Speech, January 20, 1961

This is our story—yours and mine. I share with you how we really got to this point in our evolution, starting with the foundation we have built upon. Only with this knowledge do we have the tools to undo what we, collectively, have done to ourselves. All I am asking is for you to read this material without judgment, without prejudice, and allow your heart and your intuition to guide you. If anything resonates with you in your heart center, then you will instinctively know it to be true. If it is too foreign or "out there" for you, I understand, but know that the Light contained in the messages will still affect you positively and influence your life beneficially.

Years ago, when I was a teenager in Munich, Germany, my mother asked me to join our neighbor at a classical concert at the Bayerische Staatsoper. Her bargaining chip was that Leonard Bernstein was conducting and, as I loved his musical, *West Side Story*, I agreed to go, hoping that it would be part of that night's performance. It wasn't, to my disappointment. However, Mr. Bernstein's performance that night sparked a light within me and ignited my love for classical music and I've been hooked ever since. And so, I hope this book will ignite that divine spark within you, putting us all together on our journey to create a better world.

It is not easy to break through our barriers. We all have been programmed by the ever-present powers—be it religious, political, or socioeconomic. We have been given half-truths, been manipulated, and corrupted with misinformation—all guiding us into false beliefs. The results were and still are fear, threats, and control. We have removed ourselves physically and spiritually, but also in time and distance, from the simplicity of the truth. We are far removed from our Source, the One, the Whole—or whatever you're comfortable calling God. For most, God has played second fiddle, usually only entering our lives once a week for religious services (for some, more than that), but there has been a profound separation between the spiritual and the physical elements in our everyday lives. It has been awkward for a long time to speak of God outside of religious events. Those who did speak of God were the religious freaks or zealots, New Agers, and psychics—and most people tried to distance themselves from those seen as fanatical. But, it is precisely a new way of spirituality that is needed to bring back the unadulterated messages from beyond that will help us to get it right this time around. And, yes, I said, "this time around" because we have been in the same situation before, repeatedly, earlier in our history.

Hopefully, this time we will become aware of who we are, what brought us here, and why life is always so tumultuous before it is too late. I am talking about preventing the total destruction of this civilization and severe damage done unto this planet. We not only have the power and the ability to reverse course but we are also the only ones that can do it. We are the ones that have to un-create that which we have created in the beginning. And YES, WE CAN!

My role is that of a messenger—no more, no less. I have gathered information over my lifetime, in a search for the missing pieces of the puzzle and for the unabridged, unaltered truths that have been kept from us. For years I have felt compelled to share this information in my own words, simple and truthful, to the best of my ability.

Life is a journey leading us onto the path fitting for our personal evolution. In my case, I have been blessed to be a member of a multicultural and multilingual family. I was born in Tehran, Iran, and lived there until I was eight years old, when we moved to Munich, Germany. After completing high school there, I attended college in Paris, France, for only two years as we decided to immigrate to Vancouver, Canada, where I graduated from the University of British Columbia. I lived there for eight years until I accepted a job offer in New York City. Living in so many different countries and diverse cultures broadened my perspective about people's lives and beliefs, helping me to understand that although we may be very different on the outside, we are quite similar within.

As my family was also multi-religious, spirituality became our normal. My paternal grandfather, Abdullah, was a Muslim from Azerbaijan; my paternal grandmother, Elizabeth, was a Roman

Catholic from Mainz, Germany; my maternal grandparents, Johannes and Anna, were from the Netherlands and Dutch Protestant —quite a mix; and I married a Jew from Brooklyn, NY. I am spiritual and welcoming of all religions, yet I have never been a devout, religious person. Spiritual, believing in God and the Spirit World, absolutely, but I never fit into any one religion. I questioned the authority of priests, mullahs, and rabbis as it always felt as if I were being judged and condemned. I looked at them and they were no better than I, yet they told me how to think and what to believe in. I quite disagreed with the threats of eternal damnation; I do not accept an angry-yet-loving God who will throw us into hell unless we obey and whose Word we are not to question. But question we must, because the "Word of God," as reflected in the Bible and the Koran, was written by humans. It was altered, manipulated, corrupted, and polluted for purposes of power and control. It's high time to open our eyes and investigate beyond the limits set for us.

My mother, Corry, was a highly evolved spirit with great psychic awareness who too was driven to find the truth. Growing up, we spent hours discussing paranormal and psychic phenomena, life after death, angelic guidance, and the purpose of life on Earth. Pretty heavy subject matters, for sure, considering my age. Therefore, I never questioned whether there is life after death—there simply is. It cannot be otherwise; it would be illogical, in my opinion. I also always believed I was one of God's children and was loved, protected, and guided by Him. Why would it be any different? I never believed in a vengeful, judging, or angry God, no, absolutely impossible. This raises the question, though, of why there is so much pain and agony in this, His world? For a long time, I attributed it to karma but that felt kind of lame.

It took me forever, or so it felt, until I came across a series of books, *The Joseph Communications*. I had been searching for my mother's spiritual book, *The Missing Truth*, based on messages brought forth through a spirit named Joseph by the medium Beatrice at Die Geistige Loge in Zurich in the 1950s and 60s. My mother had just passed away and I wanted to see if it was still listed. After finding it, I searched for the Spirit Joseph. To my surprise, I found *The Joseph Communications* by Michael Reccia. I read all the books in absolute ecstasy. I had finally found the answers to my questions. For me, personally, the most eye-opening book is *The Fall*. It gave me the answers to who we are, how we got here, and why this place is so unbalanced—to put it mildly, or accurately. From that moment on I was driven to write my book. I felt that Joseph's messages have to be spread by sharing them. He says so repeatedly in his books. I have based my book's core essence on the messages brought forth in *The Fall*, in my own words, condensed, to touch on the most basic information. It is this vital information that will show us how to change and thus save our world.

We start with One, you, me, and end with the One, the Whole. It's a circle and a cycle that we have disrupted, manipulated, and unhinged. If you don't believe what I'm saying, just look around you or turn on the news. Need I say more? We, as a people and a planet, are falling apart, very quickly and it seems to be unstoppable. But it doesn't have to be that way. There is hope and there is a way! We as Angelic Children have the power needed (and much more than that) to bring us out of this unending, repeating cycle. Please read the material presented to you here with an open heart but closed mind/ego and let's just do it right this time. I hope you will join me on our journey home—I need you and you need me as we all need each other to get there.

P.S. Upon completion, I urge you to read all books, in chronological order, of *The Joseph Communications* series. You, too, will become a worker of the Light.

CHAPTER 1

The Age of Chaos

The World Seems to Prepare for War

*"I know not with what weapons World War III will be fought,
but World War IV will be fought with sticks and stones."*

ALBERT EINSTEIN

W e live in a constant state of chaos. We thrive on chaos—we actually seem to need it. In fact, we live in a negative state of mind. We perpetuate negativity daily, hourly, minute by minute, dwelling on negative events and projecting them back out. The cycle of life on Earth, its circulatory system, is fueled by negative energy—our thoughts, actions, and vibrations. We perceive negative events, absorb their energy, allow them to poison us, and, then, unknowingly, send those energy vibrations back out into our Universe. On their way to the Earth's power plant (which is a sphere surrounding this planet, similar to an aura), this negative energy infects and affects all. On its circulatory path, negativity is energized through us as we are perpetuating its force by first absorbing it and then pushing it forward through our participation or sharing. Our energy gives it the charge to flow throughout. Unless, of course, we stop it.

Presently, it also seems as if time is speeding up. It seems as if our entire world order and harmony are held together by very thin strings. People are on edge and anxious about the future, their well-being, and that of the planet. After the Great Depression and World War II, survivors and their children experienced economic growth and endless opportunities for success. This has changed in the 21st century. Now, our youth are weighed down with heavy burdens such as student loans, underpaying jobs, high cost of living, and unaffordable housing. Seniors are also facing severe financial hardships due to ever-increasing costs and cuts. The "sandwich generation" is dealing with such issues as stagnating incomes and a growing cost of living in addition to the responsibility of caring for the younger and older generations as well. There has also been a widening of the disparity between the haves and have-nots, which may have had a significant role in the recent dramatic reversal of political leadership in the United States.

People in general are rather fed up with their governments and the seeming inability to improve economic and social conditions for the working class. People feel forgotten and left behind, and there doesn't seem to be anyone who can bring forth sweeping changes that will improve equality and return the hope for a better future. Leaders who have sensed the discontent of the people are rising to the top and making promises accordingly. The strongest messages are those of isolationism, anti-globalism, closed borders, fear mongering, and scapegoating. It has become a mentality of "me against you"—me, mine, and I. Sadly, that is the total opposite of Divine Law and will end in failure. Our fears and foreboding have produced the exact situations feared. It's the law of attraction at work: bringing back what we feared since that is what we are putting out.

Currently, there is such a heavy feeling about the future; it's a collective fear about events lying outside our control. Knowing what I know about the power of thoughts, negative as well as positive, I have chosen to restrict my daily intake of the news to a minimum. I have also chosen to send Light into events and people who need it most instead of perpetuating negativity. However, when we look at the world as it is at this moment, 2017, we do have to acknowledge that we're not doing so well.

The Middle East is the powder keg of the world. The area is rich in natural energy resources, thus making it an arena for power struggles. Many countries that are vying to be the ultimate winner do so to gain or maintain global supremacy. For that reason, peace is a very difficult state to reach. It also has become the birthplace of Islamic terrorism, which is an uprising against outside forces that are manipulating the region. Religion is the unifier of the dissatisfied, hopeless, and hate-filled victims of global power plays between nations. It has spread like a cancer all over the world with its distorted, hateful, and vengeful beliefs that are far removed from the true beliefs of Islam.

Russia is trying to become a major player as a leading world power and makes its presence felt globally. It is also undermining the European Union and NATO by attempting to divide and conquer while manipulating internal events in countries of important strategic value. Once again, chaos is the friend of negativity and power uprisings. The Far East is rising to power as well, both economically as well as politically, growing their military might and inventories. China, a global superpower for some time, and India, becoming one of the fastest growing economies, are both nuclear weapons countries that have become significant factors in the balance of world power. North Korea, although small, has very large ambitions of becoming a superpower with a serious nuclear inventory making it a very real global threat. It is as if the world is preparing itself for another war.

Apart from all these political events, there is a human tragedy playing out unlike any witnessed since World War II. Millions of people are seeking refuge due to the dire conditions in their homeland but the world is closing its borders. Some because they have taken in too many already, proportionate to their country's size and that of their population, whereas others are choosing to restrict or deny entry for fear of potential terrorist infiltrations. Currently, both Yemen and Sudan are experiencing widespread famine due to severe drought conditions—adding to the dire need of migration. The questions of where to go and what to do is unanswered for so many poor, suffering people, and the countries of the world, faced with their own internal problems, can only give and do so much.

Sadly, these situations are as old as the world and there have never been any real lasting solutions for them. The outbreaks and their aftermaths are somehow resolved, yet not their cause. It's somewhat like handing out Band-Aids or painkillers for deadly diseases that are still incurable. A cure can only be found if the pathology of disease is fully understood—its root cause, its symptoms, and its behavior. At some point in our evolution, there has to come the sobering moment when we take stock and evaluate our progress, or the lack thereof. In reviewing our past, a distinct pattern becomes clear: repetition, repetition, and more repetition. The same events occur over and over again with the identical results as previous events. There are the cycles of war and peace, of extreme affluence and economic downturns, excesses and frugality, droughts and floods, and so on. Wars arise on the ashes left behind from previous battles, while economic downturns usually precede the conflicts. Every cycle bears resemblance to the earlier ones, just with different players on different stages for somewhat different causes. Yet, the underlying issues have always been about perceived need, lack, greed, and fear. The cycles cannot be broken until we understand their nature and have reached a point of exhaustion, maybe even disgust, with the way things are. For this, an objective analysis of the human condition is required that identifies the root cause of our behavior, what had led to this, and therefore what is needed to correct it. Without that, no real changes will ever happen. We need to have a better understanding to make better decisions for a better future.

Another significant factor in the deterioration of our social fabric is addiction. Drugs, illegal or prescription, have become the religion of the people. Karl Marx said that "religion . . . is the opiate of the masses"; however, today, opiates are the religion of the masses. We are moving farther away from all things spiritual while being more engrossed in all things material. This leaves a gaping hole, a true void, in most lives, and voids or vacuums will be filled with something else. What follows is an endless search to find what is missing, for there is a deep longing and need to find a sense of fulfillment within all. For that matter, drugs and alcohol become such temptations—they hold the promise of finding ecstasy or at least a high, albeit temporarily, that is luring forlorn souls into their grip. There is a real need to find what is missing, for all of humanity, but it can't be found this way.

Where there is despair, hopelessness, and poverty, you can be sure drugs and alcohol are close at hand. Where there is a need and a demand, there will be a supply. Any supply needs to create a continually growing market, which is how the vulnerable become victims of their own despair. Poor, troubled, and often the very young are being seduced into a life of addiction and, sadly, today, their physicians are prescribing highly addictive pain medications—essentially leading them into it. So many become addicted of no fault of their own. They have fallen victim to the mighty dollar.

Drugs, alcohol, gambling, and sex have been used to weaken and destroy entire societies for centuries, manipulating and holding the addicted hostage. The farther we remove ourselves from spirituality, the stronger the urge will be to fill that vacuum with all forms of "painkillers" that make us feel whole again although ever so fleetingly. No illusion found in the temporary high can fill that emptiness felt deeply within. For there will always be more lack and an ever-greater need to feel complete, loved, and protected for simply being who we are. For many, this need is not found in drug addiction, but in material objects the ego attaches itself to. The fear of not having enough or running out of it—whatever that may mean to the individual person—drives the need to fill it with more and more material objects. Money and possessions give a sense of security, but they never seem to satisfy completely. As there is no real sense of security, the quest for more wealth, power, and greater influence are a constant driving force without ever finding a point where gratification is reached. The quest for more material values will always fail and mislead, as material goods are in and of themselves empty.

Although there is God in all things, animate or inanimate, material objects cannot fulfill the soul's needs on a deeper level. The only way to find wholeness is by seeking greater spiritual consciousness. And that way is by going within, in stillness and in simplicity. It is from here that we connect to our Divine Spark—the spark that directly links us to God and the spirit realms. Security, love, and purpose come from within, not without. Here lies the fulfillment that is sought by all but so many look for it in all the wrong places. Spiritual values have lasting power and keep on giving to all for a long time. Material objects, on the other hand, are temporary and of the physical plane. In death, they remain behind, while experiences and acts of giving of the self will become a part of the infinite essence.

When taking stock of our present global condition, climate change—which impacts all lives on Earth—must be mentioned. It is amazing and rather difficult to grasp that there are still many who are denying global warming. Most of them have an agenda, though, either for personal gain or corporate enrichment supported by policymakers who believe in greater profits today and the pretense of keeping jobs, without regard for the consequences of tomorrow. As Al Gore has called it, it is *An Inconvenient Truth* for those who exploit and plunder the Earth for material gain without regard to the consequences that we all have to carry. The effects of fracking, for example, include a sudden increase of earthquakes and mysterious sinkholes. Naturally, there is great denial about a correlation but it seems kind of obvious that there is cause and effect playing out here. Our belief system that greater materialistic advantages outweigh the resulting imbalances, be it in our ecosystems or our bodies, has never been accurate. It doesn't work and frankly never has or will. The Earth is the only place we have—there are no evacuation plans or routes that have been prepared for a sudden and immediate evacuation of all people. Therefore, the Earth must be treated with the same respect, compassion, and love each and every one of us expects to receive. She has been created for our benefit, so that we may experience our lives here and resolve our issues in time. Yet, we choose to disrespect and mistreat her—frankly, we do that to each other as well. By learning to respect and love ourselves first, we will grow in compassion for all, including the Earth and all that are part of it.

Presently, we are plundering the riches, harming the environment, hurting the planet, and then denying that the world is aching, is in pain, and dying. The popular children's book, *The Giving Tree*, by Shel Silverstein comes to mind. The story is about an apple tree and his love for a little boy to whom he gives all he has to give. It starts out with giving the boy his apples to sell, then branches to build a house with when he is older, and lastly his trunk to build a boat when he is very old. When there is only a stump left, the boy, now an old man, returns to sit on it, right above where he had carved their initials within a heart so long ago. The tree had given and given until there was nothing left and it died. Only then did the boy as an old man understand that he had only taken and never given anything to the tree. Yet, the tree was happy to have his love back in death. Self-sacrifice may be a noble thing but it is unsustainable in maintaining a healthy relationship. When one side only takes and the other only gives, neither can survive such an imbalanced partnership. It is this lack of balance that has created and affected our civilization.

Just imagine a child suffering through the flu—the fever and hallucinations, the thirst, headaches, and shivers erupting and going through its entire body. Now, let's look at our planet Earth and compare the symptoms. Higher temperatures have been recorded as well as warmer oceans leading to greater oceanic acidity, rising sea levels, droughts, floods, extreme weather, changes in snow and rain patterns, melting glaciers, less snow pack, and thawing permafrost. The effects of these conditions can be felt in our water supplies, agriculture and consequently our food supplies, ecosystems, energy sources, forests, and coastal areas. The planet has been poisoned by our ignorance, greed, and selfishness, and it is reeling in agony.

Climate change is predominantly human-made. We have caused the warming of the Earth by trapping greenhouse gases in the atmosphere—mainly carbon dioxide with a smaller percentage of methane, nitrous oxide, and fluorinated gases. With the Industrial Revolution came a greater need for energy usage to fuel the machines of factories and the engines of the new means of transportation. Therefore, new energy resources had to be found, such as petroleum and natural gas. Coal, which had been used before for households and local industries, had been acquired from the surface of the mines, but now required deeper and far more dangerous digging, as much greater supplies were needed. These fossil fuels were extracted from beneath the earth and harnessed to power the new age of technology. More factories, cars, planes, and trains started polluting and warming the environment while resources had to be pulled out of the earth. The imbalance here is that what is taken out of the earth is being returned in a form that only harms it. Our energy sources and resources are physical and material—therefore, negative and destructive to the survival of the planet. Only spiritual energy, or God energy, is of lasting value without the effects of pollution and greenhouse gases. The time has to come that energy will be gathered from really alternative sources. This will require a fundamental change in human thinking.

All energy has positive and negative vibrations or power charges, which must at all times be of equal value to be in harmony. On Earth, however, that is not the case. The positive and negative energies on our planet are not balanced and, thus, they are always in disharmony. Originally, the warming of the planet happened without our knowledge or even awareness. It was a side effect of our evolution into the industrial, technological, and scientific revolution—unintentional and unnoticed until recently. Now, there are scientific studies that prove with certainty that what we are experiencing is climate change, not a hoax. The abnormalities of our weather patterns are not imaginings but are very real and caused by our disregard for the well-being of our Earth. There are already instances where the effects are irreversible; however, we still have the opportunity to halt and reverse most. It will require a united approach from both the physical as well as spiritual domains.

This is our only home—where we live and work out our problems (the ones we created in the first place). And how are we treating the Earth? Frankly, terrible! But, truthfully, we are not treating ourselves any better either. By poisoning the Earth, we are also poisoning ourselves. Cause and effect! A simple example would be the usage of pesticides. They have been used in agriculture to produce more food at a lower cost due by decreasing insect infestations and increasing the shelf life of food. The consequences are that we are ingesting that poison just like all the insects that are killed. So, it should not come as a surprise to see a sudden, inexplicable increase in developmental and learning disorders, such as autism. The evidence linking pesticides to many common and deadly diseases such as different types of cancer, diabetes, Parkinson's, Alzheimer, dementia, birth defects and reproductive dysfunction, endocrine disruption, allergies and asthma, are indisputable.[1] You are what you eat, after all.

Climate changes have clearly affected our wildlife and marine life. Take, for example, the Great Barrier Reef, which has been declared dead by writer Rowan Jacobson. He wrote, "The Great Barrier of Australia passed away in 2016 after a long illness. It was 25 million years old." The cause of its death, or its dying, is the result of a chain reaction: the increased acidification of the oceans due to the increase of carbon dioxide emissions into the atmosphere, which are being absorbed by the oceans, results in water being warmed and thus bleaching of the coral. A habitat forever lost. Other animals like polar bears, penguins, and seals are losing not only the ice they live on but also the food they need to survive. They are truly victims of our brutal misconduct and rape of the Earth, but we don't leave it at that. We also hunt them for money or pleasure with catastrophic outcomes of entire species being eliminated.

Yet, we don't accept responsibility for our actions, generally speaking, for reasons of insufficient knowledge or interest given. At best, we are in denial about the events we are witnessing. At worst, we blame others, probably mostly God as being the "creator" of this world or some cosmic event outside of our control. Well, I've got news for you: it's neither God nor any cosmic event and, yes, it's real and it's our fault. It is a direct result of our original error that got us here—to the very civilization and Universe we have created. We have played with fire and now we are on fire. It is high time for us to find our way back to undo our creation before it undoes us.

---

1   Beyond Pesticides. *Pesticide-Induced Diseases Database*. Available at: http://www.beyondpesticides.org/resources/pesticide-induced-diseases-database/overview. Accessed September 8, 2017.

The first thing taught in personal success seminars is to accept 100% responsibility for the decisions we have made and the subsequent situations we find ourselves in. We have to stop blaming and complaining. We must hold ourselves accountable for what is happening and has happened to us in our lives so far. And as with everything else in this Universe, all laws apply to all things equally. They are not so much laws as they are a series of due processes or, if you will, of actions and their reactions. So, if we want to change and improve our lives, we have to accept responsibility, 100%, in order to overcome our obstacles, our stumbling blocks, and our limiting, self-constructed walls. It requires taking responsibility to change personal lives from lack to abundance, so, consequently responsibility is a prerequisite for changing the bigger picture as well. Principles, or Universal Laws, apply to all matters, big or small, individual or collective.

Accepting responsibility is the first step in any recovery, which must be followed by deconstructing limiting beliefs and self-doubt, replacing division and isolation with unification and cooperation. There has to be forgiveness, respect, and compassion to allow past events to be bygones. What has happened before cannot be undone but to dwell on mistakes made will not produce better outcomes. Therefore, it is vital to focus on the here and now, jointly and in harmonious unison. Such open-minded approaches invite alternatives from a broad spectrum to produce transformations in the existing conditions, whatever the natures of the problems may be. Positive, inclusive, and respectful exchanges of thoughts and opinions bear great results and must be applied to our current global conditions—climatic, political, socioeconomic, and religious.

So, the question that is begging to be asked is, what made the world the way it is? What happened to our civilization that we don't know about, creating the conditions we find ourselves in? If we cannot blame God for such injustices and violent conditions, then who do we hold responsible? If we are responsible, why and what did we do to ourselves to get such poor results from which we suffer to this day? And, clearly, the ultimate question is how we can stop what is happening and bring back a time of peace and joy for all.

We have never intended this experiment (for that is what it was so long ago, an experiment) to turn out like this. The intent had been to create a new world order where we, who were still very young angelic beings, wanted to experience life in a more physical way. The concept was that by adding more physicality and deducting spirituality, the result would be a condition where all form would be of a denser and heavier matter. Density would subsequently create separation from the spirit realms due to a change in the vibrational elements from the physical to the spiritual frequencies. Think of it as AM and FM radio stations—they are on different frequencies and wavelengths. Additionally, this transformation enclosed us due to the denseness and thickness of matter—we could not escape it nor receive fresh energy from the outside. So, the results were of a Universe separated, distanced, and isolated from the Source of all energy and life. We were the original builders of walls and borders, never realizing that they work both ways—nobody can enter but nobody can escape either.

We had wanted our new order to become the jewel in God's collection of experiments—His crown achievement brought to Him through our creativity. All we wanted to do was to glorify Him and make Him proud of our achievements. Nonetheless, it was wrong and so were we—and, sadly, still are. We made a mistake that has hurt and imprisoned us for millennia. Unfortunately, we can't remember that mistake anymore on account of the consequences it brought with it. Complex but logical! If one of the consequences of a given action, which was the creation of physical form due to the manipulation of energy, was the loss of memory, then it would be difficult to access that memory which of course holds the key for a safe reversal of said action. Without memory, return would seem an impossible task.

As many people have a growing sense of urgency in reversing our condition, we are receiving tremendous help from the spirit world. They have never abandoned us; it is we who have abandoned them. With great personal sacrifices and difficulties, the other side is bringing us messages through the assistance of psychics and mediums. They are working on bringing us the missing information that will lead us to greater awareness and knowledge. Undoubtedly, this will at first sound like science fiction but maybe science fiction is closer to reality than we give it credit? In other words, we have to open our minds and hearts to take in and process the information without judgment or cynicism. If it feels right, if it sounds true in your core, not in your head, then let it guide you toward new possibilities.

However, this is that moment in time when we must act. By all accounts, the effects of global warming alone will destroy the Earth and leave us homeless, as it were. This is a singularly unique point in time when the conditions for a perfect storm are forming, and all of our own doing. Any one of these individual events could potentially destroy us but here, as if in a final cataclysmic event, they are all developing at the very same time. This growing situation has to be taken seriously if we want to survive and protect our planet.

In reality, there is survival because, in the final analysis, we are always safe and protected as the children of God. As such, we cannot die as the angelic beings that we are. In this scenario, though, survival is based on not blowing up the planet and all life on it. If that were to happen, those circumstances would force us to be housed in a kind of lockbox, in stasis, until the Earth can be healed and repaired for us to start all over again. That is not what we are looking for. We have done it previously and with every new civilization we remove ourselves farther from our Source, our spiritual connection, and memory in both time and space. With every new cycle we are less connected, less knowledgeable, and spiritually gifted than before, making our return ever more difficult to accomplish. There is no doubt that we will return—the question is when, if we fail to seize this upcoming opportunity.

Every downturn can be viewed in two ways: one as failure and the other as an opportunity to succeed. In order to succeed, though, we must accept that the premise we have founded our creation on was flawed, accept that we made a mistake, and simply want to return to our original existence as angelic beings. We will explore in detail where we came from, what our mission was, where we went wrong, and what it will take to correct, or reverse, our actions. For that, we will need a united movement to create sufficient energy to break through the illusion we created so perfectly.

CHAPTER 2

The Message

Missing Truth

"Whenever you have truth it must be given with love, or the message and the messenger will be rejected."

MAHATMA GANDHI

Each one of us, by our free will, chose to come back here to fulfill a promise made to our higher selves. The problem is that by entering this atmosphere we got wrapped up in physicality, the heavy mass of Earth, and forgot what we came for to begin with. Often, even our best intentions become corrupted by the negative energy present, distorting our wishes into the very opposite of our original intent. Consequently, we need to protect ourselves with Divine Light, awareness of our true self, and knowledge to avoid being corrupted. I am referring to the knowledge of how this planet really came about and why it turned out to be so flawed. God creates perfectly but we are certainly not living in perfection. It could be called a perfection in imperfection and imbalance which can only be humanmade. The first steps in healing and in correcting our ways is to understand and acknowledge our shortcomings, then to accept responsibility and learn from our mistakes. So here, too, we need to understand that this world is off course and has always been so and, unless we change the course, it will crash. This requires knowledge of a higher truth that has not only been forgotten but also willfully deleted from our ancient records.

My mother Corry, Cornelia Shakour officially, wrote a book in 1996, *The Missing Truth. Angelic Revelations Replace 16 Centuries of Blind Faith*, which I had published. Like so many of us, my mother was looking for that missing piece in the puzzle, explaining the human condition. She was a very psychic person and used her intuition to help others and even save many lives, including mine. In 1957, my mother inherited a collection of spiritual books from my paternal grandmother that was rather unusual. Most free thinkers kept their beliefs very private as they were met with cynicism and rejection. Many were shunned from their social circles, especially if those beliefs questioned the church in any possible way. Any church, or for that matter any organized religion, was and probably is still calling any beliefs that differ, or even oppose those taught, blasphemy. It couldn't be any farther from the truth.

These books were the written recordings of the messages brought forth by a Spirit named Joseph through a medium at weekly gatherings of the Geistige Loge (Spiritual Lodge) in Zurich, starting in 1947. The group was formed by a few highly intellectual individuals whose mission was to seek greater spiritual truth. After contacting a similar group in London, The Greater World, they were able to temporarily bring over a British medium who, in a state of trance, brought forth messages from the other side transferred by the spirit Joseph. After about two years, they were able to replace the visiting medium with Beatrice, a highly intuitive psychic, who continued to be Joseph's earthly voice.

These weekly seances were never held for any frivolous purposes such as summoning up the spirits of the departed or negative manifestations of any kind. They were always opened with prayers asking for protection from lower vibrations and negative energies, thus assuring the purity and accuracy of the messages. They were held in perfect harmony and at a high vibrational state brought about through chanting and praying. The purpose of these meetings was to gain greater knowledge and help humankind. Joseph's messages covered a wide range of topics such as life after death, the various spheres in the spirit world, reincarnation, auras, health, God, angels, and all the Divine guidance and help available and given daily. However, the most important one to me was his revelations about the early Christian Church.

And Joseph states, "The knowledge I speak of is the same as that which was removed from the original record of the doctrines of Jesus of Nazareth by the early Church. At the present time, the clergy cannot explain the remaining texts logically. The number of members who have left their churches on account of this will never be known. Sadly, many have abandoned God along with the church. During the last thousand years, the Church has become encrusted with worldly influences. As such, the Church must undergo another reformation. The changes made during the reformation of the six-teenth century can again become a guiding force. When it has been decided that the time has come for the world to learn the whole truth which has been taken away, a direct connection with God's world can be reestablished."[1]

Joseph is referring to the daily contact, actual connection, that used to be established between this world—that is, an individual—and God and His world. In both the Old and New Testaments, we read of angelic appearances, revelations by prophets, visions, and prophetic dreams guiding, protecting, or advising the recipients. Those are manifestations of contact with the spirit world and they were acceptable occurrences in those times. Now, we question and are highly suspicious of such rapports or dialogues, which is what they are. However, is it any different from picking up our cell phones? We are in constant contact either by speaking, texting, or through social media, thus we are connecting through frequency, through waves. This is how it should be with each one of us and the spirit world, our angels, and of course God. Pick up your ethereal cell phone, located in your heart center, and communicate daily through prayer or meditation wherever you are. This direct contact establishes a frequency for open dialogue and guidance. No need for complexities, just a simple reaching out through the heart center in a meditative state.

It is important to mention that in the 1960s the West has opened up to Transcendental Meditation as a secular practice, but only since the 1990s, when Deepak Chopra introduced it for the purposes of self-improvement and stress reduction, has meditation gained widespread popularity. Today, it is becoming increasingly popular not only for spiritual practices, but also as performance enhancing

---

1   *The Missing Truth*, p. 12.

for athletes and executives, and as a part of medical interventions promoting accelerated healing.

Joseph continues by stating that Jesus promised his apostles that he would endow them with the living spirit after his departure. The living spirit was none other than the daily communication with God. He told them that that would guide them and give them strength after his death to face the challenges lying ahead of them. Nothing has changed in that aspect to this very day. We all need heavenly guidance through our daily communications with the spirit world. In any event, the early Church maintained this daily practice for the first three hundred years. Thus, it preserved the essential truths of Jesus' gospel in its original purity although of course some modifications were done as they had come down in the spoken word only. Jesus had not put any of his teachings into writing—it would have been difficult to put his advanced concepts into a structured, categorized format—and so they were communicated verbally. The daily contact with the angels protected the teachings from becoming corrupted and manipulated for personal advantages or material gain.

From the very beginning, the early Christians were persecuted sporadically wherever they took their new radical teachings. However, in 64 AD, after the Great Fire of Rome, Emperor Nero initiated anti-Christian policies and persecution by the Roman Empire after blaming Christians for setting the fire and devastating Rome. It had been rumored that Nero himself had ordered the fire and to dispel those allegations, he had to find a scapegoat. From then on for about two centuries, these policies were in effect and legalized by the Roman Empire.

In 313 AD, with the passing of the Edict of Milan, Emperor Constantine I and Licinius legalized the Christian religion effectively ending anti-Christian policies and persecution. Later, Emperor Constantine I would become the first Roman emperor to convert to Christianity, although probably more for political reasons than religious ones. The early Church, however, was divided over issues of Christology, and Constantine, realizing that he needed to create greater unity to solidify the power of the Roman Empire, convened the First Council of Nicaea in 325 AD. It was an important decision as it signaled the involvement of the state, or rather the empire, in religious matters.

The debate between the two Christian factions centered over the argument whether Jesus was of the same substance of the Father or if he was begotten and therefore distinct from and subordinate to the Father. Arius, a popular and influential church leader from the Greek-speaking east, believed in the latter, making Jesus a created being, of eternal substance but subordinate to God. The council voted for the first position and established the Nicene Creed, which was the first official statement of beliefs and doctrines uniting all of Christendom (or almost all). However, this meant Arius' teachings were considered heresy and a danger to those who believed in them. So, in effect, God's word and which version of it, represented in the Bible, was voted on by a council of men who did what they believed to be best for their followers and most likely for their own interests as well. It has been argued by Robert L. Johnson in his article, "The Bible's Ungodly Origins," that Constantine offered money to the various Church leaders to agree upon a single canon as the word of God and thus unifying all Christians.

The Council of Nicaea did not end the schism between the Eastern and the Roman Church, though. In 381 AD, Emperor Theodosius convened the First Council of Constantinople with the intent to unify the Roman Empire and the Church affirming the validity of the Nicene Creed. By establishing its position as the only acceptable belief, the council went further to stabilize its supremacy by adopting laws punishing all those who were in contradiction. It opened the doors to a different form of persecution, namely one against all non-Christians and anybody with alternate or opposing beliefs. This created the real threat to free thinkers for centuries to come, and severely handicapped our evolution. Beyond this, though, was the fact that this was the beginning of the end of any direct contact with God. The church had fallen victim to the same corruption, wealth, and need for power evident in all things physical and of this world. According to Joseph, the angels had warned the church leaders not to deviate from Jesus' teachings by acquiring wealth, worldly possessions, and using/abusing their power over people. Their warnings, as we know, were to no avail and the church became an institution, a real power house. However, they really needed to free themselves from the constant urgings and warnings not to forsake their original path. Joseph, unveiling a deep secret, states that the church leaders decided then to irrevocably terminate all direct contact with God and the spirit world. There was no turning back once this decision was made as they then saw to it that all mentions of such direct contact were omitted from all teachings.

In 331 AD, Constantine had commissioned, and obviously paid for, 50 Bibles for the Church of Constantinople, which possibly were influenced and edited by him as well. Joseph reveals that this was the point when Christ's gospel was actually altered so that it not only fit in with the new beliefs of the Church but also with those of the Empire. The most important omissions were those of our direct link to God, our true heritage, and divinity. Yes, our divinity as being the children of God, thus being a part of God. Each one of us and all of us. We are One with the One.

In place of simplicity and purity, the leaders created complex rituals and observances, dogmas, and doctrines, occupying the minds of worshippers with unessential fillers. Of course, they introduced threats and fear for nonobservance and deviation, cementing their firm grip and power over their followers, with monetary corrective incentives added on later. This is somewhat like buying an insurance policy guaranteeing heaven, insinuating that without it hell may be the destination after death.

The Bible was also intended to be read and studied by the clergy only, originally written in Latin so that uneducated laypeople couldn't understand it, giving the clergy greater power through their authority on God's word. Pictures and elaborate art replaced the written word, and this is how the story of the Testaments was told—the Church decided on the stories, content, and messages as it deemed fit for its laity.

Thomas Paine wrote on May 12, 1797, while living in Paris, France, a letter to a Christian friend regarding the Bible and its origins. He was a Deist—someone who believes God created the universe but left his creation in charge of it, rejecting the Bible and religion in favor of high ethical standards in personal conduct. Here are a few select paragraphs supporting the above-stated theory that the Bible was written and commissioned by humans and is not the direct word of God. He wrote:

"But by what authority do you call the Bible the Word of God? for this is the first point to be settled. It is not your calling it so that makes it so, any more than the Mahometans calling the Koran the Word of God makes the Koran to be so. The Popish Councils of Nice and Laodicea, about 350 years after the time the person called Jesus Christ is said to have lived, voted the books that now compose what is called the New Testament to be the Word of God. This was done by *yeas* and *nays,* as we now vote a law.

"The Pharisees of the second temple, after the Jews returned from captivity in Babylon, did the same by the books that now compose the Old Testament, and this is all the authority there is, which to me is no authority at all. I am as capable of judging for myself as they were, and I think more so, because, as they made a living by their religion, they had a self-interest in the vote they gave....

"You form your opinion of God from the account given of Him in the Bible; and I form my opinion of the Bible from the wisdom and goodness of God manifested in the structure of the universe, and in all works of creation. The result in these two cases will be, that you, by taking the Bible for your standard, will have a bad opinion of God; and I, by taking God for my standard, shall have a bad opinion of the Bible.

"The Bible represents God to be a changeable, passionate, vindictive being; making a world and then drowning it, afterwards repenting of what he had done, and promising not to do so again. Setting one nation to cut the throats of another, and stopping the course of the sun till the butchery should be done. But the works of God in the creation preach to us another doctrine. In that vast volume we see nothing to give us the idea of a changeable, passionate, vindictive God; everything we there behold impresses us with a contrary idea–that of unchangeableness and of eternal order, harmony, and goodness.

"The sun and the seasons return at their appointed time, and everything in the creation claims that God is unchangeable. Now, which am I to believe, a book that any impostor might make and call the Word of God, or the creation itself which none but an Almighty Power could make? For the Bible says one thing, and the creation says the contrary. The Bible represents God with all the passions of a mortal, and the creation proclaims him with all the attributes of a God.

"It is from the Bible that man has learned cruelty, rapine, and murder; for the belief of a cruel God makes a cruel man. That bloodthirsty man, called the prophet Samuel, makes God to say, (I Sam. xv. 3) 'Now go and smite Amalek, and utterly destroy all that they have, and *spare them not, but slay both man and woman, infant and suckling, ox and sheep, camel and ass.'...*

"You believe in the Bible from the accident of birth, and the Turks believe in the Koran from the same accident, and each calls the other *infidel.* But leaving the prejudice of education out of the case, the unprejudiced truth is, that all are infidels who believe falsely of God, whether they draw their creed from the Bible, or from the Koran, from the Old Testament, or from the New.

"When you have examined the Bible with the attention that I have done (for I do not think you know much about it), and permit yourself to have just ideas of God, you will most probably believe as I do. But I wish you to know that this answer to your letter is not written for the purpose of changing your opinion. It is written to satisfy you, and some other friends whom I esteem, that my disbelief of the Bible is founded on a pure and religious belief in God; for in my opinion the Bible is a gross libel against the justice and goodness of God, in almost every part of it."[2]

Thomas Paine (1737–1809) was an English-American writer, pamphleteer, and political philosopher as well as one of the Founding Fathers of the United States. He moved to America just when the conflict between the colonists and England came to a head which became his opportunity to express his ideas on revolution and social injustice. His pamphlet, *Common Sense*, written to inspire passion and be easily understood by both the common man and intellectuals, influenced the direction of the conflict resulting in the American Revolution. He argued that the colonists should fight for their independence from Great Britain rather than only revolting against taxation. He was a staunch critic of slavery, which he expressed in his writings as well, opposed social injustice and instead advocated for social security, and was a proponent of a world peace organization. However, his highly critical and radical views on institutionalized religion and the Bible, expressed in "The Age of Reason: Being an Investigation of True and Fabulous Theology," would harm his reputation irreparably. When he died in New York, during a time of religious revival, he was impoverished, reviled, and slandered as an infidel. His obituary in the New York Citizen simply read, "He had lived long, did some good and much harm."

He was a passionate, freethinking writer who was not afraid to express his opinions, even if that meant taking on the Church, and

---

2   Johnson, Robert L. "The Bible's Ungodly Origins." *World Union of Deists.* Available at: http://www.deism.com/bibleorigins.htm. Accessed September 1, 2017.

consequently governments. But that was his undoing. The Church had become untouchable since the implementation of the Nicene Creed. With it, it had legalized and justified persecution and execution of all nonbelievers, outspoken critics, as well as psychics and mediums. Any practices that went against the Church were considered dangerous and therefore heretical. This was the witch hunt, lasting centuries and spanning the globe, where false charges of heresy would suffice to bring individuals to Church tribunals resulting in torture and death at the stake or by drowning. The Church didn't want to have any "blood" on their hands, which is why they chose those methods of execution. What resulted was a fearful, subdued population that learned to not question the authority of the Church. History bears witness to this horrific crime against humanity implemented and executed by the Church.

In order to completely root out any alternate opinions or views, the Church censored, forbade, and destroyed any literature and writings deemed contrary to its teachings. Consequently, humanity has been deprived of an open forum of intellectual exchange of ideas, beliefs, and knowledge to help its spiritual advancement. Not only were the Church's teachings demanding blind faith, but they were in all actuality leading humanity on the wrong path. We were led away from the Light into darkness for reasons of might and wealth. In all fairness, though, the clergy was never given alternate views of the truth either. As stated previously, all that ended in the fourth century and they cannot personally be held responsible for what their forefathers had committed so long ago. But now is the time to search for more answers, to find better ways to improve the human experience.

For that is what life is, an experience. On this planet, the experiences are mostly of bearing heavy burdens and facing great challenges, of injustices and imbalances that are repeated over and over again. And they are not only repeated by individuals but by entire civilizations throughout history! Look back and judge for yourself. There have been so many great civilizations that all seem to have followed the same path. Generally speaking, the early beginnings were of endless battles in the fight for supremacy, power, and influence while increasing territorial boundaries, thus exporting culture and beliefs. Then there would be a time of great economic growth, bringing with it advances in and promotion of the arts and sciences. What followed would be decay through corruption, debauchery, and loss of moral values that ended that particular cycle. It's as if they ran out of steam—and they do run out of energy, literally. And so do we as individuals.

It seems we never learn from our mistakes, never gain real knowledge to change the pattern. Personally, I have always disliked the saying, "so this may never happen again," after horrible crimes against humanity had been committed which were then believed to have been remedied by the implementation of new laws and erection of memorials so we may never forget. Equally ridiculous is the saying, "I didn't think this could happen here," which insinuates that different laws apply to a particular area, which of course isn't so. Anything can happen anywhere—nobody is above the effects of our universe—and everything is repeated over and over again, regardless of what measures have been taken. So, why aren't we learning from our experiences?

Often, we don't even learn from experiences within one lifetime. We make the same mistakes again and again. That applies to personal relationships as well—how many date or marry the same kind of person repeatedly? How often do we have to tell a child not to touch a hot surface? Children, like adults, mostly learn from being burnt, yet patterns are still repeated for one reason. That reason, deep within us, is a stubborn belief that we can change outcomes when similar challenges arise. There is a disconnect in accepting that outcomes cannot be changed if they are given the same data input. If it were true that people learn from their mistakes on account of their suffering, loss, or penalties, then there would be no repeat offenders. But there are repeat offenders. This insistence that we can beat the odds is what keeps us from assessing our repeating history with a more scientific clarity.

Based on my own experiences, I am guilty of repeating decisions leading to similar mistakes, be it in business or in my personal life. No matter how hard we try, we all make mistakes and only learn from a few. It seems as if we can't successfully conclude a lesson and move on to the next level. This is not to suggest that we don't evolve at all, but that we are somewhat stuck in our evolution—we don't seem to get past a certain level.

The question is, why is it so difficult for us to learn and apply that knowledge, changing our repetitive experience? Simply put, the reason is that Earth and everything on it is imperfect by design. And it's not by God's design. God would have created a perfect world for His children to experience. He would have never created one where there is genocide, war, famine, disease, injustice, poverty, and on and on. Absolutely impossible! God Is Harmony, Peace, Balance, Love, and Light. He would never allow His children to suffer under the premise that that is how life's lessons are best learned. Apart from the ludicrousness of that statement, the evidence speaks for itself. We have not learned from these hardships yet. For that matter, the outlook for a better future is not very promising unless significant adjustments in our belief system and behavior are made.

Limiting beliefs are a direct result of the manipulation and withholdings of vital information by organized religions that would have helped humanity to progress. Frankly, religions are in it for themselves and not so much for God. God is not religion, and religion is not God. Religions are humanmade and designed to divide people by creating categories—those that are part of a particular religion and the rest who are not, the infidels. To put it differently, when one side is right, then, accordingly, the other side must be wrong, which doesn't only apply to just religious beliefs, but to basically all conflicts from politics to sports. Such fundamental beliefs of superiority force the "you're either with me or you're against me" partisanship and lead to conflict. Each side must defend its own righteous beliefs in order to protect its influence and power in its own domain. When both causes believe that they are right, that their messages and ideologies are superior, and that God is on their side, there will be war. Party convictions that are puffed up by claiming God is on their side, create causes to fight for righteousness and lead people to commit the worst atrocities against humanity such as warfare, genocide, and terror through blind faith. The consequences were, and always have been, endless wars either in the name of God, or citing that God is supportive of a given cause, demanding action.

To this very day, humanity not only bears witness to such abusive exploitation of God but is victimized by it. Terrorist attacks in the name of Allah, or God, are a point in case. There are both Islamic terrorist groups such as ISIS, ISIL, and al-Qaeda but also radical Christians, who are white supremacists and far-right militia groups, who are equally and schematically justifying their radical ideology and violent acts through their interpretation of the Quran or the Bible. They are motivated through their false interpretations of Islam or Christianity and their hateful beliefs to reign terror on all those who are not with them, not part of their sect, group, or religion. They are openly promoting religious violence against all who do not agree with them, including those of their own faith. One of the major differences between ISIL and other Islamic terrorist groups is their belief in the Apocalypse, our final day of Judgement by God, and therefore they are "selling" their version of the end of times to their recruits. The strong selling point being paradise awaiting the suicide terrorist, a far better prospect than they often face in life on Earth. Radical religious ideologies have nothing to do with any belief system or with God, or Allah, for that matter. They are just that—radical and the extreme expression of negativity only found here on Earth. God does not condone the killing of innocents, only humans in a perverted state can. The belief that the killing of those who do not share the same views will get you closer to God is nothing but blasphemy. Nothing could be farther from the truth. God is neither vindictive nor oppressive—He has no need to force anybody to believe in Him in any particular way or at all as part of our free will. I wonder how many million of lives have been lost to these false beliefs and alternative facts? A true stain on our "humanity"!

Religions are the cause of many evils—wars, prejudices, fear, power, wealth, and influence—all under the misrepresentations of righteousness. Religions do not bring you closer to God or lead you onto the right path by following their dogmas and doctrines in blind faith. There will be no salvation found in a church or temple; it can only be found by going within, becoming quiet, and allowing Him to guide you. You have God consciousness within you as you are a part of Him, but this has become rather vague and distant. Connect through the heart center so that you open the channels of daily communications. Feel and experience the Love He has for you, the strength He gives you, and the guidance He offers you. There is no need for guidebooks to tell you which way to go or not go, you will *know* instinctively what to do and what not to do.

It may be easier to sit in a church or temple and have somebody tell you how you should be acting, based on scripture or sermons. However, it is wiser to go directly to the Source of All by opening your own channels of daily communication. Trust your intuition and instincts from your heart to guide you through all the clutter and baggage accumulated daily, shed them, and find your strength from within. Become your own judge in figuring out what feels right to you from the heart—not the head for it is ego based and part of the negative powers prevailing on Earth. When hearing or reading the news, personal scrutiny is highly recommended in figuring out what's what. The same due diligence should be applied to the scriptures with the knowledge that they were written after all by human beings. They may have had the best of intentions, but most likely were directed to interpret the Word of God to support certain values and interests for certain people or groups. That is part of our human condition and problem. Unless we change the model, we cannot escape its functions.

When listening to a sermon, ask yourself if it is given with love and with your best interest at heart, or is it designed to keep you hostage by the confines of the written word and the interests of the religious organization. Do you feel fearful by the threats and promises of heaven or hell, finding redemption and salvation through monetary or other means? God is not punitive, nor vengeful or threatening. He

assists our spiritual growth through cause and effect, through what
feels right in our heart, not our mind, and through Love. God is not
seeking to confuse us with complexities or dogmas. The messages
and the paths are simple—they are in your heart and you will feel
their truths if you allow them to come through. But for that you will
have to be still, take a deep breath, and pause. In peace and quiet, you
will become aware of your within. Your true guide is there, waiting to
lead you to wholeness, to feeling complete and fulfilled. No worries,
no threats, no punishments, no need to be anxious about anything.
But, beware, you are and always will be responsible for your actions.
Be conscious of what you give out, for it will come back to you in
same, actually multiplied. So be selfish, and do what feels good and
right, give to others as much as you can, help, and send love and light
so you may reap the rewards. Simple!

God is pure, absolute love. He loves you as He loves all His
children and creations. All you have to do is to reach out and
communicate with Him daily, be it in meditation or prayer. And
you should channel His Love and Light out, send it through the
solar plexus to people, events, and places of concern to heal them
and thus to save this world. This is how you will free yourself from
the false beliefs and fears, and how you raise yourself and the rest
of humankind. You can always access this special place as you can
always reach out to God and the spirit world. There is no need to
rush over to a church or temple, just go into a quiet place and take a
time out. That is where you will tap into your Source, your essence,
and your purpose—where you will fill yourself with Love and Light
and become a beacon of hope and change.

So, you will ask, why is our world so off-track, so off balanced,
and so negative? How did we get to this point in our evolution

where it seems as if we haven't evolved at all? At least not on the most fundamental levels of our human characteristics! We have evolved from the far more primitive lifestyles at the beginning of our civilization, have added advances in technology, science, and medicine to name a few, but underneath it all, we are still the same. We are still fighting one bloody conflict or war after another, hate and mistrust one another, see only divisions and differences, live in fear and a state of eternal anxiety, and are driven by materialism and by the never-satisfied ego. Where is God? How could He allow such atrocities and injustices to occur? If God is, as I *know* Him to be, Love and Light, then our universe makes no sense at all! How would He create such imperfection as the likes of humans, or rather perfect imperfections? So, what really happened and who is responsible?

CHAPTER 3

The Fall

In the Beginning

We now know that we are missing information and, to some extent, how it has been withheld from us. Now we need to discover what it is that we don't know about our real origin and being. If we want to understand where the chaos we are living in comes from, we must first understand our true identity and the events leading into this state of existence.

Truth is still hard to find, even in an age of endlessly streaming information bombarding us from everywhere with one version or another of the facts. It took me many years to find answers to questions that weren't fully resolved for me. Explanations to queries regarding the seeming injustice and inequality in life were not satisfied with karma, for example, or that experiences were learning tools. It felt incomplete. I was confronted with this existential dilemma when Debra, a young lady who had worked for me at my travel agency in New Jersey, approached me. Her three-year-old nephew had just passed away during a fairly common ear tube surgery, which had been performed in the operating room at a premier hospital in Westchester, New York. The presiding anesthesiologist had decided to leave the child unattended during the operation while under anesthesia on account of a personal phone call. Something went terribly wrong and by the time he returned, the child was in distress. All efforts failed—the little boy could not be saved. Debra blamed God for not being there and simply letting this happen to an innocent child. What crime had this boy committed to deserve such a fate? She knew that I was "into spiritual things," so it seemed logical to seek the truth from me. Unfortunately, all I had was karma, be it for the boy and/or the parents. However, I also mentioned that our free will, given to us by God, supersedes His will on Earth. He will not break His own laws. It is our birthright, if you will, as His children, to have free will, as He has, and make our own decisions. Consequently, as we are making our own decisions, we are also 100% responsible for the outcome and our undoing. There too God cannot and will not interfere as this is the law of cause and effect. We should not blame God; it's a waste of time and energy. Instead, let us focus on how to correct the underlying cause for all the suffering experienced on Earth.

It would be fair to say that I had been searching for the truth all my life. Shortly after my mother's death, I went online to check on her book and found other books containing messages from the spirit Joseph. Among the search results, I found *The Joseph Communications*. What a goldmine of spiritual wisdom! I read all six books in the series in sequence, keeping the flow in which the messages were brought forth, having finally found what I had been missing for so long.

These books are based on the transcripts of trance sessions in which, through the mediumship of Michael G. Reccia, the "highly evolved spirit" Joseph channels his messages from the spirit world. The book that had the greatest impact on me is *The Fall: You Were There, That's Why You're Here*. The information I found was something I had never heard before, but it was the missing link I had been looking for. As it is of vital importance to aid in the understanding of why our lives are so burdened, I will, in my own words, give you an abbreviated account of the events that led to the creation of our planet according to the spirit Joseph. I will not quote any direct passages from the book, as there are many layers behind them containing more messages with deeper meanings. However, as the spirit Joseph himself urges all of us to share these messages with others, at the very least send out Light to the world and to areas of great concern, I cannot be anything else but a messenger and do just that.

I have decided to be that Light worker, to be a modern-day apostle spreading the channeled messages. When Jesus came to this world, he didn't lock himself up in a cabin on an island far, far away. On the contrary! He gave his life, asked for no special treatment from His Father to spare it, so that his messages would bring positive change to humanity. So, we must do the same today, each in our own way.

All cultures and religions have some form of creation myths with similar symbolic accounts of how the world began and how it became populated by human beings. These are sacred and time-honored metaphorical stories attempting to explain creation. They try to show us who we are, where we came from, and how Earth was formed out of nothing. Analogies have the power to describe complex subjects in easily understandable narratives to the people. As such, there are a variety of creation myths, such as the *ex nihilo*

(Latin "out of nothing") creation, which can be found in the stories from ancient Egypt, the Rigveda (an ancient Indian collection of sacred Hindu texts), the Bible, the Quran, and many cultures from Africa, Asia, Oceania, and North America. Another creation myth, predominantly an ancient Greek mythology, is based on the theory that in the beginning there was only chaos, meaning disorder, and that there was only a void containing the materials with which the world was to be created. So out of disorder, order (or cosmos) was created. Chaos would be described as a dimensionless form of water or vapor and be associated with evil and oblivion. Some of these cultures also believed that one day, disorder would gain strength over order and the world would once again fall into the abyss. Finally, there is the parent myth where the parents are the sky (male) and the earth (female) splitting up after they had been tied together and now creating their offspring. The world parent myth is not sexual in nature rather a separation of parental body parts with which the world is formed.

The biblical narrative, however, tells us that

1 In the beginning God created the heaven and the earth.

2 And the earth was without form, and void; and darkness [*was*] upon the face of the deep. And the Spirit of God moved upon the face of the waters.

(Genesis 1:1–2)

According to Genesis, God then created the Earth in six days and rested on the seventh. On the sixth day, He had created the first man, Adam, and out of him the first woman, Eve. "And God had created man in His own image," after His own likeness, and gave him supremacy over all living things. God had given them the Garden of Eden to live in with Him, but without any worries or having any needs. They were to "be fruitful, and multiply, and replenish the earth" ("and subdue it"—I dislike this part and am choosing to omit it as it is yet another impossible thing God would have had them do when He Is Love and, let's remember, this was a peaceful Paradise, not one of spears and arrows). They had everything and nothing to fear. Actually, there was no fear yet. A world without fear, only love and feeling as One, complete, and in harmony.

However, there was a tree, called the Tree of Knowledge, and depending on the religious belief, sometimes also the tree "of good and evil," placed in the middle of the garden and not to be eaten from, period. God had given a simple command, as he didn't want Adam and Eve to have the knowledge of evil. They had "good" already; they were living in the best possible way. In the Jewish tradition, eating the fruit represented the joining of good and evil for the first time. Evil only existed as a potential. God and His Universe were good, and good and evil were separate entities altogether. However, God gave humans free choice and here, Adam and Eve chose to eat the forbidden fruit from the tree of life. According to Genesis, the serpent enticed Eve to eat the fruit from the tree of knowledge because only then her eyes would be opened and she would become like God, knowing good and evil. After eating from it, she hands the fruit to Adam, who takes a bite as well. This became the transition from a state of innocence and obedience to guilt and disobedience. For many Christians, this is known as the fall and the original sin. After they ate the fruit, they suddenly became aware of their bodies,

7 Then the eyes of both of them were opened, and they realized they were naked; so they sewed fig leaves together and made coverings for themselves.

8 Then the man and his wife heard the sound of the Lord God as he was walking in the garden in the cool of the day, and they hid from the Lord God among the trees of the garden. 9 But the Lord God called to the man, "Where are you?"

10 He answered, "I heard you in the garden, and I was afraid because I was naked; so I hid."

11 And he said, "Who told you that you were naked? Have you eaten from the tree that I commanded you not to eat from?"

12 The man said, "The woman you put here with me—she gave me some fruit from the tree, and I ate it."

13 Then the Lord God said to the woman, "What is this you have done?"

The woman said, "The serpent deceived me, and I ate."

(Genesis 3:7–13)

God then "curses" the serpent and both Adam and Eve and throws them out of the Garden of Eden.

21 The Lord God made garments of skin for Adam and his wife and clothed them. 22 And the Lord God said, "The man has now become like one of us, knowing good and evil. He must not be allowed to reach out his hand and take also from the tree of life and eat, and live forever." 23 So the Lord God banished him from the Garden of Eden to work the ground from which he had been taken. 24 After he drove the man

out, he placed on the east side[e] of the Garden of Eden cherubim and a flaming sword flashing back and forth to guard the way to the tree of life.

(Genesis 3:21–24)

The consequences of their decision had catastrophic repercussions for humanity. Their choice had plunged them and all of humankind into a state of sin and corruption, creating a world of violence and pain for all time. Lost was their state of innocence and harmony, peace, and wholeness. Now they were experiencing fear for the very first time. They suddenly feared for their existence. They realized that they had been naked and now needed to be clothed to protect themselves from the elements and their awareness of form. They needed food and shelter for their survival, something that they had never been aware of or in need of. They suddenly were flooded with a deluge of needs and feelings of lack, while being isolated and seemingly left out in the cold. It is from this state of mind that worry arose. Would there be *enough* to eat and drink, *enough* material for clothing and shelter for protection? The state of *not enough* was born. Humans, from here on out, never had *enough* of anything, be it safety and security, food and shelter, or wealth and power. There would always be cause for worries and fear, in their minds. It was the beginning of the state of the ego, the "I, me, and mine" to be pursued by taking more from you, yours, and theirs as a direct result. This was to be the beginning of greed, of power-hunger, envy, and the never-ending feelings of lack and need, of never being fulfilled. It was also the beginning of division, separation, and disconnect, from God and the spirit world as well as from one another.

Storytelling makes complex concepts comprehensible to all people, educated or not, thus suitable for sharing and passing down from one generation to the next. As such, the Genesis narrative of creation is an analogy. It is not history, but theology, of both Judaism and Christianity. It contains many elements and parallels, but here is what really happened.

The Other Beginning

"The fall of man is the descent of the ladder from the dot to the circumference; the resurrection or redemption of man is his return from the circumference to the dot."[1]

MANLY P. HALL

According to the spirit Joseph, we have always existed in one form or another. In our beginning, we didn't have the form of our present physical bodies nor the space we occupy now. We were a part of God, enclosed by and within Him, but only as a concept, not yet formalized as beings. We were simply vague possibilities until God chose to analyze different viewpoints of His Whole Being through various angles. He imbued form to each possibility, so that it could move as an individualized, unique entity to inspect these different aspects of the Whole. Imagine a body of water. It is composed of individual drops of water that, as individual drops act on their own, have their own unique structures and movement, yet they are all part of and comprise the Whole. Each drop of water has its own consciousness as well as a spark of the Whole body within itself.

---

1   Hall, Manly P. *Lectures on Ancient Philosophy: Companion to The Secret Teachings of All Ages.* New York: Jeremy P. Tarcher/Penguin; 2005, p. 22.

Through movement the water drops create energy and are able to reach various locations with different positions, thus allowing them to see through a different prism. They are individual, separate aspects of the Whole containing within them the awareness of and connection to the Whole—within their center is the dot, their nucleus, containing their DNA. Although they are individualized drops, they are all joined by having the same genetic makeup and the same point of origin, therefore all water drops are tied together as part of the greater body of water.

The drops of water symbolize angelic beings—individual parts of God but imbued with and part of God. They are connected to the Source, the Dot in the Center, as individualized aspects of the One, on a mission to explore and experience. And as God Is Light, so are the angels and now "there was light," the beginning of creation.

> 1 In the beginning God created the heaven and the earth.
>
> 2 And the earth was without form, and void; and darkness [was] upon the face of the deep. And the Spirit of God moved upon the face of the waters.
>
> First day
>
> 3 And God said, Let there be light: and there was light.
>
> (Genesis 1:1–3)

At this point, the angels had no form, as they were simply a reflection of Light based on their high vibrational rate of energy. However, they wanted to become more visible and identifiable, while still remaining ethereal but having a more solidified form. In order to achieve that, they reduced or slowed their vibrational rate, which created greater density and matter. Now, having form, they created space by joining in one area, combining their auras, thus gifting a part of their "self" to each other, melting their outer limits of their forms together thus creating a defined space. By condensing energy, space had been established, as before form had been created by reducing energy. God Is Light, the angels are Light, energy is Light, and by adjusting the energy or speed of Light, by condensing it, form and space were created.

Let us return to our analogy of the water. If you have a kettle of water on the stove and it's boiling, then first, the energy of the steam is blowing the whistle and second, the water's consistency has changed into steam. It is still water but due to its high level of energy (heat), it has become gaseous, has no form but is visible, like free-flowing cloud formations that occupy space. The drops, in their gaseous form, have joined together to become clouds taking up a part of space; they are visible but intangible, free-flowing ethereal forms of energy. When they stick to the wall or microwave, they will turn back into water. As the heat or level of energy is reduced or turned off altogether, the steam or gas solidifies into water again. However, when the water is put into the freezer, it will form into ice—as it is malleable in the water state, it can be shaped into any form in its new state. Water can even be flash-frozen, creating fascinating forms and—depending on the speed and temperature—it can form into beautiful sculptures. A case in point for the various shapes and forms of frozen water are snowflakes, icicles, and icebergs.

As God imbued the angels with His Divine Spark, they in effect inherited, as part of their awareness, a desire to explore. They needed a place in which to experience it though, which is why God allowed them to co-create space, within the circumference of His circle, making it their home where they could create and evaluate different aspects of the Whole. With God as the Dot in the center of the circle, all energy moved out of and back into the dot, a cyclical flow of energy, bringing experience back to the dot, reviewing, sharing, and moving out again.

The Divine spark is our inheritance and our connection to God and, as such, we are His children and a part of Him. He not only gave us the power to create but also the gift of free will. By birthright, we have been given the right to choose our own destiny. We are allowed to choose our own dreams and illusions we would like to explore. We are the creators of our own visions and opportunities to grow by experiencing different possibilities. We are the ones who created and un-created our own experiences, as One and as a Whole. This was true then for the angels as it is true to this very day for each and every one of us.

As stated earlier, slowing the speed of light, thus condensing it into form and matter, created the Universe and the angelic beings. The angels, on the other hand, created their wishes into form through thought. They wished to create a new illusion to experience and so they visualized their thoughts into form. The architect angel, for example, would visualize a construct and manifest the thought, thus by doing so giving it form. Thoughts have ethereal form, weight, and power that result in a more physical form and matter. Although invisible, thoughts have the power to create wish into being—giving the dream or the illusion the physical manifestation of matter and form. Thus, angels are composed of two elements: light, condensed to give form, and thought, to create as well as give movement and direction to the energy of light.

Subsequently, this Universe was created by the Will of God through the condensation of His Light—giving it form—and through angelic thought—processing it into matter. Everything we see is light in a different state of condensation, which is brought forth through the deceleration of the vibration of light energy–creating form. Everything we wish for is brought through the visualization of thought creating matter. The creation of our Universe was the result of a harmonious and loving cooperation between God and the angels, our ancestors.

The Dot within the Center

What has been will be again,
what has been done will be done again;
there is nothing new under the sun.

(Ecclesiastes 1:9)

Our entire Universe is based on the Dot within the Circle principle, in both microcosm and macrocosm. It begins with God being the Center, the Nucleus of All Creation, to the angels as being an extension and expression of Him, down to us who are an expression and reflection of the angels. All form originates from the Dot within the Circle and all energy flows through the Dot in a circular motion to the outer lines of the Circle. The Circle represents infinity and eternity, within which all things are in fluid, cyclical motion ever repeating anew. The Dot within its center is the Seed, the Spark, the Source of All things in God's Creation. And God Is the Dot. God Is infinite, there is no beginning and no end. God reflects All things and Is reflected in All—energy flowing and returning to its Source in eternal fluidity. All things are in motion, ebb and flow, positive and negative charges constantly changing, adjusting, and growing in consciousness. The galaxies and the planets, atoms, DNA, and all things, small or large, operate on that principle.

Consequently, Earth is constructed on that same principle but it is unique in it being of greater density, of physical matter—a state that had been sought by the angels. Not the heavy matter we are experiencing today, but a slightly more tangible form to allow experiences in physicality. The angels and we, as their offspring, chose to explore this perspective of the Whole and how different stimuli in greater density would affect the results brought forth. Then, as part of the circular motion, they would report back with their findings to the Whole, present their data, share it for all to grow from their experiences and gain greater understanding of the Whole. The circular event here is the giving and receiving of experiences; the taking in and expelling them back out again. The purpose of experiencing and existence is to gain knowledge by appreciating God. And God Is in all things and He Is everywhere. God Is All. God Is within us and thus we are exploring Him while exploring us and our Universe—another cyclical event in continuous motion. As God Is within us all, it once more establishes that we are part of Him and that we are His children. We are all One and we all have the One in common—a uniting factor!

Therefore, we too are eternal, and we cannot ever die. Originally, we had no fear of anything, as there was no reason to be afraid of anything. We were perfect expressions of God on a mission to explore Him in physicality. There was neither violence nor pain, neither lack nor lust, and no fear of dying because we were aware that existence is eternal, moving in and out of experiences and back and forth from the dot to the outer line of the circle. We were also aware that the illusion we had created in physicality was just that, an illusion. We could still see the other reality and were aware of our connection to it. We knew that we had the ability to simply undo what we had created previously as an experiment that challenged our creative spirit in new possibilities. The purposes were the exploration of self within these conditions and in relation to others; of spiritual energies and their projection into others; of experiencing the spiritual in physical matter. Matter, unlike present conditions, was made up of equal parts of spirit and physical elements with the polarizing dot in the center. A perfect balance of energy in harmonious flow!

Everything in our Universe has duality. And here, the original intent was to blend spiritual and physical energies, in balance, to create a new form of life in which to experience different ideas. It opened up a whole new array of possibilities to be explored—the physical form on the outside, ever changing and growing, and the spiritual from within, eternal and evolving. It was the examination of the spiritual vs. the physical, from within and without. The requirements for such explorations were based on perfectly balanced charges, which were needed to maintain the flow of energy pushing forward.

Everything within the experience is forever changing—nothing ever stands still in God's Universe. Experience may be constantly changing and in flux but it is, at all times, in harmony and in joy. The reason is that the duality of the charges, positive and negative, are perfectly balanced and in harmony. They need each other to create energy and keep it in a fluid movement with direction and speed. A car needs an engine to create the motion, its pull, but must have the steering wheel within the chassis with the gas pedal and ignition to start it, then steer it in the desired direction and set the speed level. One cannot be without the other. Positive cannot be without negative and negative cannot be without positive, but they must be perfectly balanced to create the perfect joy ride. Life was to be that joy ride, an experience, evolving and forever changing. Life is change, as Is God. God Is Change. Therefore, embrace change, accept the challenges, as it is energy moving forward, pushing in new directions and forcing growth.

Earth gave the angelic beings the unique opportunity to learn in practicality instead of in theory. It is like school children learning in the lab creating an actual experiment with all the necessary equipment versus sitting in the classroom with books in front of them and learning about the experiment in theoretical terms only. First-hand experiences always outweigh speculations. But they also tend to invite for more experimentations. Previous successes egg on future experimentations. And, so too, the angels were seduced by the fruit of the forbidden tree, or rather the exhilaration of previous successes egging them on to move on to more risky ones. Challenge is after all part of our DNA, but it must be done while adhering to due processes and proper procedures for a right outcome to occur.

The angelic children were experimenting with the balance of energies, positive and negative, and were evaluating how they could tweak them to create different possibilities. They pushed the envelope and really tried to go outside of the box. We are no different in pushing new ideas and going outside of the set standards. The angelic children were experimenting with manipulating energy balances, specifically with altering the perfect mix of energy by overloading on the physical, thus creating an imbalance. Not only did they add more of the physical energy to their equation, but they also chose to increase the space between themselves and God, thus adding distance to imbalance. However, it was reciprocal as greater physicality automatically increased their distance from the center of the Dot. The distance created between them was not only one in spatial terms but also in spiritual terms—they distanced themselves from God mentally and physically!

The point of their experiment was to experience heavier matter, so they would understand how to deal with it, how to create under such differing conditions, and how to infuse it with spirituality. However, by distancing themselves from the Dot and by adding more physicality, they created a density that changed their form into one of heavier mass. Eventually, this would lead them to be actually encapsulated within their own form and space.

Growth & Evolution

Angels are like diamonds—multifaceted with brilliantly shining light illuminating their brilliance from within. They are pure reflections of the Divine. They are individualized aspects of God, each being a piece of the Whole, an aspect seen through a different prism. The angels, in return, procreated aspects of themselves into more individualized facets; in other words, giving birth, as it were, to their offspring, which were the next generation of angels. Continuing the same tradition, the offspring would carry on with what the angels had been doing already, which was to investigate new possibilities in creation and un-creation, to expand their consciousness through growth and evolve through experiences. They too would create new beings through individualizing aspects of themselves into new facets. It was the beginning of our cycle of creating new life forms and new opportunities to experience and learn from.

Everything in God's Nature is to experience and to grow. That is the essence of existence. Thus, the angels became hosts to their offspring, like parents to their children. No matter how individualized they became, they were still One, united by connection to each other and to God, unlike when in physicality, where individualization is equivalent to separation and division. As nothing ever stands still in God's Universe, all angelic beings went out to experience and when the younger generation wanted to experience physicality, they chose to do so on Earth, which they had created through manifesting their joined thoughts into form. They would project themselves into this planet, go through the desired experiences, adapt to the new set of circumstances, and learn what could be gained from this journey.

As part of the growth process, they would apply their new knowledge to improve and evolve, and when there was nothing to be added onto this particular experience, they would project themselves back to their host. Often, our sci-fi movies seem to be drawing from our memories buried deep, deep down in our consciousness. Here, the projection and retraction through thought reminds me of the "beam me up, Scotty" from *Star Trek*. It was an easy transformation from one state of being into another, changing scenarios to alter the adventure which is rather equivalent to birth and death. In any event, the young angelic beings returned home, if you will, and shared their findings from their enterprise with the others, who, in return, shared theirs. They learned from one another, exchanged ideas, and regenerated their energies while strengthening their connectivity to their angelic hosts and God. Then they would choose to experience again under a new set of circumstances anywhere they chose to be. As everything in God's Nature is cyclical, so is this a cycle of birth and death, with birth starting a new cycle. Birth is the death of an alternate form of being and the beginning of a new one, to be reversed and repeated over and over again. As cycles within a circle, there is no beginning and no end, there just Is. And all cycles are fluidity in motion, generating and re-generating energy, creating and un-creating, balancing dual energy charges in harmonious flow.

In order to give cycles new and different possibilities of experiences, the angels created this planet with its unique physical attributes. They had given form to their intent through thought. In other words, they, as a group, created visions of possibilities, of dreams, and agreed that they had great potential to provide such scenarios. They then solidified their visions and turned their dreams into reality, a form of visualization. However, the form of their creation then was one of crystalline and etheric essence. This planet, having been originated in Light, was like a jewel—radiant, colorful, and brilliant. It was in constant change, kaleidoscopically reflecting different patterns and colors, like a diamond illuminated by light. It was still in a nebulous or gaseous state, bursting with color and light reflecting the emotions and visions of the angelic beings who themselves were light beings and jewel-like.

This nebulous physicality was not only created through the manifestation of thought but also through the manipulation of physical matter and colored rays that are contained within their atoms. Color was yet another means of creating physical matter but it was also a tool for expression. The angelic beings, having no clearly visible form yet, used colored rays and bursts of color as a means of communicating their emotions and thoughts. As color was manipulated to create physicality, so were vibrations and energy fields used to manipulate even denser form. Earth had been set up with vibrational bands representing challenges through which the angelic beings moved and succeeded in. It is somewhat reminiscent of challenge courses that are popular these days in extreme sports and competitions, like the Ninja Warriors or Spartans, where the participants must master the course to advance to the next level. For winning that competition, they must also have the fastest time in completing the course while mastering each hurdle. The point of these games is that the athletes must get through the course as quickly and efficiently as possible qualifying them for the next and more challenging level. In essence, the young angelic beings designed this manipulation with the sole intent to both speed the experiences up and add new, varying challenges to the possibilities available on this physical level.

The angels, as individualized parts of God, were created through condensation—from their ethereal, vapor state into a somewhat denser form. In return, they created through thought visualization and manipulation of color and vibrational energy. The results were greater density of both the angelic form and that of space, the Earth. The angels then brought forth their own individualized parts who, as they had done before them, continued to bring forth their own offspring. All were in constant motion of experiencing and expanding their consciousness and thus their spheres. They all returned from these experiences to their host and the Source to share their discoveries. Afterward, they would move back into another challenge of creating their own new visions and possibilities. So, the Universe grows continuously, cyclically, from the Center out. It is a continuous flow of energy in the form of experiences brought back and forth, shared and learned from, growing exponentially, infinitely, and without limit. All growth was experienced in harmony and in love, glorifying God—the Whole—viewed through different aspects by the individualized parts of Him.

God's Universe Is an endless, eternal flow of energy, in perfect balance and harmony. It flows from the center dot out to return back to its Origin. It is a continuous flow of giving and receiving, of going back and forth, without beginning or end, in harmony and joy by re-energizing the individual and the Whole. As the One learns, so do all, and all learn and grow through the One. It is important to understand this flow in its most fundamental form, as these are the building blocks of our planet now. If we choose to change this world back to its original, intended form then we must have this knowledge of our past to apply, creating a blueprint for our comeback. We have not only left clues behind, but right now, we are also receiving tremendous help from the spiritual realms to assist us in our re-awakening. Just as we paved the way to get to this state, that is how we will pave it for our return. We are still angelic beings, in a materialized state, with the Divine Spark residing within us. Therefore, we too can use our thoughts and our connection to the spirit realms to undo what has been done by us so long ago, with the best intentions at heart. All creation begins from the Dot within the Center and so it is with us. Our God within us Is our Dot within our Center, and within that Dot are all the tools needed for us to create a better world, a better tomorrow. Everything we need to change our circumstances is within us—all we have to do is choose to use it. It is our Divine Gift and has been within us always and will be forever. However, we have to choose our destiny and our future but we must act upon it. Again, cyclical in nature—what we put out, we will get back. On account of our free will, another Divine Gift, it is our choice to un-create in unison what we have created before in unison.

There is always hope and there is a way to get this done.

In the Greek mythology of creation, Pandora, a most beautiful woman, who had been created by a son of the god Zeus, had received gifts from all the other gods and so Zeus gave her curiosity and a box she was to never open. Zeus had chosen this particular gift in response to his other son Prometheus' gift of fire to humans. It had greatly upset him and therefore he had devised a plan to punish all of humankind. Then he gave Pandora to another one of his sons, Epimetheus, in marriage. Naturally, one day, she couldn't resist the temptation any longer and she opened the box. To her horror, all the evils and plagues that haunt this world to this day flew out of the box. Amidst her screams, she still heard a voice coming from the bottom, saying, "Let me out. I am hope." So, Pandora released her, giving hope to humanity.

The Other Fall

Earth was conceived in Light. Its intent was to advance the angelic potential through experience whilst being connected to the Divine and each other. The experiences were transmitted back, creating new thought forms, thus new life, in the form of their children who then continued on their own quests. Earth was to be a sphere of spiritual learning amidst the effects of physicality—a different perspective from which to view the Whole.

Yet, the Earth fell into darkness. The angelic children, like most children, were impatient and wanted to do things differently. They wanted to improve upon the quality of the experiences and hasten the process by moving through them faster. It is really quite common that young people see things differently than their predecessors, as they are not confined by their knowledge or sentience. God, too, is always looking for new potential, new thoughts, and possibilities, which is what His creation is all about. However, there are right and wrong approaches and methods of doing things in a responsible manner. Experience and gained knowledge are guiding posts to lead us properly through the due processes and procedures needed to create properly. But when youth rises up to rebel against the status quo, they may decide to go against all fundamental principles, not grasping their consequences nor heeding the advice of their elders. There is always a learning curve, and although thoughts or ideas may have great potential, they must adhere to the principles and laws upon which they were built. This is another reason why experiences were shared in the spirit realms: so that all would learn and gain knowledge avoiding unnecessary mistakes and their ensuing consequences.

The angelic children had learned how to manipulate energy through their handling of the energy fields and vibrations. However, they felt that they were not moving through the experiences fast enough and that more could be learned once the process was being sped up. They wanted to do things differently, and believed that their approach would be far superior in growing Divine consciousness in an altered, advanced setting. It always was their ultimate goal, though, to do this to glorify God and to bring greater awareness to all. They had the best intentions at "heart" and wanted to implement their theories in cooperation with God and the spirit realm. However, their lack of knowledge as to the dos and don'ts in combination with that youthful swagger of arrogance, based on ignorance, led them to disregard advice or follow procedural protocol. When it comes to manipulating energy and all its enormous potential, it would be prudent to handle it with extreme caution and precision. Simply put, we wouldn't place a chef in an operating room in lieu of the surgeon, and, equally, a surgeon wouldn't understand the absolute need for precise measurements when baking a cake. In a "perfect" world, we wouldn't put an incompetent or ignorant person or an autocrat in charge of our nuclear weapons and codes, either.

Any project is built upon a specific order in which every step is based on the previous one and they are lined up in a precise order. Anybody who has ever put together a piece of furniture, let's say from IKEA, knows what I mean. If you don't follow their step-by-step instructions, you will end up with a wobbly, unsafe end result or, worse, a piece of junk. There simply are protocols and procedures to accomplish any task successfully. The same is true in creation!

The manipulation of positive and negative power had to be done in adherence of the proper procedures creating balanced atoms, which would produce the desired illusions accurately. Illusions were created to give the angels the backdrop to experience, like a set on a stage, and when done right, they could be created and un-created quickly and with ease by withdrawing equal amounts of positive and negative power. However, the angelic children insisted that by increasing the speed, they would not only improve the quality, but also the quantity of experiences mastered in a given time frame. To accomplish this, they were proposing to alter the balance of energy, namely by increasing positive energy and withholding the negative. This would result in the increased speed of the positive energy. The angelic hosts advised them that this would bring about a significant imbalance and create even heavier mass as a consequence thereof. They were concerned that this would solidify the illusions and, therefore, they would be difficult to dissolve. Coming back to my water analogy, it would be equivalent to reducing the energy of heat, which would result in its greater solidification. It would change the steam to water, and under even more severe conditions, to ice or even rock formation. A form more difficult to dissolve or pliable to mold into a new shape!

Both sides defended their positions in an amicable and loving discourse over some time, but as all God's children have free will, it was ultimately up to the angelic children to proceed or halt. They truly believed that this revolutionary new theory would produce fantastic results in the enhancement of the individual experiences and, ultimately, glorify God.

During their time of deliberations, the children chose not to return home to their hosts, thus distancing themselves even farther from their influence, and discontinuing the practice of being re-charged by the Source and instead regenerated by communal, intellectual exchanges. They lived in their own bubble and consciously reduced the flow of unwanted opinion—or, rather, criticism—thus also cutting off their life force to and from the Whole. This avoidance of following proper procedure, namely that of maintaining the flow of energy going back and forth, to and from the Source, additionally disrupted the balance of energy within the circle. They had in effect removed themselves from God and the spirit realms. It brings up images of the mad scientist, locked up in his lab, working diligently and maniacally to prove his theory right while the whole place is blowing up.

Greater spiritual distance and separation, the rejection of well-founded objections and their supporting evidence, as well as the insistence on not following due process gave the angelic children the impetus to go ahead with their experiment in altering energy fields. In order to do so, they came together, integrated as one host, and then found their new world by altering the positive and negative energies of creation, thus causing their imbalance. They had gained knowledge of how to manipulate energies from their previous experiments, but they lacked insight and comprehension of the consequences. Earth became heavier, losing its crystalline composition, which had been in harmony with the rest of the Universe, as the condensation of matter resulted in a thick layer coating its perimeter. And so, dense physical matter encapsulated Earth. The angelic children did not fare any better. As they had joined their energies together in the same imbalanced fashion, they were also encapsulated by physical mass and their ethereal forms became solidified. As if it were not enough to be both entrapped in body and in space, due to the effects of changing the positive and negative energy charges, they also lost their memory of their origin and connection to God and the spiritual realms. Suddenly, they found themselves as strangers in a strange land, stranded and all alone (or so they believed). Everything had become solidified—their forms had become bodies, and space became a physical and materialized landscape. Their illusion had become their solid, almost impenetrable reality that they couldn't see their way out of. Dreams and visions had turned into nightmares. And so, they found themselves fearful and bewildered. As they had based their creation on a formula of imbalance, the result was one of imbalance!

It must also be noted that by taking mostly from the positive energy to create, negating the negative, the ensuing result was that, from then on, there was predominantly only negative energy from which to draw. As time passed through the millennia, there was less and less positive, God energy available to draw from and the ever-thickening coating that had formed around the Earth and humans became more impenetrable.

Duality is an essential element in all things, including creation.

For example, any battery has both negative and positive charges in equal amounts producing a balanced outflow of energy when connected to the object it is supposed charge. Here, too, there needed to be an accurate amount of negative energy infusing the positive energy. Without it, the forms or illusions brought forth could not be deconstructed as before by simply retracting out of that situation. The negative needs a balanced amount of the positive, and vice versa, to create and un-create perfectly. However, now, illusions could not be simply undone and there would be disintegration and decay of form because only negative energy was projected into it.

The angelic children tried to apply corrective actions by infusing more of the positive energy but, in reality, they only projected more of the negative. For one, that was basically all they could draw on and, secondly, the solidification had obstructed their "view" and visible access to the spiritual realms and to God. They could not reach beyond their experiment, as the vibrational rate of matter was different and incompatible to a degree. It was as if they had erected a "wall" that they couldn't puncture. They had built a solid, physical sphere that enclosed them. The "wall" had also buried their connection and their channels of communication to God, which resulted in the loss of spiritual energy. "Walls" divide and separate, when all they had known until then was inclusion and unity. But they had chosen to do so, by their free will, as a joint venture and with all beings in on it, to force their beliefs into being. They were so fully invested in and convinced of the accuracy of their new energy theory that nothing and nobody could sway them off this course of action. They still believed in it, actually still do, thinking that at some point they would be proven right. But when an equation is wrong, it simply won't add up correctly no matter how many times, with however many different approaches, it is calculated and recalculated, the results will always come out as incorrect. When the foundation and the structure are flawed, they will always produce flawed results. There can be no other way. Thus, the underlying foundation must be corrected to bring accuracy to the results of the equation.

Since time immemorial, we have believed that we can change our world from within its structure through religious, political, social, and economic means but we have never successfully accomplished this. And the reason is obvious; once we not only understand but also accept that we have created a flawed structure, it must be fixed, first and foremost. We, all of us in a joint venture, have to do this together for we need the combined energy of all, in unity and harmony, to bring our God consciousness back and return our current state into its intended version. It seems to be a tall order, but what has been done once, can be done once more. For the right reasons, this time around!

We were, and still are, responsible for plunging this world into darkness, into its heaviness and stickiness, by changing its molecular structure. We plunged ourselves into heaviness and darkness as well, imprisoning ourselves physically, mentally, and spiritually, causing our separation from the Divine and the angelic hosts. The density of our Earth's firmament is not only enclosing the negative energy within its structure, but it also recycles it back into the Earth. It won't allow the negative energy to move outward or the positive energy to move inward, which would circulate the energies properly. The result is stagnation and loss of circulation, which is essential to breathe life into its very being. It's comparable to our bodies' circulatory system—if there is a blockage, the flow of blood, nutrients, hormones, and oxygen will be interrupted, potentially leading to death unless corrected through intervention—surgically or otherwise. So, it is on Earth—everything will eventually decay, unlike being de-constructed by intent, as there is no new life force to regenerate its energy. As all things in God's Universe are reflections of Him, it follows the same circulatory pattern of the Divine flow of energy. Equally, the heart is in the center of the body, as the dot, and all energy, positive and negative, is flowing in and out of it as well as through it. We are reflections, in a microcosm, of God, as Is All life and All creation. Therefore, we can safely establish that we are part of Him, His spark is within us at the heart center. And it is from here that we can connect to Him. He has never left us—we have left Him! We buried Him deep within us, amongst all the debris of our creation. All we need to do is to just reach within during our meditations, our prayers, or our reflections. We are not alone and never will be.

And There Was Fear

The actual events that led to the fall, as channeled through the spirit Joseph, are certainly reflected in the biblical fall and those of other religions, myths, and mythology. They are analogies of the true events presented in a form to help us understand the gravity of their consequences for humanity. However, unlike the Bible, it is not God, angered by our decision not to obey His laws, who has dispelled us, but we have. We are responsible for our demise, 100%, no ifs or buts about it. Besides, anger is not a Divine emotion, but a human one—a result of the effects of the fall. God Is Love and Forgiveness and all that is benevolent! With that, we must accept responsibility for our actions if we ever want to change the outcome. Taking responsibility starts with each person, individually, when faced with failures or negative events in their own lives. It is always the first step in finding solutions to correct errors and judgment. Those who choose to blame others perpetuate the negativity of the event, fail to learn and change, thereby improving their lives and potentially the lives of others. We also must stop blaming God. It is not only of no avail, it is also a waste of energy and rather negative, what else. We are, after all, living in a negative environment that only we can dissolve. Let's put that energy into changing this world, putting Light back into it, and returning it home.

So now, after the fall, when the angelic children realized that they inhabited a new, heavier landscape while being enclosed by a new, denser mass, they panicked. What were they going to do now to protect themselves from this new, rather threatening environment in their brand new shapes? And they started to worry. For the first time, fear set in! They never had to fear anything before. All was provided through the natural flow of energy, by the grace of Divine Light. There had been no lack and no need. They were always well-balanced, filled with light and love, reflecting the perfect harmony of God's Universe. Again, their forms had been of ethereal structure, mere suggestions of their cloaked substance beneath, and had been sustained by spiritual energy. Their communication was via their thoughts, their emotional expressions were via light and color bursts. Now, though, the children realized that their forms were actually physical, which meant that they needed to intake and expel energy physically. They had intentionally disconnected themselves from the spiritual energy needed to not only sustain them but to maintain their perfectly harmonious state of complete balance. Due to their solidification, they needed to absorb energy in a materialized, solidified manner—same with same. Hence, they had to physically ingest and digest energy in the form of food in combination with physically inhaling and exhaling the life-sustaining form of energy—oxygen. Their new physiques needed to accommodate their new needs and thus the human body evolved.

At this stage, their bodies were still in a more nonphysical state, unlike our current ones, but more physical than in their previous angelic state. As all is energy, then and now, they needed to place energy points throughout their forms, channeling, absorbing, and expelling energy all around. These were the Chakras and, although there are 88,000 energy points in the body, there were and still are seven major points. Chakra, which derives from the Sanskrit word and means wheel, circle, and cycle, is yet again another reflection of the cyclical and balanced energy flow of Divinity. These seven centers are lined up along our spine and are evenly divided into two groups with the heart in its center, reflecting the Dot. The three lower Chakras reflect the more physical needs of elimination, reproduction, and survival as the three upper ones are reflective of communication, vision, and spiritual being. Repeating the Dot in the center structure, the heart is located in the center, around which, spiritually, the two halves of the Chakra energy fields rotate, and, physically, from where blood, oxygen, and nutrients are circulated throughout the body. As the solidification evolved organs, operating in the fashion of the corresponding Chakras, the beings were built into solid matter with the skeleton holding the new form in its shape.

The heart and mind were originally united and charged by God's Light, but due to the lack of Light, they were separated into two centers, with the mind moving to the head. The mind became the physical aspect of creation, in the form of the brain, where incoming sensory information was processed and sent back out. The heart, on the other hand, was placed into darkness and consequently lost its position as the center of communication. The loss of Light also caused the lack of energy to maintain the heart's spiritual connection. And, so, we began to perceive through our mind, not our heart. We think through our minds and our brains operate—actually are in charge of—all our bodily functions. Consequently, all stimuli are absorbed by and processed in the brain center, through the eyes, ears, nose, and mouth. But, as a result of being purely physical, the stimuli that can be perceived are mere glimpses of what they really are.

We have deprived ourselves of true Divine Light. What we see pales in comparison to what Is, but our vibration is so low, that we really couldn't even handle its intensity. Then and now, true Light only comes from and through the heart. Nonetheless, the heart has not lost its status as being the real seat of creation. It is here where our Divine Spark is housed, connecting us to our Source. This is from where we feel and think intuitively, without the brain or, rather, ego interfering with and influencing us negatively. Like the sphere around the Earth, so has the ego become an autonomous entity running us in the direction best suited for its own agenda. It's a bit like the robot in sci-fi movies that evolves into being not only its own master but also the master of all and turning to become a threat to all.

But the angelic children had intentionally sought to separate the spiritual from the physical. They didn't want to experience the spiritual in a physical setting but rather experience the physical, without the spiritual, in a physical setting. This separation of heart and mind was just another step in the wrong direction, following their course of action and in line with their flawed theory.

With the advent of their new physical bodies, the angelic children became aware of real physical needs. They no longer were able to receive spiritual energy, and thus needed physical energy in the form of food. With that came fear! Now, there was fear of not having sufficient food and maintaining its supply, which became a source for worry about survival, lack, and need. Also, the physical need for shelter had become a necessity—one more thing to worry about. Would there be sufficient protection? Would there be food, shelter, and clothing? Would they have the weapons needed to defend themselves and establish their superiority, their power, and might over others? Fear, unknown until then, brought on survival instincts and, with that, the need for more and more power, by taking in more than needed from others. Their perceived lack of power (God energy) brought forth violence. We still fear to this day that we may not have enough, that we cannot ever fulfill our needs, and will face real lack. The underlying reasons causing fear are flawed, just like the belief this creation was founded upon. We perceive lack and un-fulfillment because of the imbalance of energies, the loss of Divine Light. We feel the need to fill ourselves with something, but can't quite understand what that may be. We are searching in all the wrong places, in all forms of addiction, and fill ourselves with material things, with riches and worldly possessions that can never fill that void. Only God's Light, in perfect harmony of balanced energies, will make us feel complete.

This was the moment when fear and violence were born and they have plagued us ever since. Spiritual energy had sustained us until the fall but from then on, flawed energy, insufficient and finite, became our resource and brought with it like results. The Earth was both conceived and influenced by humans, by physical energy instead of spiritual. It was influenced by their belief in lack and need for power, confusing them for their true need of God energy. Under their new set of circumstances, they were led to believe that they needed to protect themselves from their environment and from other angelic children. They founded communities, grouping together a number of people of similar beliefs, for their mutual benefit and protection. Now, of course, these communities fought each other to gain more power, more food, wealth, and the possessions of the other groups. Inevitably, leaders would rise from their midst promising to protect them and fight on their behalf, obtaining more power, also for themselves of course, and taking more from the others. These are the same leaders who have misguided us down the path of the fall, reincarnating, with their gang of followers, over and over again and never giving up on their fundamental belief that, one day, they will prove themselves right.

Violence begets violence, plain and simple. This was the onset of individual needs—for the I, mine, my family, my home, my team, and my country vs. theirs and the others. It brought on division and separation, walls, fences, and borders. And if history is a judge, we can state with certainty that nothing was ever gained from a fear-based society. We have never really changed any of the fundamental truths of our humanity, just the level of sophistication. Fear has, is, and always will be the opposite of Love, another negative effect of our flawed creation, and it has been running us from the very beginning. Due to the effects of the fall, we lost our faith, our knowledge that we are being loved and that we are love, and the positive energy we had discarded when we made our decision to manipulate the balances of energy.

Our endless cycle of violence then began, based on our perceived sense of lack and need for more. During the course of our history, these misconceptions have destroyed civilizations and brought us repeatedly to the brink of total destruction—an endless cycle of death and destruction, of violence, pain, and needless suffering, based on a flawed perception of creation.

Our energy, negative in nature, is stuck within the confinement of our Earth and is recycled back to where it came from. It lacks its essential counterpart to balance it through duality and give it its essential life force. Therefore, it is finite and unproductive, forcing us to repeat the same experiences over and over again, without us ever learning from them to complete the cycle and move on to the next. There is decay built in from the very beginning of an incarnation, because there is a lack of the offsetting life- and light-giving energy that would create a balanced charge to complete the cycle in its intended fluidity. As there is only negative energy sustaining us, we only channel out negative energy into our sphere, which consequently bounces off the Earth's crust and is projected right back into us as greater negativity. This outer crust, somewhat like the Earth's aura, is a dark, heavy physical sphere surrounding the planet. Like our auras, it reflects our beliefs and thoughts, which are currently mostly set to negative. Originally, the sphere was set up to serve us in terms of our energy needs. Over time, however, it has changed its intent from serving us to controlling us. It is like a parasite that feeds from its host, growing aggressively, gaining more power to secure its supremacy and in return destroying both. All our negative thoughts and emotions are projected outward, through our subconscious, into our Earth's sphere. They are swallowed by the field and regurgitated back into the Earth, and eventually back into us, with even greater negativity. We must heed our thoughts and stop adding to negativity by reflecting or dwelling on it and thus perpetuating it. Instead, we must think, feel, and see from the heart, and send out Light into all the negative events and situations that are circulating and concerning us. We must channel positive thoughts into the Earth's sphere to change its negative nature and refuel its Light energy.

Change the vision—change the world! Send light into the Earth's sphere to bring it back to its original intent. Send Light out, through the heart center, to bring about love, harmony, and peace, illuminating and changing what is dark in our world.

CHAPTER 4

The Dark Side

Sons of Belial

T he teachings in *The Children of The Law of One & The Lost Teachings of Atlantis* by Jon Peniel affirm, to a large extent, the information brought forth by the spirit Joseph. Here, too, God is defined as "One Great Being" that is All-inclusive, All-things, and No-things. God is abstract. God simply Is. This is a very difficult concept for humans to grasp since we are all about solidified form, identifying with dense matter and heavy weight. God is formless, ethereal, and infinite. In order to visualize Him, humans have given God a human form in paintings and illustrations that decorate churches and biblical scriptures. By doing that, though, God has been separated from us, as He became an individual entity in and of Himself. He is no longer within and all around us, but without or outside of us, and thus separated from us. As such, He has been given negative human traits such as anger and vengefulness, causing endless bloodshed and violence.

Separation has also created different interpretations and representations of Him through the various religions, which has resulted in countless religious wars and conflicts over the centuries. People will go to war over their version of God, considering it to be the only right one and thus having to defend it as well as propagate it. Naturally, the other side would feel just as strongly about their concept and validity of their beliefs resulting in unspeakable violence in the name of God. This is a case of many gods fighting for supremacy and survival—all un-godly values. God does not fight, nor does He have a need for supremacy or survival. By humanizing God, He has become an outside force and manipulator instead of a motivator from within and being within all things.

However, God is a "multiplicity that is One"[1] comprised of all things within One being. Just as the spirit Joseph states, here too creation is being described as a process of individualization through division and multiplication within itself. It is a similar process to the splitting of atoms. As a result, angelic beings were formed who were spiritual, ethereal beings with high vibrational frequencies. Their purpose was to experience while exploring the Universe, to create and un-create through thought as they saw fit. Again, they learned that they were capable of manipulating vibrational frequencies and slowing them down, creating the physicality and materialization of form. They also cut themselves off from God consciousness, as in the proverbial cutting of the umbilical cord. The process of materialization had gone too far though, and they were stuck in the experience, as they were incapable of simply resolving the illusion created. They were now separated and isolated from God consciousness.

---

1   Peniel, Jon. *The Children of The Law of One & The Lost Teachings of Atlantis.* Mesa, AZ: *Golden Rule Organization; 1997, p. 29.*

As we are being told, this was the first wave of materialization. Not all of us were part of this experiment and those who were left behind, watching in horror, decided to try to rescue their fellow angelic beings, constituting the second wave. They were aware of the danger they were putting themselves in, but due to their angelic nature of unselfish love and compassion, they believed that they simply had to save the others. So now, the second wavers were materialized as well by lowering their vibrations, but they too lost God consciousness as a consequence. They became just as steeped into matter as the first wavers. Some of them even lost their way and purpose, their true essence. As they separated themselves from spirituality, they became even more steeped into physicality, resulting in the first manifestation of the selfish ego. Their concerns were no longer for the benefit of the Whole nor for being One with all, but were for the one—the individual and the self. Both the first and second wavers inhabited Atlantis, but they were divided into two groups of people who were diametrically opposite of one another. One group was the Children of the Law of One, and the other was the Sons of Belial.

The Children maintained their God consciousness and their connection as best they could under the given circumstances, while the Belialians turned to the dark side, imitating spirituality and religious customs as a disguise for their dark magic. They used rituals, prayers, and visualizations to materialize whatever it was that they needed for their own self-serving benefit, their survival, and protection. They had absolutely no concern what effects their needs and consequent actions may have had on others as long as they were advantageous for them.

The Belialians were completely self-centered and self-focused. They used and abused others by whatever means necessary, from psychological to physical, social, political, and economic enslavement and imprisonment. They knew not of human rights for all, only for their own rights—their supremacy and domination of others. They had chosen to be succumbed by the darkness and had embraced their new ways.

The Children continued their mission of saving the fallen angels, but the conditions of this planet affected all. They too were losing more and more their spiritual awareness and connection to their memory. The Atlantean people were not only a highly intuitive and sophisticated civilization, but were also scientifically and technologically so advanced, that it is said their level of knowledge far surpassed ours today. However, over time, their disconnection brought on ever-greater excesses, corruption, and materiality, which led to the cataclysmic events that wiped out their entire island continent. This was not an act of God punishing them, but it was brought on by themselves as a consequence of their negativity, their dark thoughts, and selfish ways. The Law of Attraction works on individuals as it does collectively—we attract to us what we are putting out. Their negativity affected their environment and their climate, which brought on a devastating, and annihilating, natural catastrophe. Negative thoughts not only destroy the ones who are harboring them but equally destroy entire territories.

According to legend, Atlantis was thoroughly destroyed, but some of its inhabitants were able to escape before and after the catastrophe struck. They fled to many other places around the globe, and it is believed that many ended up in Egypt, becoming instrumental in the building of the pyramids. In any event, the survivors took with them their knowledge and their beliefs, influencing succeeding civilizations. The Children pursued their spiritual beliefs of unselfish love, harmlessness, compassion, and kindness, founding new "religions," mainly in the Far East. It is their mission to teach their beliefs so that we may change ourselves and thus change, actually save, the world.

Atlantis had reached the end of its cycle, lacking light energy to sustain or save itself. What happened to Atlantis can happen again and the question is whether we have reached the end of our cycle as well. Some may believe this to be only a legend and presume that this can never happen to us, or at least maybe not in our lifetime. I would like to point out the devastating tsunami of 2004 that occurred on December 26th in the Indian Ocean with its epicenter off the coast of Sumatra, Indonesia. It is estimated that it killed 230,000 to 280,000 people in 14 countries, destroying thousands of miles of coastline and even submerging entire islands. It not only caused great humanitarian hardships but devastated the economies of the entire area as well. In other words, it can happen again, anytime and anywhere. Prevention starts now and must include new thought forms founded on spirituality shifting individual and global consciousness.

Obviously, not only the Children escaped Atlantis' demise. Some of the Belialians did as well. They too continued on with their beliefs and their agenda to this very day. They are still driven by their need for power and influence over others. They must assert themselves and use others as their minions or as their forced laborers, meaning that you can either follow them willingly or be forced to through economic or psychological means. We have seen examples of such people throughout our history, and I am confident, if we look around consciously, we will find them easily in government positions, as political or business leaders, and even in religious organizations.

Their fight for supremacy and superiority has never ended, just escalated through the sophistications of their tools. They influence the masses through propaganda, brainwashing them into becoming followers, as if they were in a dream state, for, when it is over, nobody understands how this could have possibly happened. They control the people through the media, by altering facts and misleading them. They know how to create common enemies, or scapegoats, so that the people have something to focus their attention on, and therefore not paying attention to what is really going on. They also know how to keep them down, economically speaking, which creates a psychological down as the populace becomes worried and depressed about its livelihood. When people are so engaged in their own survival, in making enough money to make ends meet, then they become easy pawns in the grand scheme of things. The Belialians have a way with words, thereby fooling others so that they can take advantage of them and the situation. They must be in control and therefore keep the people oppressed and suffering. They have no regard for anybody but themselves and will walk over bodies, literally or figuratively. They have no qualm hurting or torturing others if that is the way to protect and further their agenda. They are equally disinterested in humanitarian or global causes, as they are only focused on defending their own interests at all times. They see no problem in harming the environment, animals, or even innocent children. It is all about them! The Belialians had been the instigators in swaying the other angels into following their lead to manipulate energies. Although angelic by nature, they turned to the dark side, removing themselves from spiritual energy, and embraced physicality—thus, negative energy. They were, and still are, steadfast proponents of their theory of imbalance, and have consciously distanced themselves from the Light.

Endless conflicts and wars have been fought to eradicate evil. We have to accept by now, that that is not a very effective way to change anyone's ways. We are merely supplying the Belialians with more energy to perpetuate their agenda. We have to rethink our approach and start using what works. If we continue to supply them with the same kind of negative energy that they are emitting, then we are the ones who are keeping the negative flow of energy going. We must think outside of the box, and send them that what they fear the most. And that would be Light. They are most comfortable in darkness, behind closed doors, and in secret and, by sending Light, we will illuminate their true self, hidden and buried within their selfish core. We also have to stop fighting them, as resistance creates persistence, and we have to stop reacting to them to defuse their negative energy output.

I have recently started to use non-resistance and non-reaction in situations that cause me discomfort or upset. I allow myself to calm down first by breathing deeply, then in meditation by letting go and dissolving that energy. I simply let go of what upset me and what actually invaded me like a hostile, foreign force. It may take a little bit of time, but be patient with yourself. Give your thoughts a break and move to your heart center. Feel and think with your heart-mind and forgive, both yourself and the other person. You will notice an enormous emotional well-being, an opening of your heart space, and a soothing warmth enveloping your whole being. Sit calmly and be present in this special moment, be at peace with yourself and the world. When you come out of this deep state of inner harmony, you will notice that your energy has shifted. It is no longer set to negative, that raging and aggressive force that holds you in its grip, but the other way around. Being in a state of peace, no longer attached to the conflict or in judgment, you have the ability to neutralize it by not reacting and not creating a resistance. Instead, you feel happy and complete, free from the anger and hostility that raise your blood pressure and create havoc in your body. Always ask yourself if the other person or event deserves to claim an additional gain by destroying you from the inside out. Now you can send out loving light and forgiveness, and know that you have become a Light worker. You have healed yourself with the inner light and helped bring more light to another and the world. A win–win for all.

As our world is teetering on the brink of a global crisis, it is impossible not to notice the exchange of energies between nations and their leaders. I am specifically referring to Kim Jong-un, the Supreme Leader of the Democratic People's Republic of Korea, referred to as North Korea, and Donald Trump, President of the United States of America. Both men have a great need to maintain their maniacal drive for power, for approval, and acknowledgment of their accomplishments, real or not. As one side provokes the other, their egos won't allow them to not react or resist since they have to have the last word and be more powerful and threatening than the other. This kind of approach will have only one way and one direction: an increase of aggression and conflict.

Although there is little we, as bystanders and nonpoliticians, can do to stop what is occurring directly, we can indeed stop it indirectly. Believe in a peaceful, harmonious world—see it in your imagination as if it were real and send light to those areas of concern. Visualization works like magic—what you perceive to be happening will happen. It never fails, but be sure to visualize positive things instead of wishing that bad things won't happen. Do not judge either side, do not hate or be angry, just send thoughts of love and pure white light into the situation and the hearts of the people involved. There is no need to overthink this; it's actually really simple. Our thoughts can and will manipulate vibrations, as they had in creating this Universe. Let's apply this magic to create the miracle of healing this world, and protect us all from further violence and suffering. Let's alter the current energy, which is set to negative, by infusing it with positive light. By bringing in more light, we are correcting the imbalance of our energies and bringing them back to a neutral state.

"The world will not be destroyed by those who do evil, but by those who watch them without doing anything."

ALBERT EINSTEIN

Einstein is right insofar that we do have to become involved and do something, but not in the traditional way of picking up our arms and marching onto the battlegrounds. This is a bloodless revolution from within, being supported by our spiritual helpers, to rise up and bring an end to our violent, ego-driven civilization. This is our time to rise up against the evil in our society, and bring back freedom and harmony. And we need as many light workers as we can possibly recruit to join us in avoiding total chaos. All we need is You and for You to change your thoughts.

CHAPTER 5

The State of Being

I Am that I Am

*"Thus men will lie on their backs, talking about the fall
of man, and never make an effort to get up."*

HENRY DAVID THOREAU

Now we know who we are: Angelic Beings. We also know what we are: Fallen Angels. We know how the Earth was created: via manipulation of energy and vibrations. We know what happened as a result: the fall. And we know who did it: we did. We also know that everything we see is energy and is based on the dot-in-the-circle principle, with God being both the Dot and the Circle, and that everything within has a frequency and a vibration. We are light energy but in a condensed state, as is everything we see and touch.

However, energy needs to be propelled by another force to find its direction, like the engine in your car, and that is thought. Our thoughts are the operators of the engine—starting it, steering it in the desired direction and hitting the brakes when needed. Our thoughts are the operators of our being, are the creators of this world, from the smallest to the largest element in it. We are both the operators and creators of this Universe, brought into the state of being through the power of our combined thought form. By pulling together our forces, we created a huge energy field, a magnet, which attracted more and more angels and joined us together. Our forms became One, our thoughts and goals were One, and thus we managed to create this Universe, built on a false premise and against the advice and warnings from the spiritual realms.

Now the question is, once we feel this to be true within us, how do we bring about change or, to be more specific, how do we undo what has been done so long ago? There are so many people in this world, there are so many languages, cultures, religions, and countries, and the sheer physical distances between us! It may seem insurmountable, but it is not! It all starts small, with you and me. We need to keep it simple, no complexities, we have to know what we want and believe in it unwaveringly to re-create our New World.

People around the world basically have the same dreams and wishes—we all want happiness! We interpret happiness differently, based on our backgrounds, family, race, and religion but we all want to fill our lives with joy and abundance, feel safe and secure, create new experiences while we challenge and are being challenged. We always want to raise the bar and shatter the glass ceiling. Happiness is the one constant in humanity that connects us—we are all the same at the core of our being. We have different cultures and traditions, but our core values, the very essence of our being, are based on our fundamental right, our birthright, of being in joy and peace.

*"Happiness is when what you think, what you
say, and what you do are in harmony."*

MAHATMA GANDHI

So, I ask you, "What do You want most in life? Are You happy, truly happy?" How do we define happiness? Happiness, as per the dictionary, implies experiencing pleasure and satisfaction, resulting in a state of being pleasurably fulfilled as well as possessing or having attained something considered to be good. Our individual definitions of *good* vary, but most people equate it with feeling secure which indicates financial security. There is the belief of finding happiness in owning a house, having more money, a better paying job, a new car, and all the possessions that promise to create our perfect dream. And once we have all those perfect material things, we still feel empty, dissatisfied, and keep on acquiring more, because we are empty and void of spiritual wealth. It's much like the addict who is looking for the next fix to get high while trying to find that feeling of being complete. We are all looking to feel whole and fully satisfied, of being able to blot out all our troubles. It's a never-ending cycle of filling our lives with things money can buy, objects and possessions that may be fabulous, but they are empty in the final analysis. For when we are lacking in emotional values, objects cannot fill that void. Although all things have spiritual essence—as all things have within them the divine spark and the dot within the center—if we are all about lack and need, we imbue that onto these things and therefore they are as shallow as we are. They are also temporary and fleeting in nature, and are bound to decay or breakdown at some point. It is fair to say that nobody, and I mean nobody, has left this Earth with all their money and possessions, nicely wrapped up, to enter the other side after their passing. Material values are of this physical plane, but our actions and our thoughts will always be with us and be a part of us. They are what define us and they either elevate or lower the level of our true inner beings.

Another state of happiness is having love in your personal life through relationships with your partner or spouse, children, family, and friends. It is about giving and receiving love, respect, forgiveness, compassion, and kindness. And it starts with you. You have to love and respect yourself first in order to give out love and respect to others. Love and respect should be unselfish but not selfless. For those who cannot love themselves, they limit how much they can love somebody else no matter how much love they receive. There is an imbalance blocking the flow of energy. In those situations, we cannot force our love upon them but can only channel love and light to heal them from within. We should not take this personally or feel anger and resentment toward them. It is best to let go and to forgive for they cannot give what they do not have yet.

Happiness originates from within and has no need for any material values. It is simple but it does require an understanding and acceptance of who you are. You have to start with honoring your feelings as you would honor the feelings of others for you are equal to all. You have to know that you are a worthy individual, no matter what your thoughts or past may have been. You are an aspect of God and, thus, know that you are worthy. Change starts with you and therefore it is you who has to believe in yourself first if you want others believe in you. If you want to be loved and respected, then you have to be open to giving and receiving. Set your intentions for what you want and then send out those vibrations. The energy you put out to other people is the one you will receive back. If you want love, then give love unselfishly. It's not a bribe to the Universe, though. You will get it back but not always in the form you expected to receive it.

There is also selfish love, which brings no happiness or satisfaction. It is just that—self-serving. It is abusive as it denies the rights of others, their feelings, and emotions. It is a power play of the stronger suppressing the weaker or needier individual. That kind of love lacks spiritual qualities. It is purely physical, ego-driven, possessive, and, in the end, stifling. As it is not love in the true sense but an abuse of power, it is therefore of this sphere and has no lasting values. It is another expression of feelings of lack and need that cannot be fulfilled through a physical approach.

Our society has become very materialistically oriented. We admire fame, wealth, and possessions above intangible values. We are driven by the quest for more of that and have gotten lost through the constant noise and busy-ness in finding what we believe will bring happiness. It cannot be found in worldly goods for they are of this world, thus flawed. We can only find it within, no money or fame needed. No fear or lack either, as the love we find fulfills all our needs. However, it starts with us bringing love back into our hearts through our connection to the spirit realms. Respect and believe in yourself, know your worth as a being, and honor your beliefs and be willing to stand up for them. However, honor those of others as well and be open to their new ideas and ways of seeing things. Do not block yourself off as that would restrict you from growing, expanding, and refining your vibrations. Never forget who you are at your core and remember that you count as a valuable member of God's circle. You are special as you are unique. You are the dreamer who can change the world into heaven on Earth. Your contributions are needed and ever more valuable the more God Light and Love you put into them. You have the power to change others as you are changing yourself—you will motivate them to become more loving and open to new ways. You will be the Light helping them to identify who they are and what powers they possess to bring about change as well.

We can either fall prey to worldly temptations, pursuing a life in darkness weighed down by heavy burdens, or you can choose to be that shining Light illuminating the darkness, leading away from the worldly temptations. But one thing is clear: we cannot do it alone. We have to reach out for the help that is there, waiting for us to ask. Reach out and ask and it shall be given to you. God is always there for us, reaching out His Hand but we must reach our own if we want to touch Him. A handshake requires both hands to be outstretched and touching each other.

We must take action if we want to see change. Without action and the flow of energy moving forward, there will stagnation and a continuation of the status quo. We cannot stick our heads in the sand and pretend we're not part of the human condition. Change starts today and with You. We cannot look to others and expect them to take charge while we're choosing not to do anything. We have to change trickle-down negativity into trickle-down positivity. You are the head at the top of the trickle-down, not the politician or minister, and it is up to you how you influence your environment. The more light and hope you have, the more you will transmit into your circles. And it will grow from there, becoming a movement of positive energy. If you want to change the negative climate of our society then you have to be the one who will start the movement by creating a positive environment. It has to start from the top down, which would be you—and not the politicians or ministers—healing the great divide.

We have to start with ourselves by becoming aware of any possible negative attitudes. If or when we detect negative feelings or emotions, we have to fill them with love and let go of them without judgment. Our peaceful, loving radiance will affect others even if they are not aware of it. It has a calming, soothing, and healing quality toning down the prevailing anger and hostilities. We need duality and opposing points of view for us to grow and expand upward. Therefore, we must be not only open-minded but also welcoming to new ideas and thought forms. We have to encourage dialogue and the exchange of beliefs. Most importantly, we must respect and love the other for they are as much the children of God as we are. If we disagree with their message, then we have to respectfully distance ourselves instead of insisting to convince them that our beliefs are superior. Rather than stirring up turmoil, we bring harmony to possibly bridge the divide. Each one of us has a responsibility in transforming this world into heaven on Earth.

Fear

We are constantly living in a state of fear—we worry about not having enough money, not having a job or being successful, of getting sick maybe because of some genetic misfortune, of losing a loved one, or never finding true love. We live in a constant state of anxiety and total stress. As everything is circular in the Universe, this too is a non-ending cycle that feeds on itself. The more we worry, the more we get worry back and worry more in return and on and on we go. We feel that we are not protected, that we are not safe unless we build walls, either for our homes or our borders. We believe to be vulnerable against a host of intruders and invaders that want to destroy and harm us, be it physically or emotionally. The standard response is that of fighting! We fight the intruder, be it a burglar, a foreign power, or disease—we fight it out! We live in a world of violence so it seems to be a normal reaction to fight violence with violence, intrusion with intrusion, pain with pain. Yet we are part of the Universe and all the applicable laws pertain to us in equal stature. As the law of attraction applies to all things, we all attract the same of what we are sending out or what we are doing. It's like an echo—what you holler into the woods comes back multiplied. The law cannot change and, thus, what we fear and do in response to it will come back—in this case, to haunt us.

Any worries, fears, or anxieties we may have and send out in thoughts or beliefs, we will attract back to us. If we believe that the normal state of being is one of suffering, pain, and loss, then we will draw that to us. If we fear that we are carrying a genetic disease and that it will affect us one day, then it will become so. It's a self-fulfilling prophecy. However, most people are not aware of their own thoughts or of the power that their thoughts have and hold over them. Let's not forget, we created this Universe through the power of our combined thoughts. Our thoughts have power, have weight and substance, and can change this world. On the other hand, that means that we have to become aware of our thoughts and have to heed them. Every thought carries with it a frequency and vibration, either positive or negative, and it affects the Universe. There is no way around it. Heed your thoughts and become aware of them. Once you are, you are in control and can direct them for the greater good of all.

The reason we have always felt the need for more is based on the fear that we may not have enough. This is a direct result from having cut ourselves off from our Source. Our Source of energy is what gave us the feeling of being safe and secure, of knowing that we are loved and taken care of. We lost our faith in what has been given to us, what is ours as a birthright, which has been and will always be ours. We are the children of God. He has never forsaken us and never will. We have cut the umbilical cord, severed the connection to the spiritual realms, which had been our support team. That is the emptiness we feel, the lack of being One with God, of being within His Circle and being near Him. He is still with us; we just need to peel away the layers in meditation by going within. We have to quiet our minds, our egos, and find Him in our heart center. The feelings of unsurpassed love, warmth, and incredible joy will fill you with hope and faith, and the knowledge that you are taken care of. Pure feelings of harmony and utter peace will flood your being, giving you a sense of being complete and Whole.

However, there are instances when fear is pathological, still a result of our altered states of energy but also being affected by the Law of Attraction, as in my late mother's case. She had almost always been a bit paranoid, maybe as a result of her distressing childhood and youth. She grew up during World War II, with wars raging outside and inside her home. Her parents were always fighting and arguing, causing her great pain and unhappiness. She got married when she was only 19 years old and moved from Holland to Iran. She learned to speak Farsi, German, and English, read philosophical and spiritual books, but also *The Inside Detective*, which certainly added to her growing sense of fear.

I recall that she would obsess about a particular subject for days, if not weeks, poisoning her entire being, driven by the enemy within.

She would look at all possible aspects of a situation, illuminating it and dissecting it ad nauseam, until the energy died and she would let go. This was the case in her relationship with my father and, in later years, with her second husband. Her fears and suspicions became obsessions about infidelity, dishonesty, and driven by a lack of trust. She was split between two polarities—love, kindness, and compassion vs. fear, lack, and distrust—her spiritual essence vs. her physical being. With time, her state of imbalance progressed, imprisoning her in fear and altering her state of mind. She was haunted by vivid hallucinations, threatening her physically and torturing her mentally, without the possibility of reprieve. There were so many hidden figures luring in the nooks and crannies of her brain, threatening her every waking moment. I believe that her saving grace was her fundamental belief in God and her spirit guides, protecting and guiding her out of the depths of suspicion and anxiety. Her condition deteriorated at an alarming rate leaving me at a loss of how to help her. It seemed as if I couldn't reach her anymore, couldn't break through the protective barriers she had placed herself in. She imprisoned herself physically, paralyzed by fear, while her dysfunctional brain was holding her hostage. As she became more fearful, she only attracted more fear to herself, as same attracts more same.

Fear and paranoia brought on an increased attachment to objects, a form she could identify her fleeting self with. That was her reality—an illusion, like our reality is an illusion on a different wavelength. Shortly before her death, she reached out to all those she had wrongfully accused of trying to harm her and asked for their forgiveness. She kept saying that she simply couldn't understand what had made her feel and act that way. She was diagnosed, postmortem, with Lewy body dementia, a form of dementia that causes hallucinations, and Parkinson's disease. A brilliant mind taken hostage by the effects of the human condition, yet the spiritual side awakened and rose above the darkness of the delusion.

The Power of Thoughts

Most people either dismiss the power of or are unaware of their thoughts. The average person has 50,000 to 70,000 thoughts per day! That's a big number. In order to harness their positive benefits for ourselves, and the world, we have to become aware of our thoughts, beliefs, motivations, emotions, feelings, and desires. Most of us not only let our thoughts run amok but actually also allow them to own us. They run our lives and we aren't even aware of it. They cause us to make decisions and to take action, which is a really good reason as to why we should pay attention to what we are thinking. Otherwise, we may not like what kind of reactions they may produce.

Remember that our thoughts were originally seated in the heart center and were combined with our feelings. The separation of heart and mind occurred as a result of the fall, moving the mind to the head center, its new physical home. From there, the mind and the ego took charge of our thoughts, and haven't relented since—unless we consciously work to change that state through awareness. By being aware, we learn to understand and accept our own personalities, who we really are, and what we believe in. We appreciate our own uniqueness as a point of strength not weakness. In honoring and respecting ourselves, without being either too egocentric or too humble, and in standing up for our own beliefs, we are reaching to become the best we can be. This is how we can use the power of our thoughts in a positive way, with kindness, compassion, and respect for other people. We will therefore no longer be insecure about who we are and how others will perceive us, or our beliefs, thereby taking away any power they hold over us.

During meditative heightened awareness, which is when we perceive our thought processes in slow motion, we learn to focus and be in the moment. From here, we learn to exclude all the noisy chatter of our brains that is solely there to distract and confuse us. Hence, we see and feel with great clarity; being truly present in the moment allows us to develop the ability to influence, change, and guide our thoughts. Now, we are in charge and by doing it through the heart center, we are guided by our feelings and emotions, our true self.

Being in a state of heightened awareness is the first step in understanding what we want our life's purpose to be and what we want in life. It assists us in mastering the turbulence of our daily challenges with all the ups and downs and confusion. The clarity in knowing what we want, rather than what we don't want, brings us closer to attaining it. Through concentration, focus, and stillness, we allow our heart-mind to steer our ego thoughts and us in the right direction, in harmony and unison. We will bring toward us that which we have put out in thought-form and will attract experiences that will help us to get to where we want to be. We may not get exactly what we asked for at the time of expressing that thought and wish, but we will get what is best for our growth in that moment. Be patient and surrender to the greater wisdom of the Universe in loving gratitude.

Our thoughts are the most powerful tools we have at our disposal, to not only change our own lives but also change the world. Use your thoughts to bring healing into our planet. Visualize a perfectly harmonious, peaceful existence dwelling in the beauty and magnificence of our Earth. Heal it with your loving thoughts. Respect, honor, and be grateful for all it has given you. Give back through the powerful energy your thoughts provide, sustaining us in the end as well. Use your heart-mind to heal yourself.

When you start your meditations, focus on being grateful for all your blessings, for we all have something to be grateful for. Then, see yourself as being perfectly healthy—visualize it as if it were already reality. Create your own reality. It starts with your mindset. So, set it to positive and make positive affirmations. In gratitude, start with stating your wants and wishes as already being part of your reality now. If you want to be wealthy, see yourself as being just that. Make positive affirmations with very specific images of precisely what you want to see becoming real. If you want peace, visualize what kind of peace you have in mind and truly see it in your imagination. You are the creator of your own visions through your focused and clear thoughts.

Think and see yourself as being in a perfectly blissful state—which is your birthright, by the way—and eliminate all fear and worries. Do not expect the worst-case scenarios unless that is what you would like to receive. Stop the negative mindset; stop the negative merry-go-round! Pay attention to the higher mindset and intentions, and the lower, negative ones will simply fall away.

Be not deceived; God is not mocked: for whatsoever a man sows, that shall he also reap. (Galatians 6:7)

Unfortunately, we are active participants in adding more negativity into our climate through our destructive thoughts and beliefs. Additionally, we are also mostly unaware of it. We are oblivious of the great effects our thoughts have on our own lives, our environment, and all our global events! We influence our climate through our negativity—it's not only our irresponsible environmental behavior but also our active, negative thoughts. We affect peace in our home as well as around the globe. The same negative thoughts that influence our personal lives pervade all aspects of our existence, from our governments to climate change. Thoughts have no borders, walls, or blockages of any kind—they are free to roam and spread their inherent messages, positive or negative, as far as our imagination will allow. Their ethereal essence is a remnant of our divinity, which we are either misappropriating or not using effectively for the greater good of all. Our lack of knowledge pertaining to the power and quality of our thoughts has supported our negative state of being. Unbeknownst to us, we are perpetuating negative thoughts countlessly on a daily basis, actually from one split second to the next. We are the transmitters of unguarded and uncensored thoughts sent into the Universe. We have been our own worst enemies, until today. As we now have the knowledge, we can become the transmitters of positive thoughts, lifting our low vibrations and increasing our frequencies.

Thought transmission is actually a very simple process; as we send out thoughts or vibrations, they are propelled out into the atmosphere, affecting those they touch, and are eventually absorbed by the Earth's sphere. As nothing penetrates its thick crust, the negative or positive vibration of the thought bounces back to the sender, again affecting people and things in its path. Thought forms travel in circular motions with the flow of energy we activate. Right now, we predominantly feed the field negativity—and it thrives on it. Strengthened, it sends it right back to us manifold. It has become a force of its own that will manipulate and influence us negatively. As do our minds and egos. Both macrocosm and microcosm, or the field and the ego, have the same mission, reinforced by our negative thoughts, and that is to keep us confused, divided, and imprisoned in our darkness.

Although we have caused the spiritual darkness we find ourselves in, we are at this moment truly ignorant of those events and their ensuing consequences. Additionally, knowledge that could have helped us to advance faster has been willfully destroyed, keeping us incompetent. However, times are changing, as are we. There is far more information brought to us from the spirit world than ever before and we have become far more open-minded to often quite challenging messages. We have reached a point in time where we are painfully aware of our negative climate and the far-reaching and devastating results that come along with it. It has always been our responsibility to correct our present condition because we were responsible for creating it in the first place. However, it is difficult to do so without awareness, which is why we must strive to learn more daily and to spread our knowledge so that others can do same.

At the same time, we are also witnessing an escalation in divisiveness and separation, creating greater isolation for the individual. Thus, we have two movements occurring at the same time: one that is guiding us toward greater spirituality or pulling us upward, and the other toward greater physicality or downward. The negative forces on this planet have, from the very beginning, been the more prevalent and stronger ones. This is, after all, a planet conceived as more physical— first, eliminating spiritual energy and, then, adding greater distance between that spiritual energy source and us. If left to its own devices, the physical (therefore, negative) energies will infiltrate our thoughts and behavior so discreetly that we will suddenly find ourselves completely corrupted and destructive without our knowledge. For that reason, the spiritual world is bringing us these revelations so that we can change and save ourselves from the threat of being thrown into complete darkness.

It is our responsibility to bring about change and that change begins from within. Until now, we have believed that change comes from outside, thus physical in nature, through new philosophies, policies, laws, and even punishment—yet no improvement can be detected to date. If anything, it seems as if the level of toxicity is increasing, poisoning every fiber of our being every day. There seems to be nothing that can be done to stop this until it runs out of steam. Yet there is, and it is to simply send out the Light into the toxicity. It requires so little of us but has such a great positive impact.

We are certainly active participants in spreading negativity. Currently, our political climate in the United States is extremely hostile, so much so that their supporters regard members of the opposing parties as the enemy. Hostilities are fueled by social media posts, negative rhetoric, and by the media reporting incessantly on breaking news, which incenses people. All this adds even more to the prevailing negativity driving many to lose themselves in the disturbed flow of its powerful wake. Apart from that, our government seems to be incapable of working together toward the goal of making life better for the people by using the strength of different points of view. Duality, in its divine form, propels energy into new directions, but in our physical environment, it blocks it through resistance based on self-serving motives. What we are witnessing right now is the onset of chaos, which always had but one purpose: to lead us farther and farther away from the truth.

On a personal level, we are ever more preoccupied with survival. For some, the pursuit of making a living is taking up every waking moment of the day, whereas others have become infatuated with the pursuit of wealth and possessions. In the end, both approaches serve the same materialistic purpose. Our society has become increasingly materialistic. The "simple life" has seemingly vanished forever; the appreciation of the joy of living and doing things that nurture us is lost. We are driven to make ends meet, pushing ourselves and trying so hard all the time yet never feeling that what we do is enough. We even forget the reason why we were working so hard in the first place. We never have time to enjoy the pleasures of life by spending time with others—all we do is rush around. That is not the path to joy. We have the right and the power to align our priorities with what is best for our true self. Follow your inner flow instead of the flow of worldly values. Enjoy, relax, reflect, and take time to be silent, finding there what truly matters.

The materialistic pursuit of happiness is derived from the feelings of lack and need after the fall. Ever since, there have been times when they were more pronounced than others. At the beginning of a new cycle, usually founded on the ruins and ashes of the previous one, there is a prevailing sense of soberness. The pain and suffering are still etched in the memory of the survivors but in due time, they are forgotten and so are the lessons that should have been learned. And so, the pendulum swings ever so slowly the other way towards excess and decadence, without sounding an alarm warning of the repeat experience.

Now, materialism is the driving force of our existence. Success is being measured in the amount of money we earn and in the possessions we own. We dwell on our looks, driven by the desire to look perfect, whatever that may mean, but it is something that is impossible to attain. There is neither perfection nor staying forever young, no matter how hard we may try. It is our birthright to live in joy and experience life in harmony, without fear or needs, but our circumstances here have altered that promise. Again, this is a result of our own actions. We have created a physical world with material values and goals. Our thoughts are so preoccupied with fulfilling our needs and attaining our dreams or fantasies that there is no time left to think spiritually. Our egos and fears dictate to take care of our needs, cluttering our heads with existential busy-ness. We are just so preoccupied with the self that we overlook the bigger picture.

The motives of the ego are survival of the self regardless of the impact our decisions may have on others, be they people or things. Ego-driven thoughts lack emotion and empathy. They are all about the self yet not grasping that we are all a part of the whole. It is not all about the I, me, or mine but about what is good for one should also be good for all. We are not alone and must respect others as we respect ourselves. If our pursuit of happiness denies others to do same, we violate their rights. We have to include the rights of our planet—we must treat it with respect, otherwise we may not have a place left where we can even attempt to fulfill our dreams. Actually, this planet is where we have the only chance to reset our beliefs.

What good are the mansions we dream of if we have destroyed the ground to place them on or the people we meant to share the dream with? What good is anything if we destroy our planet, our home, and extinguish life? We must start thinking of the bigger picture. We have to start treating others and our planet as we want to be treated ourselves. We need to love and respect all, through our thoughts, emotions, and behavior. The way to a new beginning starts with us.

We have to change our thoughts, become aware of their power, and start believing in the fact that we are the change we want to have. We are Creators, we are all powerful, and we are changing this world by changing our dreams.

When boarding an airplane, the standard safety precautions and emergency rules are presented to brief all passengers on the required protocol under any potentially threatening circumstances. In the event of a sudden lack of oxygen, we are advised that the adults or competent people must first take care of themselves by applying their own mask and then assist children or persons who need help. The logic being that we can't help anybody if we're unconscious due to insufficient air. So, it is with our spiritual rescue operation. We have to take care of ourselves first by changing our belief system and our thoughts. We also have to change our dreams and our goals. For doing that, we must be aware of what it is that we do and what we don't want. The change has to start from within by substituting fear with love and faith, doubt with belief and knowledge, dis-ease with ease and harmony, depression with joy. Positive thoughts are also a habit that we need to simply acquire—we need to work on them consciously. Often, it may feel easier to be complacent or to allow bad habits to linger, to dwell in self-pity, envy, or even hate. There is a sense of unease and discomfort when we go against the majority of prevailing mindsets. Free thinkers, such as Voltaire and Einstein, and open-minded people, like Lincoln and Gandhi, have always faced the predicament of cynicism and ridicule. Where would we be without those people who dared to stand in opposition of mainstream thinking? Those who choose not to rise up against all odds when their heart and their intuition tell them to will miss their opportunity to achieve their purpose.

We must take charge of and change our mind! Not fight our mind, because that would create ever-increasing resistance. As part of becoming more self-aware, we need to analyze who we are, without judgment or prejudice. We need to understand who we are and learn to love ourselves. Most people are highly critical and judgmental about themselves, setting the tone of how they treat themselves and others. Instead, we should be grateful for all the blessings we do have, for all the gifts that were bestowed upon us. A change in attitude will change the day, and all those it affects. Start your day with positive affirmations and most definitely gratitude.

Often, by the time we get to work, we are already heavily endowed in major negativity. Traffic, problems at home, endless negative chit-chat on the radio station, overwhelming schedules ahead, and so goes the day. Again, we are not in charge at this point. We're simply floating in a stream of negative energy. Awareness will get us out of the negative flow and stop the cycle. Once we stop, we need to start by loving ourselves more and giving ourselves enough time to breathe, to reflect, and to be actually in the moment. The more we run around, thoughtlessly and aimlessly, the more we play into the negativity of the field and the ego. We don't have a minute to think about nothing, to sit still, to go within, and to simply cherish the moment, to be there fully. We don't take time to enjoy the beauty in the flower or the glory in the music we hear. Our eyes are glued to our phones, tablets, and even watches. We're running around in a comatose state.

We are obsessed by the innuendos and small talk of our social media feeds instead of being fully present in the moment. A couple of years ago, I attended a businesswomen's luncheon where the topic was how to successfully manage social media. I needed to learn more about this marketing venue for my business. One of the speakers shared her secret of how she managed her time between her daily job and being in charge of the social media marketing department. Amongst many ideas on how to double task, the most striking was her recommendation of how we should make use of our bathroom time. She suggested that we should do our tweets or Facebook posts while being in the bathroom! The first thought that came to my mind was "gross"; second, and more profoundly, was that our last bastion of privacy and a moment to ourselves was being torn down in order to get some tweets or posts out. I was honestly mortified. Sadly, she is not alone in tweeting or posting during bathroom breaks as even President Trump shares this practice.

It's time to stop the insanity of being connected all the time, potentially miss the most important moments in our lives, and not allowing ourselves time off to reconnect with our selves. We believe, falsely, that we are more connected and informed than ever before, yet we are the very opposite. We don't talk to each other anymore; we don't make time to see each other to truly connect face to face. We are manipulated and held captive by our own inventions that were to set us free. We are becoming more isolated and lonelier than ever before—the consequences of which are being unhappier, less fulfilled, and needing more. It's a never-ending cycle of chasing our dreams and losing ourselves in the chase. The problem is that we are dreaming the wrong dreams—we believe that material values are our dream, but they are only as fleeting as the dream itself. We need to look elsewhere to find true fulfillment of our wants. We need to envision a better future for all, in peace and joy. We need to envision a planet that is sparkling with brilliant energy, working with us to achieve ever-greater consciousness, wisdom, and love for all.

CHAPTER 6

Easing Conflicts

"I alone cannot change the world, but I can cast a stone across the waters to create many ripples."

MOTHER TERESA

It would be fair to state that we presently live in very chaotic times. The Middle East is volatile, the Far East is playing with nuclear might, Europe's unity is being challenged, and the United States is deeply divided and governed through chaos—unpredictable, incomprehensible, and irresponsible. Our planet is reacting to our political and economic negativity, as well as carbon emissions, through climate change, catastrophic weather occurrences, cataclysms, and rise in global temperature. Our governments are, to a large extent, ineffective and corrupt, so are our financial institutions and large corporations. Our societies are disintegrating into the haves and have not's and there are far more have not's, creating a huge imbalance in the wealth distribution. Any imbalance creates a disturbance, as every action has a reaction. As Sir Isaac Newton stated, "Every action always has an opposite and equal reaction."

We have to acknowledge our current predicament without judgment. We must observe it in order to take inventory of where we are at this point and what has to be done to correct the course we're on. I am not here to judge or critique, just to bring awareness to our collective minds. Throughout the millennia of our civilization, we have found and tried multiple forms of government, from monarchies to democracies, totalitarianism to anarchism, dictatorships, oligarchies, and, under the umbrella of socioeconomic idealism, communism, socialism, and capitalism. Some have fared better than others, but in the end, they have all failed. All great civilizations have risen to power, fared many wars, and, ever so slowly, their star stopped shining so brightly and soon diminished. And this holds true for every single civilization, large or small, throughout history. For one thing, decay is built into everything on Earth as a result of the effects of the fall. Decay is the involuntary method of dissolving form, be it animate or inanimate. It signals the end of a cycle, regardless if we have gained knowledge and greater consciousness from the experience or not.

Deconstruction, on the other hand, is a voluntary form of moving from one successfully completed experience into constructing the next to evolve into higher awareness. As angelic beings, we visualized another possibility to experience in and then manifested that vision. When we had gained all there was to be learned, we de-constructed the illusion and moved on with ease, as it was all in the ether. On Earth, however, we move from one cycle to the next without resolution, which is why we are endlessly repeating the same patterns. We are stuck in our illusion because we are encased in and surrounded by heavy matter.

People, like civilizations, are also affected by the power they hold. Power is like a beast within that gets stronger with every victory, and with every successful act it requires an encore. As John Dahlberg Acton, first Baron of Acton, stated so well, "Power tends to corrupt, and absolute power corrupts absolutely." We have to make ourselves feel good all the time! To do so, we believe that we need more power, and the more we have, the more we want. It is not even need any longer but absolute greed. Countries feel the same need for more power and wealth as individuals do and so they take from other countries.

In an ego-driven society, the rights of one are superior to the rights of all. Thus, my or our superior needs justify any acts of aggression against others in obtaining what we want. Such mindsets believe in taking only, rather than giving and sharing, and hence need to protect what is theirs. As a result, walls, borders, and fences are built to protect what is within and hold others outside with the conviction that they would only diminish our wealth. They would rob us of our resources and threaten our survival, if not even our way of life. Yet, what is not being considered is the wealth they bring with them in terms of labor, new ideas, and opportunities for growth. Closing in is equal to blocking the flow of energy, the give and take necessary to produce new forms of energy. Without new energy, we cannot sustain life. This holds true for an individual, an institution, a country, and our planet. In isolation and separation, new energy is restricted from entering, thus only existing energies can be used until they run out of supplies. Death, in whatever form, is the imminent result. All energy must flow in a circular motion—taking and giving in equal measure to maintain a healthy balance. Therefore, building walls will be the demise of the country or person that erects them. It is equal to stagnation. The Berlin Wall is a case in point—West Germany flourished and rebuilt their country and economy after World War II, while East Germany, as part of Soviet rule and responsible for erecting the wall, continued their demise and economic collapse.

And, whom are we keeping out anyway? Our spiritual siblings! Let's never forget that as we are all Children of God, we are all connected to one another, are all equal, but different aspects of Him. In other words, we are keeping ourselves separated from ourselves. ironic and counterproductive! We need one another if we want to succeed in saving our world and us. We can't fight against them because they are us. We need to stop the culture of "us against them" but think of all of us in it together.

Many people fear the unknown, be it people from other parts of the world or a fear of foreign places, cultures, or religions. They fear what is new to them as if it were an invader and a thief stealing what they hold dear. The old brings with it a certain element of comfort and a false sense of security, for nothing can or will remain the same. Closed-mindedness is yet another blockage of new energy stopping growth in its tracks. God Is Change, and so are we, whether we accept it or not. We have to embrace new thought forms and ideas, which bring change along with them. Many resist change, but without it we cannot be.

Certain new thought forms may sound extremely foreign and downright bizarre, yet they only feel that way because they are new to our limited understanding. If we want to direct our future in a better way, we must remain perceptive. We also have to take an active role and take ownership of our future. We cannot sit by and allow others to take charge of our future and that of the planet's. We cannot sit on the sidelines and just push it off as the responsibility of politicians or statesmen. We have to become our own defenders for a better future—a better, more harmonious, peaceful, and joyous existence. And we cannot repeat the same tactics from the past. The same procedures will get the same results. It's the garbage in, garbage out principle, and so we need to rise up in peace, from within and with God Light as our tool.

This too starts with the individual—you and me! We have to start by changing us first, by being aware of our thoughts, and the power and effect they have. Start by observing your thoughts and analyze them, without judgment. Most are simply bad habits that we are totally unaware of. Many years ago, I would visit my brothers and their families in Pennsylvania for birthdays and special events. I packed my two children and my mom in the car; my husband usually chose to stay behind in New Jersey to take care of the dogs. Most of the time, we left late. I knew that the drive would take us about 2.5 hours without significant traffic, but, invariably, for whatever real or not-so-real good reason, we would leave late. At first, I was relatively calm, but as we reached the time we were supposed to be there, I became more and more nervous and agitated. I'm sure you've all been there. So, my mother asked if I was helping the situation by getting so upset. The answer was obvious, and got me just a notch more upset, until I allowed it to sink in. All I did was perpetuating more negativity, upset myself more without changing the outcome or estimated time of arrival at all. However, it made me feel righteous—it was the traffic, not I or we. In other words, I didn't take responsibility of my tardy departure and thus closed the possibility of correcting the action for the future. I, of course, was poisoning the day and all of us with my negative response. A bad, non-thinking habit that can be easily changed, once we start paying attention to our thoughts.

It starts with you as the center of your universe. It starts with how you treat yourself and how you think of or view yourself. Know and understand your flaws, we are all perfectly imperfect, and take responsibility. By doing that, we take away the power of negative thoughts, and the destructive, judgmental, and poisonous power they have and hold over us. Now we have the ability to learn to love our faults, put love and light into them, and work on correcting them. We need to change our negative thoughts into positive affirmations of love and hope while visualizing a different possibility. No matter how much I may weigh, I always think I'm too heavy. So, I call myself fat, yet all I attract to myself is precisely that, being or becoming fat. Once I realized that, I quickly changed my mind! But I do have to actively work on changing my thought patterns daily. It does require work to bring about change.

You will also have to learn to forgive yourself. Again, none of us are perfect in an imperfect world. It cannot be any other way, yet we can deal with our mistakes in a better way by owing up to them and forgiving ourselves. Forgiveness is an act of love and light and the first step to healing. As you are as valuable as the next person, you must do this for yourself as well as others; all energy is circular, so the vibrations of your forgiving thoughts will permeate the Universe. It often may seem very difficult to forgive those who have hurt or harmed our loved ones or us. We look for punishment, evil with evil, to pay back in same for what we have received. Again, the law of attraction works here too. It can't be otherwise. The law of gravity won't stop in your neck of the woods, it just won't. And neither does the law of attraction. We have to understand the consequences when we penalize the committed offenses. Do we want to change the perpetuators and help them become better individuals, or do we want to push them into more anger, hatred, and pure rage, continuing on their path of violence? As a case in point, Germany treats their prison inmates with respect and dignity while giving them considerable freedom and privileges during their incarcerations. Their model is based on human dignity being an inviolable right of each citizen with the aim to rehabilitate and educate the prisoners. The government's goal is that once the person is released that they lead productive lives, free of crime. The system emphasizes rehabilitation, not retribution, and accountability for both prisoners and corrections officers. If a released prisoner relapses, the officers, who have to qualify for the position and are required to go through a two-year training, try to figure out what went wrong and what they could have done better to prevent this from happening. The results of this model speak for themselves—Germany has about 63,500 inmates with a population of about one-quarter of the United States, which represents about one-tenth the amount of ours. The United States incarcerates about 2.2 million people, with significantly longer sentences than the German model.

When we learn to forgive, we have taken the first step in healing and taking away the poison from the act committed against us. If we continue to fight same with same, we will succeed in getting back the very thing we don't want. It has to start with having compassion because perpetrators are victims too, often of their poisoned minds or from horrible events in their past. I understand that it may seem difficult to forgive for the pain and agony afflicted on the victims and their loved ones. Still, we cannot allow ourselves to become part of the hate, for it will destroy us with certainty.

One extraordinary example in forgiveness occurred as a result of the events that happened on October 2, 2006, when a lone gunman, Charles Carl Roberts IV, stormed the West Nickel Mines Amish School in Lancaster County, Pennsylvania. Roberts had entered the school under a pretense, walked out, and returned with a handgun. In the ensuing confusion, one of the teachers managed to escape and ran to a neighbor's house to get help. Roberts made the boys help him carry in more guns, lumber, chains, and other items from his truck and then proceeded to barricade the front door. Afterward, he had all the girls line up against the chalkboard, released the boys, a pregnant woman, and three parents with infants. Another young girl managed to escape with them as she didn't understand his commands in English. She only spoke Pennsylvania German. He had taken 10 young girls hostage. Police arrived at the scene and immediately began hostage negotiations and asked him to throw out his weapons, which he refused to do. The girls understood the danger they were in and talked to each other throughout their ordeal. Just before the shootings, two sisters stepped forward and asked to be the first ones to be shot sparing the other girls' lives. They were both shot, only one of them survived. In the end, Roberts shot eight girls between the ages of 6 and 13, killing five before he turned the gun on himself.

When the police stormed the barricaded schoolhouse, the scene was one of pure horror. Glass, bullet holes, and blood everywhere with the bodies of these little innocent girls scattered throughout. They immediately attended to the survivors who were rushed to nearby hospitals. It was a heart-wrenching scene of the most unthinkable crime committed for no apparent motive. Roberts was

mentally disturbed and had stated in his suicide notes that he feared
he would molest young girls again, which he believed himself to
have done so when he was a young boy but apparently never did. He
left behind a wife and three children, his parents, and parents-in-law,
who were shocked and shamed over the crimes he had committed,
yet they too lost a member of their family.

The most amazing and unforgettable turn of events occurred on
the day of the shootings, when a grandfather and a father of one of
the killed girls warned the relatives and community not to hate the
killer or to seek retribution. Instead of hate, they wanted to forgive
the man who had murdered and wounded their daughters and they
wanted to reach out to all who suffered loss, including the family of
the shooter. They went so far as to comfort his widow and father over
their loss, some even attended his funeral as the widow in return was
permitted to attend the funeral of one of the young victims. They
were even given donations to help them through their hardship. The
Amish have understood the most basic of all principles—love! Love
heals all, love helps all, and love will make this world a better place.
And love comes from the heart, not the head. We should be thinking
more with our hearts than with our heads!

When conflicts occur, and they always will, we should approach
them from the heart-mind, not head-mind. The ego will always try to
interfere either in the form of self-doubt or superiority. In conflicts,
there are no winners or losers if the conflict has not resolved the issues
at hand, just moved them to the next stage. One side undoubtedly
will concede after a certain amount of time but that doesn't mean
that the issue has been resolved, it may just be transferred into the
next conflict. This holds true within the family, office, or global
setting. No war has ever really been won—one party will usually

concede as it has depleted its energy resources. However, unless the underlying issues are resolved as part of the peace negotiations, the next war is already in the making.

Every conflict and every war has different perspectives that need to be taken into account so that real peace can be made. World War II was, without a doubt, born in the ashes of World War I. The Peace Treaty of Versailles officially ended the war between Germany and the Allied Powers on June 28, 1919, but it didn't end the conflict between the nations. Germany had to accept responsibility for all the losses and damages occurred—in other words, accept the guilt for causing the war, make major territorial concessions, disarm, and pay substantial reparations. Germany was humiliated, not pacified, and it wasn't totally defeated either, only temporarily weakened. The harsh and severe penalties imposed, as well as the perceived injustice and bias of the treaty, gave rise to voices rallying public sentiment, anger, and lingering resentment leading to the rise of the Third Reich. A tragic example of the law of attraction at work—the harsh punishment brought forth harsher feelings of resentment instead of resolution.

Resolution starts with compassion and with emotions—and we only become conscious of these emotions when we activate what is within. We need to find clarity in the face of calamity, giving us distance and calmness from its intensity. By meditating, we will reconnect with our true self, our soul, and our Source, thus giving us guidance and putting light into any given situation. If practiced on a daily basis, we build up a foundation of strength and support that we can draw on in crisis. If a conflict still overcomes us, it is best to remove ourselves temporally, and to go within, letting go of all that is upsetting us. Our focused mind will bring us clarity and allow our compassion to forgive ourselves, and those who have pained us. We will learn to think from the heart with true feelings, allowing us to resolve issues and put them into the ether.

Anger or hatred is far worse than possibly not winning an argument. We are all equal players and we all have free will, so as long as we have made our perspective and objections clear, we should let go. Are we the ones who have to be right and are we always right? Nobody is always right and, remember, we are here to experience different aspects of being. But it is important that we work to keep the peace and harmony in our daily lives. That is another step in bringing more light into our Universe and into everybody around us. That's how we start to set our vibrations to a higher frequency.

CHAPTER 7

Hardening of the Outer Shell

The Ego and the Field

The Ego and the Field have a lot in common—they are both forces that constitute the energy behind our actions, individually and globally. The ego defines itself by possessions, beliefs, emotions, and experiences. It is the thought form that separated itself from the heart center and moved to the head center, a separation between being and thinking. The heart-mind center was where feelings, emotions, and thoughts were One, with love as the core value. Actions derived here were based on intuition and compassion, uniting and appreciating all as Being part of the same Truth. That Truth is our Divine Spark that unites and connects us all to each other.

As the ego moved into its new position and status, it needed energy for fuel, which is derived from fear—concealed by anger and hostility—complaining, faultfinding, and reactivity. However, nothing strengthens the ego more than being right, which makes others wrong. The ego needs conflict to survive and needs drama to assert its identity. Being right establishes a much-needed sense of superiority—morally, ideologically, and emotionally—and enhances the ego's position. Therefore, it must defend and protect its standing through aggression, be it verbally or physically. It is also constantly struggling to survive and enlarge itself for which it requires an opposite charge of thoughts or actions. The I-thought thrives on name-calling, labeling, and blaming others and any reaction is the fuel that amplifies further actions. For this reason, no reaction to other egos is the most effective way to dissolve conflicts. It should not be confused with weakness as it comes from strength. You can identify negative people easily, as they thrive on chaos, animosity, resentment, complaining, and faultfinding in others—they need that energy and responses to empower their own egos.

Not only does the ego need to be superior and righteous, but also unique, setting itself apart from all the other egos. It establishes this through its attachment to beliefs and possessions as they define its identity—a further step toward separation and increased individualization. No longer was the individual part of the Whole, but a singular, detached being separated from all. A totally contrary perspective from that of God's Universe of all being One where all are connected to each other and thrive in unity. The ego, however, thinks in more physical terms and cannot exist in nothing. It must attach itself to something that can define it, unlike God who Is No-thing, therefore All Things.

The ego expresses itself through personal belief systems, experiences, and possessions that set it apart from others. In order to maintain its position in society or family, it must defend its opinions based on its beliefs at the expense of another with opposing views.

Defense and even offense is essential to its concept of survival. In extreme egocentric and egotistic individuals, the ego cannot allow another to express, or even have, a different point of view. It is viewed as an act of hostility and defiance. The breakdown of our society has its root cause in the false power and preponderance given to the ego.

Our society has raised the level of the ego's importance to new heights. It is all about the rights of the one versus the rights of all. Gone are the days when we would allow and actually welcome the expression of other, or even opposing, opinions. Now, the egos won't have it. They feel threatened and respond in anger and hatred. Over the last few decades, we have witnessed the collapse of civility in our interactions and dialogues. Our rhetoric is becoming increasingly hateful and incendiary, where truly only one opinion is allowed to exist. The opinions of others are viewed like the enemy threatening the very foundations of our civilization or our own self. Through our increasing connectivity via social media, everybody not only feels empowered but also emboldened to express their opinions freely, or beyond the scope of civility. Anonymity has given rise to the expression of hatred but also of insults, inflammatory speech, personal attacks, and psychological bullying. It is alarming to watch the disintegration of our society. We are becoming more and more imbalanced, divisive, disconnected, lacking spiritual God energy, and playing into the dark forces of our particular environment.

This is the moment when we have to recognize what is occurring and take the power away from the physical forces. Those of us who have greater awareness also have a greater responsibility, and have to start the movement of taking the power back. We have to take charge of our destiny again and the only way to accomplish that is by infusing more spiritual energy into our world. We need to bring down the temperature, not raise it by spreading more incendiary thought forms or more anger. Our egos are not that important, but our heart centers are. We have to become the calming forces that do not engage in ego competitions, do not insist that we have to have the last word and always have to be right. On the contrary, we allow others the right of free expression, without hate and bias. We have to become the ones who soothe the infuriated and the angry who feel they have been forgotten. They are the ones who need our help most as they are easy prey for the dark frequencies to rile up and confuse even more. In our current political climate, it seems to be appropriate to attack members of the other party, be it verbally or even physically. We, those of us with greater consciousness, have to put an end to that and bring mutual acceptance, love, and compassion into our relationships and discourses. We need differing ideas and beliefs if we want to create new energy to produce new thought forms. It is what the Universe is based on.

Our raised social temperature is reaching a boiling point and will explode unless we take measures to bring it down. As all things are energy, vibrations, frequencies, and wavelengths, our increased heat is affecting the level of heat of our global climate. Coincidentally, as our social temperature has risen over the last few decades, so has that of the Earth. As we are all part of the same energy source, we do influence one another. As we become more negative, hostile and vengeful, so is the Earth. It is imperative that we lower our temperature. Let us bring back spiritual energy and let us channel love, light, and compassion to those who need it most. That is how we can start the healing process and return balance to our world.

The heart-mind knows that I Am That I Am—God Is, and I Am. I Am a part of God, and thus I am Love, I am Light, I am Joy, I am Change. What I own, nor what I think incessantly, is not who I really am. Those are simply constructs of the heavy materiality and physicality we have entrapped our true self in. The ego seeks to divide and conquer, to separate and isolate, to create superiority and righteousness for itself. It derives its energy from negative emotions—like anger, resentment, injustice, and so on; it needs those to feel superior and defend itself from a possible invasion by the other I or them, "hostile" perceptions and perspectives. It feels threatened by others because they either think or look differently as that would question the belief set created to define it. It has to define itself by form, as it is the physical, material expression of thought and emotion.

The ego is easily frightened by loss of possessions or people as those are the very things, physical things, that put form to the identity of it. It differentiates itself by describing who the 'I' is through visible and tangible elements. If or when these possessions have been taken away by accident or on purpose, by an act of God or humans, or simply through loss, the ego has to respond. And as we have seen with all forms of energy, there are two different reactions to loss: one is positive and the other one is negative. In the negative response, there is anger, faultfinding, complaining, hostility, aggression, and retaliation, which are all adding to feeling more grief and pain. However, in the positive response, there is almost a sense of peace, inner peace, and absolute faith that all will be well. There is a freedom and an unknown inner strength from deep within that is allowed to come through as the outer restraint of materiality falls off.

I have personally experienced this feeling when I was faced with a terrible loss. Many years ago, my husband's business had significant tax problems and, sadly, he was unable to resolve them. This had been going on for years, but had finally come to a head in 1993. At first, in March, the IRS shut down all his businesses and froze all corporate accounts. The loss of our income was most certainly stressful but what was worse was the unknown. How were we going to pay all the bills and salaries still outstanding? But, staying calm and collected, we found a way. The obvious other questions were of course how would we find another form of income and what would be the legal repercussions? We had hired attorneys and were working with them to find resolutions to our problems. However, on a clear Monday morning on September 13, the IRS came to our house in New Jersey with warrants to confiscate all of our possessions except for the most essential items like our beds, etc.

By then, I was six months pregnant with my son and the sight of about 25 to 30 agents, all dressed in black suits, white shirts with black ties, and black glasses, was intimidating, to put it mildly. They looked like "Men in Black," just not as humorous. After the shock wore off, panic set in. On account of my pregnancy, I was allowed to leave the house with my 2-year-old daughter. Before leaving, I quickly took all the cash out of the safety box and put it in the diaper bag and, thankfully, nobody checked it. Hysterically, I called my mother from a public phone (there were no cell phones yet) and she was able to somewhat calm me down. After I took care of my obligations, in sending enough money to my mother to last her a few months and taking care of other responsibilities, I returned back home. By sunset, they were mandated to leave the home, though not quite finished with the job yet, which meant they couldn't take all the items they were hoping for. However, they did just fine. The house was basically empty—bare walls, empty rooms, empty cabinets—it felt like we had just been robbed. Everything was gone!

When the day was finally over and we went to bed, my husband was going to set the alarm but turned around to look at me. Well, I cracked up! *Why bother?* I asked him. There was nothing of any value left behind that anybody would care to steal. We started laughing—the best medicine to reduce stress! We lost most of our possessions that day, and there was more to come. However, what I got in return was far greater. I found peace and enormous strength by going within. I found, under duress, my spiritual connection to God and I have never given up my special daily connection to Him since. As a result of this event, I changed the way I looked at possessions—they no longer define me or reflect who I am. They are there to be enjoyed and used and, in the final analysis, we are only temporary custodians of anything and everything. Nothing really belongs to us other than the experience it gives us, emotionally, and what we do with it or what we will get out of it. What matters is what we do with the experience or the objects that define us, not they themselves. You have to become aware of who you really are, your true self, the deep Truth within, not this or that thing. That's the lesson that should be taken out of emotional experiences.

I am aware that I am not the only one to have ever lost anything and it is never pleasant, yet it is part of life. It's a mechanism to teach us to not be run by things and, instead, to fill them with light and spirituality. It is in the giving that we receive. Others who experience loss of any kind may have the opposite reaction and, instead of turning to God, they raise their fists, figuratively or literally, against the heavens and blame Him. The ego finds strength in blaming and complaining by creating opposite charges that provide the energy needed for its survival. In order to protect the ego, it needs to find fault in others, raising its status to one of superiority, thus it turns to blaming and shaming others. It finds great pleasure in feeling that it is above others, superior and always right, regardless of any perception but its own. The results are all negative—anger, hatred, and resentment endlessly fueling the ego with ever greater power. The ego needs negative emotions to defend its position, its territory, and boundaries. It seeks to separate us against them, whoever *they* may be, creating enemies and outright hostility. Now the ego has something or somebody to fight in order to defend itself, because outside of physicality it has nothing—it's empty of all spirituality. Things give it form and substance, thus it must have them. The more negative the ego becomes, the harder it gets to penetrate its outer shell, its protective barrier, and the more rigid and cemented it becomes in the selfish position it has adopted. Now, it becomes ever more difficult to penetrate, to bring light into that ego, or to open it up to other possibilities or perspective to consider. Negativity abounds and is released into the Universe and absorbed by the Field. As the sphere around the Earth soaks up our collective negative energy, it too hardens its shell—like concrete that makes it impervious to alteration but subject to cracking and deterioration. The Earth's and the ego's encasements limit, if not imprison, us—both physically and spiritually—because nothing can penetrate the crust, thus blocking the flow of energy. Is it possible that the increasing rigidity of the Earth's crust is a major factor of our global warming? Nothing can escape its boundaries, while no new energy can penetrate it, either.

As there is always duality present, the two approaches available to us are to either fight or to let go. In order to let go, you have to become conscious of your thoughts, emotions, and feelings. You have to become aware by being still and going within. Just listen to your spinning thoughts, no judgment, just observe to become aware.

Then, in stillness, from you heart-mind, put love and light into your thoughts to change them. It will take time, but with patience and no pressure or force, they will break up and be released, thus freeing you from the negative possessiveness of the ever-aggressive and controversy-seeking ego. The fight approach will bring back the same as what has been put out. It will create bitterness, self-pity, and deep resentment, resulting in division and separation. In opening up to awareness, you actually find new possibilities and understand what it is that you must do to get through this situation. However, in closed awareness, all communication from your inner truth is blocked and the ego has entrapped your real being.

Negative people need drama, anger, resentment, and grievances like the air they breathe. Without negativity, they lose their purpose of being because they have not looked to find their true being within. They love creating discord amongst others—love riling them up to put them on the defensive, and thus having to fight for themselves. In the energy of fighting, negativity simply flourishes. And this is not only true for one individual or individuals, but also for nations, religions, races, ideologies, and societies. There is ample material that can be found on this planet to create grievances of any kind, fueling uproar and uprisings against one another. We are all different, yet equal; no two perspectives will ever be entirely the same. In reality, that is what and who we are, and we should celebrate our uniqueness as the basis of our being. However, the ego, collective and individual, cannot allow that, as it feels threatened in its position of righteousness and thus moral superiority. One side has to be right, and must defend its position by faultfinding and blaming. And so, have all conflicts and wars begun! Each side must be right and must protect itself, and its people, by fighting the other side. And when it's all over, the energy of the struggle has deflated itself, run out of fuel, and everybody has to start picking up the pieces. There are never winners; all are equal losers—today more so than ever before!

At all times, it is dangerous to believe that you are right and the other person is wrong—it closes the mind and the race to defending your ego—your believed persona and your standing—is on. It creates separation, division, and conflict, resulting in weakness. Not for nothing, the saying goes, "Divide and conquer." Our beliefs can be so strong and thus so blind that we are willing to not only kill but also annihilate the other. This is truly insane when you understand that the death of One is the death of the Whole. We are all One, aspects from One God, One Source. However, due to the effects of the fall, we have forgotten our heritage and our connectivity. How else could we explain the violence and brutality we afflict upon one another?

Religions are a prime example of the divide and conquer philosophy. Naturally, religions insist that their beliefs are right and leading to God, that their God is the right one and the only one. It therefore must define those who do not believe in that particular religion as wrong or infidels. Its veracity is supported by books, such as the Bible or Quran, documentations and collections of stories, and by preoccupying the individual through dogma, doctrines, and rituals. It blinds and corrupts the minds of the believers to the extent that they are willing and honored to kill nonbelievers of their God. More blood has been shed in the name of God, in His defense, and the protection of His territory than for any other reason. A very sad chapter in the annals of our history, and it is not over yet.

The belief that only our way is the right way opens the door to unimaginable acts of violence against humanity with the least amount of consciousness. The notion that we are the "defenders of the realm" justifies our actions against human life and human rights. Not only are religions guilty of this but also governments, terrorist groups, and big business, to name but a few. In the end, who is right and who is wrong? Those who choose to use force and aggression to defend their position, violate God's Laws. He is Peace and Harmony, not aggression and bloodshed. Nobody is above that law nor above another human being. We must learn, finally learn, to solve our disagreements lovingly and allow others to exist peacefully. The one has no greater rights than the other. One religion is not superior to another; it is simply another way of communicating with and celebrating God.

The way to God is simple and doesn't require being part of any particular religious group or institution. There are many paths to the same goal and to God. Regardless, those who choose to find deeper awareness and truth, will have to go within to connect to their Divine spark in stillness and in solitude. No egos or constructs, only You and God sharing a moment in time, being connected. This is the most direct and sure path to God. No complexities or complicated rituals needed to take you on to the path of enlightenment—all that is needed is becoming still, taking time out, and connecting through the heart center. The true self—our true identity and not the illusion created by the ego—will be guided by love and compassion. There will be no need for rules and regulations, laws and commandments, because the Law of Love and Light is the essence of our Being and we will live by its simplicity.

The way to get to this state of being is through awareness. Only then can we see and perceive other perspectives, and empathize with other people and their opinions or the situations. It allows us to be open-minded, to allow our intuition to guide us. Resisting or fighting the things we oppose will bring more resistance and fights. As Mother Teresa brilliantly said,

"I was once asked why I don't participate in anti-war demonstrations. I said that I will never do that, but as soon as you have a pro-peace rally, I'll be there."

She was clearly aware that attacking and fighting would draw more aggression and counterattacks, in reaction to our action. In today's society, we pretty much fight everything, starting with wars on drugs, poverty, illiteracy, animal abuse, global warming, and all sorts of diseases. The law of attraction is always the same—like attracts like. In order to change what we don't want, we have to ask for something we do want. We want peace, good health, and balance so then we have to focus on those instead of their opposite. We have to create positive affirmations of what we want to see or happen now. We also have to stop reacting and contributing to the spreading of negativity. By not reacting and not perpetuating, we will withdraw the energy needed to sustain and grow the ego's power. This is true for the individual and collective egos as well as for the Field.

The Field is the reflection of our collective egos. It acts and reacts very much like our egos, looking to establish its own identity. It was supposed to support us, to work for us, not against us, by becoming an entity in and of itself. Just like the ego, it stiffens and becomes more and more rigid with the increase of negativity. Therefore, less and less Light can penetrate its heavy crust, encapsulating our planet within its field of energy. It feeds on negativity as it lacks any other energy intake. So here, as with the ego, we cannot fight or resist it but send it Light in our meditations. Light is the God energy it lacks, and by sending it, we can improve the energy imbalance it exists in. Also, any positive changes in our thinking will influence and raise the Field's energy levels. We can effectively start poking holes in its thick crust to allow the Light to penetrate its darkness and heaviness.

Awareness of the ego's and the Field's roles, specifically their need to be in attack mode protecting their survival and proliferation, will free us from the power they hold over us. We can finally break free from our entrapment, our self-imposed prisons, in which our true self has been buried. The ego and the Field cannot exist in awareness, as their purposes are its opposite. Awareness seeks to set you free and allows you to perceive through feeling from the heart-mind, being conscious of who you truly are within, whereas the ego seeks to rule by conflict, by closing the mind to other possibilities and perspectives, defined by physical form and thought.

Fairy tales and allegories can often explain a complex concept far better—actually, they are there to do just that. So, it is this concept of the selfish ego, the entrapment of form and its ever-increasing rigidity, that can only be released through awareness of self, or rather be freed from that encapsulating outer shell. One such fairytale is *Beauty and the Beast*. It tells the story of the handsome, but selfish prince who, on a very stormy cold night, is offered a rose by an old haggard woman in exchange of shelter for the night. He refuses the offer and ridicules her for her looks, but just before he throws her out, she reveals herself as a beautiful enchantress. She punishes the prince by transforming him into a monstrous beast and his palace staff into household objects. She leaves behind an enchanted rose that will slowly lose its petals and, when the last one falls, the inhabitants of the prince's castle will lose their humanity forever.

The only way for the prince to break the spell is to learn to love another and to earn her love back, while still in the form of the hideous beast. As time goes on and as the petals fall, all members in the household become stiffer and more rigid as their hope fades. Their forms are solidifying and, unless a miracle happens, they will become the very objects they have been turned into. The prince is falling into despair, but, in the course of time, his personality has changed from who he had been before the spell. He has found his true self within, and on account of his predicament, he was able to raise his consciousness. In the end, the Beast is saved in the nick of time through the power of true love.

We, the people, are the servants and the beast, entrapped in our heavy crust, hiding our true perfect selves beneath all that physicality as a result of bad judgments and poor decisions based on a need to be right. We are not yet aware of our true essence and our endless need to prove ourselves right, then and now. Once we get to that awareness, we too will be saved, and the blinders will fall from our eyes, seeing and grasping what has been hidden for so long. We will infuse spirituality into physicality, return balance to our energy sources, and restore the light, thus illuminating the darkness from which we will be freed.

CHAPTER 8

Believe in Change

Your Infinite Power

"The world as we have created it is a process of our think-ing. It cannot be changed without changing our thinking."

ALBERT EINSTEIN

Infinite power seems so far-fetched when we look at our seemingly insurmountable problems and our minuteness in this vast Universe of ours. We think we are but a leaf in the wind, being swept up in the rush without the power or position to change our course. We believe that we have no say and are only bystanders in a world gone mad. However, we are neither innocent, for we were all participants in the events that brought this world into being, nor powerless. We have the power to change but are as of yet lacking conscious awareness thereof.

We doubt our strength. We doubt ourselves. We live in doubt and act out of doubt. When doubt defines us, it limits us. It reduces us to what our doubts are. It makes us live in fear—fear of the unknown, the future, disease, poverty, war, or whatever else may weigh us down. When we pay attention to our doubts and our fears, then we give negativity even greater power. We all hear those little voices in our head that cloud our thoughts with doubt and insecurity. They are telling us that we are not good enough, which, if give heed to them, will hold us down. The lower vibrations will always try to put us down, but we have the power to not follow that path. Pay no attention to the voices that fill you with anguish and self-doubt; instead, acknowledge them and lovingly let go of them. Without the fuel of your attention, they will cease to exist. Instead, allow your positive voices to build you up to the loving, kind, and successful person you truly are. Be your own motivator and generously give yourself Light and courage. That is true power, the power of positive thinking.

Mind you, we are inundated with doubt-producing thoughts all day long. All we have to do is listen to the news, read the newspapers, or spend time on social media. There is enough negative information covered to throw us into despair. We are living in very uncertain times. The world is in turmoil—everywhere we look! There are more and more politicians who run their campaigns and policies on fear, creating division and conflict. They rile up popular sentiment against perceived invaders who will rob our jobs, invade our homeland, and threaten our way of life. Their doctrines are founded on the basis of "me against you" or "us against them." Their rhetoric is inflammatory, disrespectful, downright cruel, and comprised of falsehoods for the sole purpose of inflating their own egos, while creating instability and public confusion.

Slogans like "America First" encapsulate, in a nutshell, the underlying sentiments—self-interest, indifference, superiority, nationalism, narrow mindedness, and uncaring—that are all opposite polarities to spirituality. No nation and no human being can do it alone—we cannot exist in a vacuum or in isolation. In a state of vacuum, no oxygen can either enter or escape, leaving stale and stagnant air within. Oxygen is a form of energy and, without new forms entering and old leaving to be re-circulated, no new creation and ideas can be born. Within a vacuum lies stagnation, leading to decline. We are all interdependent and interconnected and need one another to be successful. Those who only strive to serve their own needs will invariably fail in the end. Nobody will ever thrive or last at the expense of others or disregard of another's needs.

On a political scale, it would be considered a form of extreme nationalism, which always leaves behind utter devastation in its wake. This was the case after World War II when Europe understood that it had to integrate its nations as an antidote to future nationalism. Therefore in 1949, European and North American nations established NATO, a military alliance of member states, with 12 countries (membership now stands at 29 countries) that agreed to mutually defend each other if attacked by another power. Europe also formed the European Economic Community (EEC) in 1952 with only six countries but, when more and more countries joined, it led to the creation of the European Union. Under the leadership of the EU, nations joined in signing the Paris Agreement in 2015 making the alleviation of climate change a top priority. Not only did the European nations attempt to unite, but there was also a global movement toward solidarity.

As a result, the United Nations was established in 1945 in order to prevent another horrific war. Its role as an international governmental organization, which has currently 193 members, is to promote global collaboration and to create and maintain order. For more than seven decades, the world, under the leadership of the United States, had the prudence that strength, prosperity, and security are founded in union and collaboration between a network of allies and partners. However, President Trump has chosen not to reaffirm America's commitment to the mutual defense of the alliance's members when he addressed NATO leaders in May 2017. He seems to disregard NATO and considers it to be obsolete. His intentional omission to reaffirm the so-called Article 5 sent shock waves through its member nations, and for the first time created a rift in the Atlantic Alliance. Europe can no longer rely on the support of the United States, which undermines the stability and security of the continent, especially considering the resurgence of Russia's power and interference. Combined with President Trump's decision to withdraw from the Paris Climate Accord, a tone of separation and isolation has been set.

That tone is heightened by plans to build a wall between the United States and Mexico, and verbal attacks on and threats to other nations, be they friendly or hostile, and on members of his own or opposition party, while incessantly tweeting. Washington, DC is the headquarters of instability in the world. Doubt and anxiety in uncertain times undermine stability and give other, hostile nations an opportunity to sow even greater discord and create more confusion and distrust among allies. Russia is both benefitting from this situation as it is instigating it, while North Korea is seeing it as an opportunity to test its strength on a global level. As all things are cyclical in the Universe, so is this one—from unity in plurality we are down-turning toward individualization, separation, and into discord in singularity.

In recent years, there has been an ever-increasing focus on singularity, leading to detachment among people. The heightened importance given the ego is reflected in our product names and uses, take our iPhones, iPads, and selfies as an example. Social media is also geared around satisfying the need of the ego, publicly sharing personal issues and experiences, down to the most menial of daily occurrences—all supporting the inflated sense of self. As much as it pretends to connect through sharing and informing, it has the opposite effect of disconnecting and isolating us. Real experiences and direct contacts are replaced by illusion of social media. On the dark side, it has also become a tool for incendiary posts, hateful comments, and cyber bullying—all of which are made in anonymity and give a greater voice to malevolence. Recently, I liked a Facebook post and commented on it, which I usually refrain from. However, in this case, I had knowledge on that particular topic and so I agreed with the writer. I started getting responses but one stood out in particular. Not only did the person disagree with me, which is obviously his or her prerogative, but the response was personally insulting and truly vicious. I chose to tone down the rhetoric by responding that there was no need to be disrespectful as this was a discussion and should be about facts. It went on for a bit but I did not engage in return attacks and it lost its steam. In the end, the power of appeasement was stronger than that of indignation.

It is important to understand the true nature of positive power. There is no need to shout, attack, or brag to be powerful. On the other hand, there is no need to be too humble, either. Both are extreme opposites on the power scale where both sides need corrective repositioning. It is for you to recognize who you are and which power picture you would like to emulate. Many believe that power is only negative, associating it with powerful people who have abused their influence. That kind of power is finite, albeit it may be turbulent and destructive, yet it has no lasting qualities. However, true power influences and inspires people to reach greater heights on their paths of growth and self-awareness. People who use their positive power will motivate, love, and assist others in recognizing their own strength, yet they may be modest and gentle. These are not qualities of weakness but of strength. Knowing who you are will help you to find your inner strength, and allow you to own it. If you are too humble and lack self-confidence, you may not be doing others any good for you are hiding your true power and gift within. The gift is your Light, the ability to help others in growing and evolving, bringing out their own power and Light.

Surround yourself with people who will bring out the best in you and will guide you on your path to Light and Love. As you grow, so will those who you assist on their path. Your positive power will trickle down and cast greater and greater splashes. There is no harm in motivating and inspiring children from an early age. Instead of building up their egos for self-serving purposes, allow the nobility of their souls to emerge at a young age. You will help them to evolve and recognize the gift of their positive power. They will learn that the greatest gift is in sharing and in giving, in helping others—be it with a kind gesture or word, or be it on the sports team supporting others to play a good game. It is unfortunate and a sign of the "Me Generation" that we watch children who are only interested in what they perceive to be in their own best interest. On sports teams, the good players aren't interested in the group effort of having fun as a team player, but they're only in it for themselves. They need to stand out and often play the game for an ulterior motive—scholarships or professional futures. Coaches go right along with this kind of approach as it is all about winning and what it entails for them. The young generation is learning that it is no longer about team play, but about the individual play, missing an opportunity to learn the power united forces hold.

There has also been a great emphasis on winning or succeeding. Yet, failure is an experience and an essential component of learning. It is essential that we learn from our mistakes and figure out how to deal with failure. We can choose to be defeated, or we can consider it an opportunity for growth and a challenge to find inner strength. Everything that has happened to us in the past is for our greater good. We have to learn to love all our experiences, good and bad, for they are there to help us evolve and give us a greater understanding of life.

Whenever you remember a painful event in your life, change your focus to the good it has brought you. Change the narrative from a negative point of view as a victim to a positive learning opportunity and be grateful for it. Learn to love the events of your life and what you have made out of them. Only in loving can you let go of something. Do not give your bad memories power through your negative thought forms. The more you hate them, the stronger you are tied to their negative connotations. Love them and set yourself free.

You should also forgive those who have hurt you as you forgive yourself for hurting others. Forgiveness brings healing to all parties no matter how long ago the painful event occurred. In healing, there is hope for a better future because you put an end to your negative mindset. You replace negative images from the past with projections of a brighter future. It also stops the cycle of repeating a pattern as you have gained all there is from those experiences and can now move on.

Everything we go through has a deep purpose, with our best interest at heart. It may not seem that way at that point in time, but the more evolved we are, the better our acceptance and actually appreciation of these events. That does not mean that we only learn through pain and suffering, but it is part of our learning experience here on Earth as a result of our imbalance between spiritual and physical energies. Originally, it had been our birthright to experience through joy and harmony.

We can improve the nature of events by our attitude and our positive perspective. When we allow fear, anxiety, or worry to overcome us, then we seceded power to the negative thought forms. We are controlled and victimized by them. When I went through natural childbirth and allowed the pain to roam free, even if it was just for a second, it was as if it had invaded every cell of my body. The pain became truly unbearable and so overwhelming that I thought I surely would die. I would immediately correct my brief lapse in feeling sorry for myself, and start using my breathing technique. The pain dropped instantly. I had taken control and focused on the positive outcome of this labor of love. It was also faith-based—I knew I was in good hands and would be safe.

There is a deep knowledge within us all, and it knows that we are safe and secure. We also know that we are never alone and are being helped by our spirit guides and God. When we allow doubt in we give up faith, and that makes our journeys all the harder. It is up to us whether we undergo pain and struggle to learn our life's lessons or if we, through our positive outlook, choose to grow through ease and joy. We need to have faith and optimism again, especially when there seems to be so much darkness around us. Instead of being washed up by the wave of negative emotions of fear, lack, and violence, we have to consciously change our thought forms. Let us be full of hope and optimism. Let us be the peace and love we want to see in our future. Let us change our mindset from negative to positive by our sheer intent. We have to be the change we want to see.

You can tap into your infinite power through the practice of meditation. It will take a bit of perseverance and patience but given time and the sincere desire to change, you will be able to access your true source of strength and energy. As you will calm your mind and stop the merry-go-round of ever-repeating thoughts, you will learn to focus and find clarity. It broadens your perspective from the immediate, as if you were removing yourself emotionally and physically from the scene of events. It's as if you were above it or watching it from a distance, which gives you a more objective, wide-angle perspective. From here, you will be calm and optimistic— transforming negative, fear-filled thoughts into absolute positive beliefs.

You have taken charge and set the tone for your beliefs, moving them from the head-space to the heart-center. You are the one who has the most to gain from changing your negative views into positive ones as you raise your vibrations and thus elevate your radiance. You will improve your mood and emotional balances and reduce your stress, depressions, and feelings of lack. You will draw positive images you have envisioned, while releasing those that no longer serve you.

As you become this positive Light-filled person, you will radiate that vibration out to others. You will also become a different person, as you are no longer thinking from a negative point of view. No longer will you focus on what is wrong with other people, on problems, on differences, and divisions, but you will see the best in others—solutions, cooperation, and respect. You will bring the good out in others and calm any troubling situations. This is not to say that you will have to agree with everybody's opinions or pretend anything. It means that you do not need validation that you are right, but that you would like to focus on the positive and celebrate your differences. You will help others to become positive influences, motivating others to do the same.

This positive attitude and knowledge gives you such deep, inner peace like you have never known before. You could be in a tempest but you know that no harm will come to you. This assuredness will give you the clarity needed to lead you to the path intended for your growth. You will find that your higher self will lead you to find the right answers and solutions. Intuitively, you will take the best course of action in all situations and attract to you what you need to learn. You will draw to you the situations you need so that you can make the changes you want to see in your life. As always, you will attract that which you see in your mind's eye and what you receive will be what will prepare you for your next step. Therefore, be positive, have faith, and fill yourself with love and light. Then, share your positive energy and optimism, be the hope and the light leading others to higher spiritual elevations.

You can and will affect reality—it is up to you whether it is for positive changes or negative. You are not only the master of your own life but also for the world entire.

Whoever destroys a soul, it is considered as if he destroyed an entire world. And whoever saves a life, it is considered as if he saved an entire world.

Mishnah Sanhedrin 4:5

Stop thinking from your limited perspective and believing that what you see is all that there is. There is so much our eyes cannot behold on account of our physicality, so much we cannot hear or feel either as our vibrations are on a far lower frequency than the spiritual ones. Just dare to imagine, dare to believe, but if you feel uncomfortable in the public eye, dare to imagine in privacy. I have been a "closet spiritual" for many years. Now I have accepted who I am and what I believe in. I have found my confidence and my voice. I will never want to make anybody else feel uncomfortable, shamed, or bullied by my beliefs but I have changed my opinion on being reclusive. I feel that I must share the message of hope and actions needed to save our planet and us. It is not necessary, though, for you to do the same. The effects of light and positive affirmations can be done from wherever you are and in the utmost privacy. The results will be the same.

Never believe that you cannot bring about change, that you are too insignificant and powerless, and therefore choose to be a bystander. You shouldn't believe that the politicians will solve our problems and deal with our issues just because we voted for them and it is their job. You shouldn't push off to others the change that must occur—it has to start with you. Change must come from within and start with You. For any change to be effective, it has to be from the spiritual source of energy instead of the physical, human, and rather negative energy.

Change starts by not focusing on what you don't want. We don't want war so we must start by being for peace. We have to visualize peace, as we would like to see it, as we would like it to be. Visualize the world at peace and in harmony. Stop harboring thoughts of the negative imagery you are witnessing or are being bombarded with. Right now, feelings of pessimism and fear pervade the atmosphere, and scenarios of doom and gloom are filling our minds. We cannot help but take in the stream of visual images but we can choose to react to them in a positive way. Instead of focusing on the negative event, thus perpetuating that negativity even more, we can put light into the scene we are observing. We can visualize God Light flooding it and lifting the weight off the event and affecting the emotions of the participating people. You will not be able to see what difference your Light thoughts have had, but you can rest assured that they are bringing forth positive effects. Your Light will contribute optimism and hope to people and change the emotional climate of the Earth.

If you want peace in the world, you have to start with your own peace of mind as well as keeping the peace in your own home. We cannot judge or criticize conflicts elsewhere when we ourselves can't stop them within ourselves or within our four walls. As Mother Teresa has put it so succinctly,

> "Everybody today seems to be in such a terrible rush, anxious for greater developments and greater riches and so on, so that children have very little time for their parents. Parents have very little time for each other, and in the home begins the disruption of peace of the world."

The way to create peace within is through conscious awareness by becoming still, in meditation, and stopping the insanity of the incessant thought activity and the endless rush. If left unchecked and in the unconscious, we get swept along for a downhill ride. However, we have to first become aware of it to be able to change. We have free will and it is our choice which thoughts we allow in and which we choose to gently push aside. Don't fight negative thoughts because that will not only produce resistance but will also give them the necessary energy for survival and superiority. Remember, fight begets only more fight. Change your thoughts to positive visualizations and positive affirmations. Let go of the endlessly racing thoughts in your mind—the revisiting of negative events until they have contaminated every single cell of your being.

We have all experienced upsetting events or have been humiliated by painful comments made against us. Only you can decide how you deal with that negativity! Will you choose to perpetuate or to release that energy into the ether? Will you choose to give that negativity what it is seeking—more negativity? Whatever you choose to do, never forget the law of attraction: what you give out will come back to you in same. So, anger begets anger, violence begets violence, hatred begets hatred, and so on. Negative emotions don't even end there. When you choose to hate somebody, that hatred will affect the person you are focusing on and result in greater darkness for his or her soul. Your negative actions will make that person even darker or more troubled. As you are intentionally sending out hateful thoughts, you must accept responsibly for the negative impact they have on the other person. You are adding to the existing problem instead of alleviating it. But it will also come back to you, amplified, as all energy is circular. Do you really want that in your life? Are you really going to give that person or event the ammunition it is looking for? I don't believe anybody wants that but, as many of us are unaware of the effects our negative and our positive emotions, we don't know that we can change and put an end to them.

Negative energy is like a poison that contaminates the mind and the body. It creates disease in both: mental and physical illnesses as the result of harboring negative states of mind. I have learned to react with a non-reaction! I choose to remain in neutral, which gives no energy to either side. It's exactly like neutral on your gearshift in the car—it goes neither forward or backward, unless the terrain dictates the direction. The neutral state dissolves the energy that is needed to perpetuate the flow of any charge. It is also nonresistance—just let it be and it will lose its steam. Just don't fuel it.

It is not always essential to be right. Our ego will probably disagree with that statement instantly, but, then again, we are aware of its characteristics by now. The ego is selfish and self-preserving, only doing what it feels to be best for itself. No one else exists outside its realm. Our dysfunctional lives and times are bearing witness to the power of the ego—the individual and the collective ego of nations, religions, races, corporations, and societies. If everybody needs to be right all the time, then somebody will have to be wrong, or at least made to feel that way. And so starts the conflicts we don't want. We need to start with ourselves and not overly dramatize every slight or wrongdoing. We shouldn't allow our egos to feel so threatened and needing to defend themselves, which makes everything a declaration of war. The ego always feeling threatened and needing to survive is a result of the effects of the fall. In physicality and in dense matter, the ego has taken charge to protect us from any perceived danger to ourselves—our outer selves because the inner self is always protected. Our essence is always safe, but our physical forms are not, which is why the ego does what it does. So, it is up to us, our true self, to release the ego from its negative role by loving it and infusing it with faith.

Let go. Not everything is worth arguing or fighting over. Frankly, it would be best not to argue or fight at all. We will only increase the resistance and willpower in our opponent. We need to learn to apply nonresistance, non-reaction to defuse the crisis. Mahatma Gandhi is most likely the most well-known proponent of this theory. He was the leader of the Indian Independence Movement in British-ruled India and, by employing nonviolent civil disobedience, he led his country to independence in 1947. Gandhi's example has influenced and inspired many civil rights and freedom movements around the world.

"Non-violence is the greatest force at the disposal of mankind. It is mightier than the mightiest weapon of destruction devised by the ingenuity of man."

MAHATMA GANDHI

Learn to forgive—and to forget. Nothing can be more poisonous than negative memories that invade our thoughts and run havoc. They eat us alive—they destroy every moment and all happiness in our lives. They are your greatest enemies. I remember my mother telling me that my grandfather, on his deathbed, recalled images of his tough childhood. At the age of 86, he was still holding grudges against his father for the harshness he had to endure as a child. He told mom, vividly, how his father had woken him at 3 am to carry him into the fields so he could help with the work. Just think of the baggage he carried all his life. And what did it do for him? Other than poisoning his entire life, his marriage to my gentle, kind grandmother, and inflicting emotional pain on his two daughters, it did nothing beneficial for him either. But he couldn't let go. He allowed his memories to haunt him all his life, and he couldn't forgive his father. We need to learn to let go of things we cannot change and, through awareness we will understand which those are.

As you forgive, you will also learn to be grateful. Instead of seeing the pain that caused you to forgive, see the blessings in the act of forgiveness. You have now become the giver, the light, and relief of all that darkness. Be grateful that you have the awareness, the wisdom, and wealth of positive, compassionate feelings that you can do that. Be grateful for the sunrise and the sunset, the food, the family, and all the blessings you receive daily. The more grateful you become, the more you will be grateful for. It's as simple as that. Gratitude shifts your awareness to a very special place within. It is filled with love and joy that can only be experienced by doing and feeling—it can't really be put into words effectively. It's a natural "high." Best of all, we can be "high" all the time, whenever we choose to be grateful. I have also learned to be grateful for the tough times in my life. Those were the moments I have found the greatest enlightenment, the best books, the most remarkable coincidences, the most unbelievable help and guidance. I learned to open my mind and my eyes to new possibilities, learn and improve something about myself, and, above all other things, it helped me to deepen my connection to God and my spiritual guides. I consider those to be blessed events.

As you are learning to change your negative thoughts, you will most likely encounter roadblocks. The ego and the Field won't give up easily on what they consider to be theirs. Expect it, don't resist it, and put light into them. Send light and love back and defuse their power and potential grip over you. Check with your heart center for the right guidance to approach those blocks to your higher spiritual self.

Expect roadblocks on your path to spiritual enlightenment. Pessimism and skepticism will be there to challenge your belief that you can bring about positive change, that you can benefit your future and that of the Earth. Most people, if you dare to publicly challenge traditional mindsets, will consider you to be at best naïve, at worst out of your mind. And, yes, that's what we really want to be, out of our minds and in our heart space instead. Sometimes it is important to do something different because what has been done traditionally has not worked. The world has practiced the same beliefs and principles for thousands of years with the same outcome over and over again. Do we really feel that now, all of a sudden, we can apply the same violence-based thought patterns and produce peace? Now that would be a miracle! Garbage in, garbage out; violence in, violence out! Only now, we would be facing nuclear weapons if there were a global war. It is time to try a different approach to heal the ills of this world.

And, the world needs You! It takes a village to raise a child and it will take the village of humanity to raise the world out of darkness into the light. We will all have to do our parts by accessing the light within through conscious awareness, and sending that light into the world and into our neighbor. You will have to activate that light within as if you were switching on the light in your room. By switching on the light, we will illuminate others, and we will bring light into their heart centers. Where there is light, there is hope and there will be healing for all. We can no longer fight the violence of this planet with ever-greater violence—we can't fight the battles at all. We must create change from within.

It has to become a movement, a happening, where we lay down our weapons, our negativity, and go within to affect that which is without. It must be an uprising with light, love, hope, and faith as our support system. Every positive thought from the heart–mind center counts. Even the smallest change will affect the bigger picture. Every kindness, every act of light emission into the darkness will bear fruit. Those who are the darkest will need the most of our light. Send light into prisons, war zones, tyranny, and oppression as well as weather patterns, thus promoting the reversal of global warming. By helping others to become lighter, we help the Whole to be lighter. What light we send out and give will come back to all of us multiplied. As a result, we increase the levels of positive energy entering our currently shrinking power supplies, returning much needed balance. With every person we attract to be a part of our silent uprising, we tilt the scales in our favor. We need to bring about a greater balance and set the scales to neutral. Whatever we can do to bring in more positive energy through light and love, the greater and faster our recovery will be. Just know, Light and Love are the most powerful energies in the Universe, far outweighing the energy of hate and fear.

"You must be the change you wish to see in the world."

MAHATMA GANDHI

Suffering and Violence

It is our belief that suffering and violence are part of the human condition. So much so that we actually expect it! We expect to get ill and to experience pain. We expect violence in one form or another in our lives. Violence has many forms—it can be bodily, emotionally, or psychologically. You can be the perpetrator or the victim, but violence and suffering are part of this experience on this planet. However, you can choose to believe differently. You can set your own goals to exclude suffering and instead expect joy in all things you are doing now and in your future. Both suffering and violence are fear-based and result from the effects of the fall. You need not wait for the fall's reversal to change from a fear-based experience to one based in faith and love. Take your own life back by being positive.

Recently, I attended a small lecture by a couple who had written a book about the wife's journey of suffering through severe depression and inexplicable physical ailments at the hands of dark spirits to her healing through the light. Light workers, shamans, and avatars from the spirit world guided her to be healed physically, mentally, and spiritually. By sharing her experience, the couple wanted to enlighten and bring greater awareness to others. At the end, they opened for questions and I brought up Joseph's revelations about the fall and what had caused it. I thought that this would help them to understand the cause behind their experience but also to illuminate the fact that we can and must use Light to bring about healing change.

To my amazement, they were quite taken aback, and so was another person in the audience. They felt that if we were to reverse the effects to the fall, life would become boring, without challenges. They argued that life without challenges, albeit violent challenges would create lack and they would lose interest. In other words, life without painful challenges would be too boring. I really didn't get that, at first. I had to think about the meaning and, frankly, what they were afraid of. I realize that facing the unknown is quite often rather unnerving but I only suggested being in joy, harmony, and peace instead of being in violence, suffering, and pain. I was thinking of the millions of people who had been tortured, and are still tortured, the horrors of the concentration camps, the Cambodian Killing Fields, the soldiers returning from war having witnessed the most horrific aspects of our "humanity," the refugees, and the suffering of innocent children and animals. How can we justify that with the argument that we may not be challenged enough? That it would make life a bore?

I started to reflect on it, without judgment, trying to find an explanation to this incredible paradox. Finally, it dawned on me that we so deeply identify with being human, knowing only this human condition, that we can't imagine being without the constraints and thus the pain that comes with its solidified form. We can't think outside the box we have placed ourselves in, can't imagine a life without heavy, dense matter. We think in physicality, not in spirituality. We only believe in what we see, which is physical. The notion of potentially experiencing in joy is considered less challenging and, thus, not as meaningful as experiencing through pain and suffering. In other words, it's too easy. We are programmed to assume that life has to be difficult and burdensome for us to grow. We are brainwashed to believe that what we see is all there is. Restriction of any kind will prevent open-mindedness and disallow possibilities in new thought forms. There is an element of stubbornness in believing that our current way of experiencing, no matter how violent or painful, is superior, faster, and more efficient than the one in joy.

Not so long ago, people believed that children would learn better and faster if corporal punishment was part of the education structure. It was thought that fear of physical punishment would create better results and that children would learn faster so as to avoid it. Yet, the opposite is true and, thankfully, the horrible practice has been discontinued in most parts of the world. It has been widely accepted that positive reinforcement and happiness create the best students, guaranteeing the most successful outcomes for their education.

We need to open our minds and allow ourselves to imagine experiencing without suffering, without pain or fear. God never intended that kind of experience for any of His children. We have designed this form all by ourselves. Let us not forget that God Is Change and God Is Love. That being the foundation of the Universe, it contradicts the notion that suffering is a tool for achieving greater enlightenment faster. It is but a falsehood we must discard. Change your experience through Love and Light.

Elkhart Tolle describes the state of human suffering in his book, *A New Earth: Awakening to Your Life's Purpose*. He states that without suffering, children (or we) "would not evolve as human beings and would remain shallow, identified with the external form of things. Suffering drives you deeper. The paradox is that suffering is caused by identification with form and erodes identification with form. A lot of it is caused by the ego, although eventually suffering destroys the ego–but not until you suffer consciously. Humanity is destined to go beyond suffering, but not in the way the ego thinks. . . . Suffering has a noble purpose: the evolution of consciousness and the burning up of the ego . . . The fire of suffering becomes the light of consciousness"[1] (pp. 101–102).

Suffering and violence are a part of this Universe, are part of humanity, and cannot be separated from this, our human condition. Therefore, if we want to end this, we must change the condition. We must evolve back into Spiritual Beings and leave our heavy human forms behind. Our so-called "humanity" has not been able in all its history to eradicate the pain and unnecessary suffering. It is up to us now to start thinking differently, from the heart center, and to seek better, kinder ways to elevate to our higher and better selves. Let us free ourselves from such dark notions and wake up to better opportunities. Learning in squalor and confinement is not

---

1   Tolle, Eckhart. *A New Earth (Oprah #61): Awakening to Your Life's Purpose.* New York: Plume/Penguin Group; 2006, pp. 101–102.

only limited but also incomplete. We can no longer accept violence and cruelty as a status quo. Now we have the opportunity to offer change through the knowledge that Love and compassion are the best motivators. Let us dare to imagine a better today and future by changing the status quo to love and kindness.

Human Resistance

The attachment to form is human and ego-driven. We cannot separate our existence from form, doubting the existence of all that is formless. We need proof, endlessly, yet there is no tangible proof regarding spiritual matters, because it is formless. It's in the ether and cannot be beheld by the physical eye. There have been innumerable accounts of life-after-death experiences, for example, which have been brought to us by near-death survivors and through psychics and mediums. Still, it requires an open mind to accept that there is a vast Universe we have little knowledge of. Many of the great intellects and minds of our civilization, such as Socrates, Plato, Kant, Nietzsche, and Bertrand Russell, to name but a few, have believed in the super natural and in metaphysical theories because they have always tried to challenge the state of normal. Yet, no matter how much information is presented to us, if we choose to doubt and hang on to traditional beliefs, we cannot see beyond the physical—thus, evolution will be restricted. For the skeptics, there is never enough evidence to convince them to probe further.

Unfortunately, most people can only believe in what they see, but thankfully there are more and more who are not satisfied with that narrow perspective. They will be the influencers and motivators who push us to broaden our minds and accept alternate thought forms, bringing much needed positive change. It would have helped humanity if the scriptures had not been altered because they included clear references to our life in the spiritual realms. Now, with only fragments remaining, they are rather obscure and open to many interpretations.

As we only identify with form, we are attached to it, inseparable from it, and have an intense sense of pride for what we have accomplished in our history. It is an ego-stroking, self-aggrandizing emotion that camouflages our true incapability and incapacities, our tremendous shortcomings, and real spiritual void. Our accomplishments are measured in our scientific achievements, our culture, philosophy, literature, music, and art. We are also proud for our culinary achievements, our fashion—in other words, our way of life. Most are created to enhance life by endowing it with joy and beauty, helping us to get through our adversities, others to share wisdom and knowledge to elevate our souls and lift our spirits—all very redeeming factors. As great as our feats are, we are still immersed in our restricting beliefs that hold us back in perceiving a far greater reality. By allowing our insatiable egos to dominate us while being grounded in physicality, we have closed ourselves off to a far better and brighter vision of our potential. We still resist the notion that there is far more to existence than what we can perceive from our limited perspective.

There is a resistance to exploring the unknown, especially when it has to do with spiritual matters. For centuries, we have been constrained from probing into these super natural subjects so much so that it has become ingrained in our minds. It is as if we would cross a forbidden threshold, with severe repercussions. There is of course truth to that since many people have been punished and even burned at the stake for believing in the existence of other dimensions. Many, however, subconsciously hold on to their beliefs that our society represents a new form in experience and will, at some point in time, work out. This subconscious knowledge that insists our theory of life in the physical realm will be proven right permeates all other experiences and beliefs. Therefore, we are constantly repeating the same events, over and over again, resisting accepting the fallacy of our convictions. We resist accepting that we were wrong and that we have to change. We also resist that change has to come from new sources and different inputs. When something does not work, we must change our minds and think differently. Resistance only creates persistence of what is.

What a Wonderful World

"I see the world being slowly transformed into a wilderness; I hear the approaching thunder that, one day, will destroy us too. I feel the suffering of millions. And yet, when I look up at the sky, I somehow feel that everything will change for the better, that this cruelty too shall end, that peace and tranquility will return once more."

ANNE FRANK

Change starts with you, and me. We don't just wake up one morning and say to ourselves, "Well, this is the day I will change the world." Change has to begin within us first, by changing our story. And the story can only be changed when we change our vision and *really* believe in that vision. We start with baby steps, one step after the other. We may not be able to see the entire path, but it's really not even necessary as long as we take each step in the right direction. Be in the moment, embrace it, and don't worry about what is to come down the road. Right here, right now is where you begin your journey, where the future has its source and takes its direction. You decide your destiny one day at a time—find your purpose and set your goals in the now. Don't be consumed by the past and don't over-think the future. It is delivered to you in small, bite-sized portions.

Ever since my childhood, growing up in Munich, Germany, I always knew that one day I would live in Paris and in New York. I had absolutely no idea how I would get there but I knew that somehow or other I would end up living in both cities. And, so it was. I had applied and been accepted by the American College in Paris, staying there for two glorious years, and many years later, while living in Vancouver, BC, I got a job offer in New York City. It took world-changing events that I certainly had neither control over nor any foresight of.

My father—who was, by the way, dead set against my New York dreams—passed away in Tehran, Iran, in 1978. My mother had to settle his estate, which was expected to take about a year. In January of 1979, the Shah of Iran fled the country, and in February it became the Islamic Republic of Iran. My mother had unfortunately not been able to settle the estate in time and was therefore prohibited from taking out any money. She had no other choice that she could come up with, but to buy and export Persian rugs to Vancouver. The understanding was that the monies from the sale of the rugs had to be returned to Iran for the purchase of more goods. That's how we started our Persian rug business in Vancouver, which unfortunately didn't do very well and we had to close it after a few years. However, a former competitor hired me who later took me on a shopping trip to New York. I had threatened to quit unless I was going to accompany him, arguing that all his previous managers had done so, but secretly, an inner urging drove me.

He tasked me with visiting as many stores as possible so that I could learn how the big retailers displayed their rugs, what their merchandise was comprised of, and where the fashion trends were heading. I did as I was asked and visited Einstein Moomjy, The Carpet Department Store, where I met one of the owners, Mr. Ted Einstein. He heard my German accent and we instantly connected to one another, speaking German, of course. A few days after my return, I got a call from Mr. Einstein, offering me a position at his New York store. My intuition had become reality. I was moving to Manhattan, following my dream and inner guidance that had been pushing me to have the courage to stand up for myself and face the unknown. What happened to me shows that following your path to your destiny doesn't come in a lump sum, but in small increments. However, it also shows that you do have to follow your instincts and not be deterred by roadblocks. Follow your heart, and trust your instincts and divine guidance.

Changing the world starts with changing your own world first. Consequently, as the center of that world, you have to start with yourself. The first thing that you should do is to learn to love yourself. Some people need to work harder on this than others (I am referring to egomaniacs whose self-love, although superficial and thin, is ever-present, camouflaging a deep void). True self-love originates within, around your heart center, and can be found in stillness when the endless chatter of the brain is turned off. Go within and accept who you are, accept your faults and your strengths, for nobody has been solely gifted with flaws. Don't fight your faults, as you will only strengthen them. Love them as they are a part of you and in love you will be able to work with them, correcting and neutralizing them. It will require patience and time, but you can do it.

In loving yourself, you must also have compassion for yourself. Nobody is perfect on this earth and everybody has a story. Yours may be far more difficult and heavier to bear than mine, maybe it's karma, or a choice you have made before you were born to advance faster in this experience. Regardless of the reason, some people have unbearable hardships and tragedies that have formed them into who they are, but with love, compassion, and forgiveness the form becomes malleable. Slowly, the hard outer shell will fall off as the need to protect the inner being is broken down.

Recently, I watched a report about young, underprivileged children who suffered from very tough hardships in New York. On a weekly basis, dogs would be brought into their afternoon center where they could interact and bond. The counselor praised this program's efficacy highly as she said, "The children close their hearts to protect themselves," but the dogs open their hearts and allow them to love and to be loved. The point is that through love and compassion we allow ourselves to open up to others, to love and be loved in return, but also to be vulnerable. We allow ourselves to experience to the fullest—to feel and to be open instead of putting up barricades and walls, imprisoning ourselves. No happiness will or can be found in isolation and protection by being shielded from life. We all get hurt, it's part of life and the physical experience, but we can't ever lose our true identity of being love and light. We have to see it within us, as we have to see it in others. Underneath it all, we are all Light and Love.

Forgiveness will follow once we show compassion to others and ourselves. As we accept and love our flaws—in other words, stop resisting them—we learn to forgive. In forgiveness, we find peace and healing. When I owned a nurse-staffing agency, I obviously had a lot of contact with my nurses. I used to take call during nights and on weekends in the beginning of my business, and for about two years it was a 24/7 operation for me. Certainly, there had to be fatigue. One night, I received a phone call from a beyond-irate nurse claiming that her paycheck was not in the nursing office for her to pick at the end of her shift, which was customary. There was nothing that I could do or say that could have calmed her down and, finally, I lost it, too. I was yelling and screaming just like her, it was a terrible scene. I was shaking, and finally had to simply hang up on her. My night was over—I was shaking with anger and hostility.

We both fueled the conflict by responding, attacking, and defending our own perspectives. I should have said nothing and taken my beating. A couple of days later the problem had been resolved, the nurse called me to apologize as I apologized to her. I asked for her forgiveness for losing my temper when all I had to do was to be compassionate and to keep quiet. After that episode, she became one of my most loyal nurses and we held each other in great esteem. By forgiving each other, we were able to let go of our futile anger and instead embrace the true essence of the person underneath the physical constructs, which gave us the opportunity of developing a great relationship based on mutual respect. Also, this shows how destructive uncontrolled thoughts and emotions are and, if left unchecked, how lethal they can become.

Change really starts with you as you see yourself and your world with greater clarity. By going within, you will be able to peel away layers and layers of protective coating, like the peels of an onion. Slowly, you will deconstruct what painful memories and experiences have created, to shield you from more of the same, without being able to resolve the issues and to put them into the ether. By covering up, we're not allowing the pain to be deconstructed, an essential part of creation, and we're not opening ourselves up for new experiences without the baggage and fear from past negative events. We are also not allowing hope to enter our lives to lighten our burdens and let our true Light guide us onto the right path. By flooding yourself with Light, you will feel unconditional Love and compassion, which negates all dark vibrations that have adhered to you. Light and love neutralize negative thoughts, emotions, and memories, thus allowing you to open up to both receive and radiate positive vibrations. You will become the bearer of hope and faith in a never-ending flow of positive energy.

When you have become One with yourself and your greater consciousness, you are able to connect to others on a far higher level. You will see them through different eyes, peeling away their layers of protective coating as well and sensing their true self. You will see with great clarity that we are all the same deep down: we are Light Beings and we are all connected. You will become aware that basically all of us have the same dreams and fears at our core level. This is when you can learn to love the other for who they are, and accept them with compassion.

In every home, there is some level of dysfunction. Same with every workplace! These are the best places to start bringing Light, make peace with your loved ones and the not-so-loved ones, and create harmony through the emphasis of compassion and empathy. Be loving, unconditionally and unselfishly, kind and compassionate with your family, your spouse or significant other, your children, parents, siblings, friends, and coworkers. It's not all about "what's best for me," as this ego-driven world makes it to be, but it's about all of us, and each one of us. As we care and feel for others, we open up a whole new level of awareness. A change so profound will occur in us, awakening our true self and flooding us with deep faith and conviction that we are safe and deeply loved. What a wonderful return on giving and loving!

At all times, try to make peace and bring love to a situation. By being a beacon of Light, you will bring Light to others and give them hope. They may not know this and you may not see the effects, but it is so nonetheless. We also don't see that we age daily, but it is so nonetheless. Only after time passes do we see the effects of aging, just as we will be able to see the effects of our love and compassion have had. You know what havoc negative people can create in a home or office and on a global level. Most of the time, we can feel their negativity emanating and poisoning the atmosphere. There are times, though, when we are not suspecting it and therefore are unprotected, when we allow the negative radiation to invade us and linger for days. Usually, our gut instincts warn us if we are in imminent danger and need to protect ourselves by either leaving the situation or putting Light into it. We should learn to heed their advice.

Many years ago, when I danced with a young man, I felt as if a dark force was overtaking me. It started in my back, crawling through my arms and legs into my veins. I felt it as if I could actually see it happening. As quickly as possible, I ended the dance and left the room. When inquiring about the young man, I was told that he had a long, dark history and a rap sheet to match, and it was rumored that he may have killed people. His negative vibrations were palpable! Equally palpable, though, are good, positive vibrations and their benevolence can be felt and actually seen. When I see Pope Francis, I feel that he lights up the world. I have never met him nor am I Catholic, but his presence of loving kindness reach beyond religious boundaries. He expresses deep compassion, utter humility, and a boundless capacity to love. The Dalai Lama shares these qualities of nobility at the soul level and both do much good for humankind.

Our spiritual leaders have come to show us true spiritual power through humility and unselfish love. They need not try to impress us by showing us how powerful they are. We can sense their power, and that they are full of light. They are influential through their love for others and they motivate others to recognize their true self. There is a great need for more spiritual leaders and role models. Many of us are very evolved and need to express our qualities as spiritual leaders, positively influencing others who are attracted to our light. Spiritual power links itself to the higher will for the greater good of all in healing and lifting others into higher spheres of being.

Just look around yourself, and you will be able to feel the positive or negative vibrations of others. Choose to focus your attention on those who will lift you up and send loving thoughts to those who need your positive energy. As you grow in consciousness, your intuition will guide you to those people that will lead you to a path of greater light, sending you on your way to fulfill your life's purpose.

Just as Mahatma Gandhi had a vision to create an independent India through nonviolent civil disobedience and Martin Luther King had a dream to advance civil rights using nonviolent civil disobedience, so do I have a dream that one day we will all be One with the One, live in peace and harmony, in equality and liberty through the means of a nonviolent civil disobedient uprising. We can no longer remain silent bystanders to a world spinning out of control, driven into sheer insanity through the negative dark vibrations and energy forces. If left as is, choosing to let others do what may seem to be the right course of action, we will run out of time and it will be too late to shift gears. There will be a point when no correction is possible anymore, when nothing can affect a course shift any longer and no Light can penetrate through the encapsulating shield around the Earth and us.

In other words, we will have hardened our structure due to the increase in negative energy, thus becoming even more solidified and rigid. Simultaneously, our elevated states of negativity are contributing to the upsurge of ever more detrimental global events on all levels, such as political, social, economic, racial, and religious. Thus, we are increasing the level of discord as the tumultuous situations are heightening our fears and dark thoughts. This could result in another catastrophic world war or wars with extreme casualties to all life forms and horrendous damage caused to the Earth. At the same time, our negative energy is harming our atmosphere and consequently speeding up global warming, which will bring forth cataclysmic weather—again, causing death and destruction. According to the Spirit Joseph, in the event of such devastating destruction, making this planet uninhabitable, our immortal souls will be placed in stasis while the Earth is healed by devas, which are nature spirits. Then, we will return to start another cycle when we hopefully will achieve enlightenment to undo the effects of the fall.

I realize that this is a very pessimistic outlook where annihilation is entirely possible, unless we start correcting our energy imbalance immediately. What has to happen now, through our internal change, is that we alter energy levels to restore balance by setting them to neutral (like the scales of justice). By visualizing and manifesting Light, we return spiritual energy into the equation, replenishing the drained reserves of positivity. As the positive or spiritual energy levels are raised, our physical forms will become lighter and more ethereal again as will the density of the environment we live in. It will be as if our physical disguise will fall off us revealing the angelic beings we really are. Moreover, our planet will be restored to its crystalline, jewel-like essence again. We will then understand that the reality we have lived in was but an illusion solidified through our collective thoughts and materialized through a significant lack of spiritual energy. Now that the heavy veil has been lifted, energy can flow freely again, returning harmony, peace, and joy to all.

Now is the time to act. And your action is required to bring about change. Start today or, better yet, start right this moment. Make this the wonderful world of your dreams. Believe in it through your heart; see it through your inner eye as the perfection of creation. See it in all its glory and beauty, filled with bliss and hope. Feel the gratitude from your heart for such a world as if you had achieved it already. Make it real by seeing it in the now. That's how we will make a change!

CHAPTER 9

Duality

"Wisdom tells me I am no-thing.
Love tells me I am every-thing.
Between the two my life flows."

NISARGADATTA MAHARAJ

There is duality in all things, as one charge must have an opposite charge to create a flow. If the flow is to be harmonious, there must be an equal mix of the two polarities. The most basic, fundamental duality is between within and without, between the person you see in the mirror and the one that is not seen. In this, our current existence, we value what we can see—the physical, the material, and the form. We are mostly unaware of the spiritual—the ethereal, formless, and the invisible. Yet, both must be in harmony for one needs the other in this, our experience here on Earth. Without the awareness of our essence, our inner self, we are imprisoned by the physical side of self, and are condemned to suffer. Why do we suffer? Because we lack the other ingredient, as we are only half of who we really are. For we are angels (that is, our spiritual inheritance) in human incarnation (that is, our physical condition)! Here on Earth we are both, but at our core level, we are all Angels and therefore God's Children.

When there is too much matter but too little non-matter to sustain the flow of experience, then we stop, or at best, slow down the flow. This is why we are endlessly experiencing the same things, over and over again. We are repeating history and human experiences infinitely, without ever completing the cycle and moving into new experiences. If, for example, you take a toy plane and you load more weight on one wing span, let's assume the right side, then the plane will fly in right circles, over and over again. When you take some of the excess weight from the right and add it to the left, balancing the plane, you can steer it into any direction wanted. As we are right now, we cannot escape our circles unless we change the balance by filling the lack of positive energy with our innate Divine Light daily.

Imbalance created our solidification, leading to the creation of self as a form, tangible and visible to identify that which lies beneath. But the physical form has decay as part of its DNA, built in from the very beginning of this illusion, which is the life we are experiencing. Physicality is a temporary state and, therefore, the soul must return to its starting point in the spiritual realms, where it will begin its spiritual side of life. However, when a soul chooses to experience another life in physicality, it will reincarnate for a pre-set period of time. At the physical birth, the soul is endowed with a blast of vibration that will expand outward and grow until about mid-life. Then, intuitively, the soul contracts and pulls back from its physical attachment to the body and the Earth. As the soul is preparing itself for its return home, it withdraws energy from the physical body, ensuing deterioration and culminating in death. So, at the mid-life stage, our two energy sources are beginning to operate in duality—the soul, our spiritual energy, is pulling upward while it is incrementally withholding its energy from the physical body. Without it, the body lacks spiritual, positive energy, a form of starvation, and thus ages and decays, which means that the body is pulling in the opposite direction, the physical one. The body is naturally attracted to the vibration of the Earth, as both are physical and have negative energy. As the soul is pulling upward and the body is pulling downward, there comes a point when the cord that connects body and soul ruptures, much like the umbilical cord that is severed at birth. That is the moment when the physical body dies, as if the outer shell is falling off, and the eternal soul is reborn into the spiritual world, beginning a new cycle there.

Here on Earth, the physical body is the tangible evidence of the separation from the ethereal self and the Source, from where we can identify with our physical identity. As individual entities, we have not only separated ourselves from our own essence, but also from God and all other angelic beings as they have also chosen the same individualization process. Instead of us seeing ourselves as a part of all existence, in unity and harmony, we see ourselves as single, disconnected, and alone.

This perception, creating divisions and boundaries, impairs our vision and leaves us unable to see through this created illusion. We can only change this limiting view through greater awareness. Then we will discover the path to the state of selflessness, or less of the materialized form around the self. We will be able to detach ourselves from identifying our innermost being through the visual aspects of material things, such as our bodies and our possessions. Self-awareness will allow us to expand our perception of reality, broaden it and free us from our current limitations.

Attachment to the physical dimension will give it greater strength, pulling us down into lower vibrations. Form is created through the condensation of a gas or liquid by lowering its vibration; therefore, the more attached we are to form, the lower our vibration. The lower the vibration, the more unlike or un-matching we are to the higher, spiritual ones—we are simply on different wavelengths, making it more difficult to communicate with each other. Therefore, we are creating greater distances and boundaries between our higher states of being and us. Dissolution and detachment of form are necessary to reach higher levels in our evolution here on Earth, which we can attain by letting go in love and with compassion. Just to be clear, we always evolve, be it in the physical or spirit world, just in different ways. There is more to us than what we are able to perceive with our limited physical vision. We are so much more than the bodies we are in and the possessions we own. There is a whole Universe out there that we cannot see yet, but it is waiting to welcome us back home.

The origins of our spiritual and physical duality have been the subject of interest as far back as Greek mythology. Plato wrote in *The Symposium*:

> "According to Greek mythology, humans were originally created with four arms, four legs and a head with two faces. Fearing their power, Zeus split them into two separate parts, condemning them to spend their lives in search of their other halves."

As per Greek mythology, humans were originally endowed with both sets of genitalia, creating a complete being. The god Apollo added to the absolute separation by giving each half one set of genitalia, creating male and female beings. He then sewed them up, leaving the navel as the only part of their original unity. From then on, each human being was on the search to find the other half of its self, in search to make him-/herself whole again.

The Spirit Joseph, in *The Fall*, concurs with Greek mythology and states that we were split apart into two, the male and the female, as a result of the fall. Before that time, we were unified angelic beings, neither male nor female, but one whole complete being that worked in harmony creating and experiencing as one. In our current state, we are separated from our other half, our soul mate, and are no longer a harmonious unity but instead opposing polarities. For that reason, we will forever seek to find our other half to make us whole again.

We have, through our own free will, separated ourselves from God, from our angelic siblings, spilt ourselves in half and, to top it all off, distanced us from the spiritual realms and encapsulated ourselves into our physical bodies in a physical environment. We have also altered the energy balances to such a degree, depleting the spiritual energies almost totally, such that we are stuck in this creation. We can't see beyond the materialized boundaries to see the glory on the other side. Therefore, we cannot grow through knowledge and absorb the messages from the lessons we are going through. We repeat, search, and stubbornly believe that someday very soon, we will get it right and prove our theory of imbalance. We insist, at a soul level, that instead of having perfectly balanced energy levels, our theory of imbalanced energies will eventually come through and prove its efficacy.

In the beginning, we invested predominantly positive energy into our creation, while at the same time we were withholding the negative, believing that that would increase the speed with which we could experience in. The intent was to get in, experience, learn what could be learned, and get out. However, it didn't work out that way! The consequence was that it threw us out of balance and made us physically heavier. The illusions we were accustomed to experience in and then dissolve through the withdrawal of equal amounts of energy had now solidified like cement—very hard to break up. Our vibrations slowed down, which weighed us down physically even more and enclosed us into heavy, dense mass that stuck to us like glue. Along with that, it buried our connection to and our consciousness of God and dissipated our memories from the spirit world. Additionally, as we had chosen to use up most of our positive energy reserves, we were and still are left with only negative energy to draw on, which explains the urgency to infuse the world with spiritual Light. Spiritual energy in the form of light will ultimately tip the scales back to neutral. Our theory of unbalanced energy cannot ever work out as it goes against the laws of Creation, the Universe, and God where all things are in perfect harmony and in a state of equilibrium. It's time to rethink our position and start reversing the experiment!

No wonder that there is so much loneliness, sadness, depression, and feelings of incompleteness in this world! We are looking in all the wrong places—in materiality, power, drugs, and violence—to find a way to feel better, more complete, and whole again. We have been suffering both mentally as well as physically from the very beginning of our civilization. We have caused so much pain, both here and in the spiritual realms, as they are grieving over our condition. They cannot interfere, as we have been given free will and it was our free will that got us into this situation. Consequently, only we can get ourselves out of it. All they can do is to try and influence us positively to guide us back. In the end, it's our problem. If we want to heal the symptoms, we must go to the source of the disease and must heal from the inside out. We need to return to greater spirituality and allow God's Light back into us, so that we light up the world.

It is not naïve to believe that that is possible. In Jack Kornfield's book, *The Wise Heart: A Guide to the Universal Teachings of Buddhist Psychology*, he shares a story of one of his teachers and revered Buddhist elders, Dipama Barua of Calcutta. He writes that,

> "her selflessness bloomed in her smile, in her care for others, in her openness to whatever was needed. She was both empty and radiantly present. Dipama's heart seemed to pervade her whole body, the whole room, all who came into her orbit. Her presence had a big impact on others. Those who lived nearby said that the whole apartment block became harmonious after she moved in."[1]

Each and every one of us has the potential and possibility to give kindness, compassion, and love to others. Each one of us has the Light within that needs to be shared and broadcast. We have it in us to change the vibrations of our community, of our world, each and every moment. Every moment and every day is another opportunity to start anew, to reverse and reset our energy depletion. Open your

1   Kornfield, Jack. *The Wise Heart: A Guide to the Universal Teachings of Buddhist Psychology*. New York: Bantam; 2008, Chapter 5, Loc. 1194–1205.

channels of communication at your heart center and let the Light radiate, heal, and bring love to our world.

"Only in love are unity and duality not in conflict."

RABINDRANATH TAGORE

CHAPTER 10

Health

*"There is nothing that wastes the body like worry, and
one who has any faith in God should be ashamed
to worry about anything whatsoever."*

MAHATMA GANDHI

Imbalance creates toxicity in body and mind, as it does in all things. As the body is the physical construct for our essence, we are dealing with the duality of both physical and spiritual balances. They are represented by the physical intake and expulsion of nutrients—food and oxygen—and also spiritually by our thoughts, emotions, and feelings. Today, most people are well aware that if they choose to consume poor quality foods, smoke, abuse alcohol or drugs, that their bodies will reflect those choices with poor health. Equally, the body's condition is affected by too little or too much exercise—for example, resulting in sports injuries or in weakened

173

muscles and bodies. Sleep deprivation will without a doubt cause great damage to both body and mind.

What is still not well known yet is the role our thoughts and emotions play on our health. As Gandhi says, worry is the body's worst enemy, but it is actually more than only worry. All negative thoughts and emotions will affect the body with poor health. Be aware and heed your thoughts if you want to be both healthy and happy. Consciously focus on the positive and what you want to attract into your life. Pay no attention to negative thoughts and emotions, acknowledge them only and set them free with love and compassion. Same with the little nay-saying voices in your head: tell them that they no longer serve you and lovingly set them free as well.

We need to change our minds. We have to consciously be aware of our thoughts and learn to guide them where we want them to be. Allowing your thoughts to have the upper hand and take control will make you a victim of your own thinking. You will hand over control to the negative vibrations that will affect all aspects of your life, from your health, relationships, finances, to your overall wellbeing.

Our bodies are the reflections of our thoughts. The nature of our thoughts and emotions directly affects our bodies—its physical function, structure, and substance. Consequently, we need to heal our thoughts and emotions, our within, to heal the physical structure of our bodies. The origin of disease is within. Therefore, the cure and healing process must start within, too. As it stands right now, medicine treats the symptoms, and not the underlying cause, deep within our essence. Medical science is starting to understand the correlation between thoughts and emotional states, and their effects on the physical body that determine health or illness. It is undeniable that there is a body–mind connection affecting our state of health.

When I was about 18 years old, I developed lower abdominal pain, which over the course of a year became so severe that I decided to see my OB/GYN. During the examination, my doctor seemed rather alarmed and asked me if I had any plans of having children in the future. What a question! Of course I wanted to have kids. He told me that unless I was operated on immediately, I might not ever be able to become pregnant.

The exam had revealed a grapefruit-sized tumor that had attached itself to my right ovary and uterus. This was in late August and I was planning to move to Paris to attend the American College there. This would definitely interfere with my plans and my admission schedule. He urged me to discuss this with my parents, which I didn't do for three long days. After my mother asked me one too many times what was wrong with me, I broke tearfully down and told her about my diagnosis. She freaked out, understandably, but remained calm and collected in deciding what treatment course we should pursue.

The prognosis was dire; the possibility of a complete hysterectomy, based on a suspicion a cancer, was very likely. My father, other family members, and the doctor urged for an immediate operation but they were up against a mother protecting her child. There was no way that my mother would ever allow anybody to lay a hand on me without first looking for an alternative healing method.

Coincidentally, she had read a story in one of her spiritual magazines about a healer, Mr. George Chapman, who then lived near London and performed "surgeries" on his patients' spirit or etheric bodies with tremendous success. Mr. Chapman was a medium and, while in a state of trance, allowed the spirit of the deceased Dr. William Lang to operate through him. Patients from all over the world and all walks of life, including celebrities and physicians, flocked to him to be treated of all kinds of diseases, reporting unbelievable healing.

Dr. Lang (1852–1937) had been an ophthalmic surgeon at London's Middlesex Hospital from 1880–1914 and was by all means a very sophisticated and cultured gentleman, unlike Mr. Chapman, who was originally from Liverpool with working class roots. Mr. Chapman had been unaware of his psychic gifts until the death of his first daughter who passed away at only four weeks old. In their devastation over their loss, he and his wife were seeking answers through something like an Ouija board. They did receive spirit messages from their deceased daughter that she was well in the other world. The reassurance that there was life after death set him on his life's mission to share this knowledge, while healing the sick as Dr. Lang's physical body.

My mother had contacted Mr. Chapman immediately with an urgent plea for the earliest possible appointment. In the meantime, I had moved into my apartment in Paris and had started college but within the month we had an appointment with Mr. George Chapman/Dr. Lang. So, my mother flew to Paris to pick me up and then we both continued on to London. We had to take a train to the small town and then a cab to his home. As we got into the cab, my mother was fumbling in her purse to retrieve the address but after hearing that we were going to visit with Mr. Chapman, the driver didn't need any further information. He told us that many people made this "pilgrimage" and he drove to the Chapman home at least a few times per week.

As we entered the driveway of the home, a few Rolls Royce's were parked with their chauffeurs waiting. An impressive sight! We entered the modest home and sat in the waiting room filled with people from all around the world. I still remember the woman with bandages over her eyes, the elderly man in the wheelchair, and a young child afflicted with some nerve damage. There were patients who had traveled very far to be seen by Dr. Lang in the hope for a cure, which hadn't been possible through mainstream medicine. Now it was our turn and we were led into Dr. Lang's room.

It was decorated in a very old-fashioned way—dark wood paneling and dark, heavy wood furniture. Although Victorian in appearance and feel, it also had a very calm and otherworldly aura. It was softly lit in warm, soothing light, radiating a warm, loving energy. Mr. Chapman was sitting behind his desk, but of course he was now in trance, and therefore it was Dr. Lang who was temporarily residing in his body. Dr. Lang asked us what had brought us to him and so my mother told him about the diagnosis. He looked at me intensely, asked me a few questions, and then he concurred with the diagnosis. He also said that now there was so much fear and anxiety about any possibility of cancer that, most likely, they would perform a hysterectomy. He told us that he could cure me by operating on my spirit, or astral body, and that within three months the tumor would be gone. It would be passed through my menstrual cycles and I would notice real texture, which would be parts of the tumor being expelled. He then asked my mother to sit in the back of the room, while he led me to an examination table, upon which he asked me to lie down fully clothed.

Now Dr. Lang was beside me and his hands were hovering over my stomach and he was talking to his invisible assistants who were handing him invisible instruments with which he was operating on my etheric body. He must have had his hands about 10 cm or a foot above my body, and I could hear him snap his fingers when he needed a new instrument from one of the nurses assisting in the operation. The atmosphere in the room was what I would consider holy, as if this room had entered a different plane of existence. When it was all over, he asked me to sit at his desk again and asked my mother to rejoin us. He told me that I would be very tired that evening and that I must take a long hot bath, which I absolutely hated and still do to this day, but I followed his instructions. He also told me that I needed to drink a lot of water and that I wasn't drinking enough anyway. Then he stated that the young girls "these days" were simply too engaged and needed more time to relax and reflect. Yes, he was definitely speaking from the past. However, he did urge me to take it easy, to rest a lot, and not to strain myself unnecessarily.

I did as I was told and I took a bath when we got to our hotel room. I was utterly exhausted and went to sleep right away. The next morning, I returned to Paris and my mother went back to Munich. When my next cycle occurred, I understood what he meant. There were actual large pieces of the tumor being expelled, and I was extraordinarily fatigued and weak. The cycle after that was lighter and, by now, it was already Thanksgiving and since I was attending an American college adhering to standard holidays, I went home for the break. I had made an appointment with my OB/GYN for a checkup even before my departure as we had tentatively scheduled an operation during the winter session break. I had never informed my doctor that I was going to see a spirit healer nor did I tell him about it afterward, as I knew he would only dismiss it as foolishness.

I watched him intently as he examined me and noticed that he checked his notes after the physical exam, looked perplexed, and then proceeded to examine me again. He was dumbfounded! All he was capable of saying was that he must have been wrong with his original diagnosis regarding the size of the tumor. He also assured me that I did not need to rush into making any decisions right now. When I returned to see him after Christmas, the tumor was completely gone; it had disappeared into nothingness and was now categorized as a large cyst that had dissolved itself.

At that time, I was not ready to discuss my otherworldly treatment with my doctor, or, for that matter, with anybody else outside of my family. I knew I would be either ridiculed or be labeled a freak. Therefore, I chose not to talk about my miraculous spirit healing. I simply was not ready to argue with the skeptics who would question the original diagnosis and would argue that the healing method was nothing short of quackery. Skeptics would find it difficult to comprehend healing through the hands of a medium guided by a deceased ophthalmologist! I must assume that he gained greater knowledge in the spirit world of the complete body so that he could astral operate on all parts effectively. People would argue, I felt, that I had been brainwashed and that my mind had healed me through my beliefs. As we know, that is possible but, in this case, it was the operation performed on my astral body that removed the tumor.

The cause of my illness had been a medication, DES (diethylstilbestrol), a synthetic estrogen that my mother had been prescribed during her pregnancies with my older brother and me. It was intended to prevent sudden miscarriages, which, unfortunately, remained unchanged and also sadly affected the embryos. Young adults who had been exposed to DES in utero developed—during their late teens and early 20s—serious illnesses such as a variety of cancers (breast, cervical, and vaginal) or noncancerous testicular tumors. Additionally, most would also be affected by infertility as well as complications during their pregnancies. Dr. Lang agreed that DES had led me to become so terribly ill.

After this event, I had no doubt that there was so much more to us than we were capable of perceiving with our limited earthly vision. I knew that there was life after death—or, rather, that there is no death at all but transition and only temporary separation. Death only occurs to the physical body, our outer shell, which falls off releasing the soul back to the spirit world. Upon arrival, we are taken care of and greeted by someone we have known in life. As most souls will be still in shock when they realize that they are alive but no longer attached to their bodies, they are greeted by familiar souls, helping them to calm down. Then they are moved to holding areas so they can disconnect from physicality, be cleansed from negative thought forms, convalesce from trauma, and start raising their vibrations. For those who are spiritually aware, this step may not be necessary and they transition straight into the sphere that corresponds to their vibrational rate, which is determined by the soul's experience, spiritual evolution and the history of the life, or lives lived. Every soul is placed into a sphere that is determined by the quality of its life and its thoughts. So, those who have dark and even monstrous thoughts and lived accordingly will be placed into a sphere matching their low vibrational rate. Same attracts same, which applies in both the spirit as the physical world! You are placed with souls who are just like you, not based on judgment but rather on similar energy that you are attracted to. There are a great many spheres from the really dark, to the mundane, to the very ethereal and spiritual areas matching the status of each soul. You will be there for as long as you choose and you will evolve spiritually, even on the lowest levels. The key to existence on both sides is to raise your vibrations and that holds true for all souls regardless of their status. The length of our stay in the spirit world depends on us – we can choose to be there 'forever' or decide to return to Earth in a new incarnation. Both experiences serve to enlighten the soul, help it grow and raise its vibrational rate. But here's the thing: both our physical and spiritual worlds are contaminated with our particular energy imbalance and thus we are in a form of quarantine. Ours is not the only one of God's universes but we are singular based on our low and dense vibrational states due to our unbalanced energies. Therefore, we are being segregated from the angels in the other universes so that we do not infect them with our flawed beliefs. Raising our vibrations with divine Light will set us free on both sides and allow us to reintegrate into our vast cosmos.

My experience helped me to understand that healing can come from many sources and different applications, that there is so much that we still have to learn about spiritual healing or healing the spirit. As we become more aware of the relationship between negative emotions and disease, we realize that illness is often a reflection of what is occurring at our soul level, which we are usually unaware of. In my case for example, I can't say that I was negative in any way, but I was most certainly affected by the hormones that were given to my mother during pregnancy. We are also susceptible to pesticides and hormones treating our food sources, the water we drink, pollution or our genetic inheritance, thus unrelated to our emotional states. However, it is equally noteworthy that people with very positive and optimistic attitudes heal faster and their prognosis to overcome their condition is far better.

This is a fascinating subject where many studies have been done on the effect optimism has on both physical and mental health. Studies have shown an undeniable connection between having a positive outlook and the resulting health benefits, such as lower rates of depression and distress, lower blood pressure, less heart disease and healthier blood sugar levels, greater resistance to infections and the common cold, better psychological and physical well-being, better coping skills, and, consequently, increased life spans. When facing a health or life crisis, an optimistic attitude can boost the immune system and ward off depression. There is no question that what happens in the brain influences what happens in the body.

In 2012, researchers from the Harvard School of Public Health[1] concluded that optimism makes you happier and helps you to live longer. In this research, they used data collected from 70,021 women who were part of a massive and long-running Nurses' Health Study. In 2004, the women (whose average age was about 70 years old) were asked a series of validating questions to establish their level of positivity. Then they were tracked from 2006 to 2012, monitoring their health and mortality. Researchers allowed a lag of two years to avoid including women who were already seriously ill. They found that the most optimistic women were 30 percent less likely to die from any serious or chronic illnesses than the least optimistic. Specifically, cancer rates were down by 16 percent, stroke by 39 percent, heart disease by 38 percent, respiratory disease by 37 percent, and infections by a whopping 52 percent.

For those who are not born optimists, there is no need to despair: positive thinking skills can be learned. Start by self-analyzing whether you are an optimist or pessimist. Is your glass half full or half empty? Winston Churchill put it very succinctly: "The pessimist sees the

---

1   Dwyer, Marge. *Optimism May Reduce Risk of Dying Prematurely Among Women*. Harvard T.H. Chan School of Public Health; 2016. Available at: https://hsph.harvard.edu/new/press-releases/optimism-premature-death-women/. Accessed September 13, 2017.

difficulty in every opportunity. The optimist sees the opportunity in every difficulty." There are skills you can acquire that will foster positive emotions.

Judith T. Moskowitz, a professor of medical social sciences at Northwestern University Feinberg School of Medicine in Chicago,[2] developed a study for people with new diagnoses of HIV infection in which the participants were asked to learn eight new skills and practice at least three daily. She and her colleagues found that those who practiced these skills had a reduced viral load count and the need for antidepressants to cope with the illness was less likely. The eight skills were to acknowledge one positive event each day, cherish that event, start a daily gratitude journal, name a personal strength, evaluate a minor stressful situation, become aware and practice small acts of kindness as well as mindfulness, and set a realistic goal and chart progress. Similar studies have concluded that being optimistic was the most significant factor in extending and improving the quality of life, but that it was also important to have characteristics like altruism, a good sense of humor, and having a meaning in life—or, rather, something to live for. It is good to know that if we put our minds to it that we can learn to turn negative thinking into positive thinking. The process is simple, but it does take time and practice—you're creating a new habit, after all.

What we think, good or bad, positive or negative, we create and we become. It's as basic as that. As we are angelic beings, it is our birthright to be healthy. It is up to us to maintain a healthy balance between our body and our mind, and to protect ourselves from

---

2   Brody, Jane E. "A Positive Outlook May Be Good for Your Health." *The New York Times.* March 27, 2017. Available at: https://mobile.nytimes.com/2017/03/27/well/live/positive-thinking-may-improve-health-and-extend-life.html. Accessed September 13, 2017.

negative influences poisoning our entire being. We live in duality, but we can influence the two polarities of our opposite energies to work in harmony and unity.

Negative thoughts affect every cell in your body, creating an imbalance and a blockage in the circulation of positive energy. As you focus your thoughts on the illness and fight it, you create greater endurance. In resisting you will create persistence, maintaining the same negative frame of mind. Instead of fighting and resisting, reframe your thoughts from negative to positive. Send Love and Light to it, changing its frequency, and let go of your attachment to that illusion of yourself. Instead of being upset or dismayed with your ailment, love it as you love every other part of yourself, and then detach your thoughts from it. Recently, I had severe pain in my lower back and knee but chose to accept them as a new part of me. I also sent love and light into the areas of discomfort and, within a short period of time, the pain subsided. I never forget to be utterly grateful for my health and appreciate my blessings.

Disease separates us and sets us apart from others as we become unique in our particular pain and suffering. But, in effect, it is a sign of lack—a lack of love and completeness. It is a symptom of unhappiness, anger, continued emotional upheaval, and imbalance. Obviously, not everybody wants to be sick, most people are simply victims of their uncontrolled thoughts, feelings, and emotions— unaware or in denial of their power. They choose to surround themselves with lower vibrations and perpetuate their negativity. Every part of the physical as well as the astral body is affected by this negative energy. It darkens the aura, hardens the area around the heart, affects the skin, and dulls the color of the blood. As we cannot measure these effects, most will choose to dismiss the power our beliefs and our thoughts have over us. Most people have no conceptual idea how bad it is for their soul and their physical well-being to be in a constant state of fear, distress, flight, or fight.

When I lived in Vancouver, my mother's friend experienced the physical evidence of a broken heart. Her son had committed suicide, which had broken her husband's heart, literally. Two years after their son's death, he suffered a fatal heart attack in our driveway. He had never gotten over his son's suicide, blaming himself and mourning his loss. Another case in point is my grandmother's battle with cancer. She died at the age of 53, losing her life on account of an unending battle with my grandfather that simply poisoned her every cell.

You need to become selfish when it comes to harboring negative thoughts. Consider the consequences, and understand that your thoughts have weight and impact. Learn to let go and to forgive. Also, do not hate others, do not wish them ill or seek to destroy them. For what you send out will come back to you. Guaranteed, no question about it! Unless you're a glutton for punishment and enjoy ill health and unhappiness, I suggest you change your ways. Instead, we need to get rid of the lower vibrations that pull us down.

Right now, our vibrations are heavy, thick, and sticky and make it difficult for the refined and higher ones from the spiritual realms to penetrate through their density. As in all things in the Universe, if this law works for little things, it will work for big things alike. We have the ability to affect emotional states, diseases, and world peace all through the seat of our soul.

It is essential for us to learn how to maintain balance and harmony in life. It will require becoming aware of your thoughts, without judgment or resistance. As you start noticing your thoughts, you will realize how often you are thinking negatively. By that I mean being worried, anxious, angry, hateful, and doubtful. Pay attention and you'll see for yourself. As we notice these thoughts, we can take action and stop them. Let go of the constant barrage of little negative flashes producing self-doubt, insecurity, and worthlessness. Talk to yourself, and lovingly tell those thoughts to give you a break. Quiet your mind, take control, and replace those harming thoughts with positive, loving, and compassionate ones. It's a bit like bait and switch. Change the narrative and create a new vision. It will take some effort in the beginning to change this sometimes simply bad habit of allowing your negative thoughts to roam freely.

It is also essential to quiet your mind and to de-clutter it. The world we live in is filled with distractions, noise, and complexities. We rush through busy schedules that don't allow us much time for reflection. Everything is geared to keeping us so busy that we don't have a minute to come to our senses. That is not accidental, but it is by design. Complexities confuse and mislead us, cluttering our mind with unessential ballast that gives strength to the negative powers at work. The speed in which we live, creating a sense of insufficient time, by endlessly rushing from one thing to another, adds to the blinding effects of negative energy.

We have to become still. We have to stop being run by our day, controlled by the wrong frequencies. Set the channel to a different frequency and observe the difference. For this, you will need to learn to meditate—make it a daily practice. It will affect your whole body, your relationship with yourself and others, and your sense of optimism and deep gratitude. It brings about a shift in your vibrations, actually lightening them and you. It will feel like a burden has been lifted from you, and it has. You will learn to focus on what is important and to become the master of your thoughts. You will decide what it is that you want, what you would like to attract into your life, and then you will think those thoughts, become those very thoughts, and emit their frequency, which then attracts more of them to your life.

When I meditate, I first flood myself with white light, going through me from above my crown chakra, through my body, and into the ground. I release all my negativity, and cleanse myself from all the negativity that has attached itself to me. Negativity is dark, sticky, and clings to you, so it requires cleansing. I follow my breath, and become still. At the end, I send out white, divine Light into the Universe, into places of great concern, people who are sick or troubled, into people I may not necessarily like but who need it most, and then I visualize and manifest whatever it is that I need to work on. I always make sure to be grateful for all my blessings, including my hardships, and to personally thank all my spirit guides, my family, and God for all the help I am receiving daily.

As it is my purpose to change the world from within, I am intentionally sending out white Light and Love to radiate outward, changing our vibrations to higher, finer wavelengths. And as all energy is circular, I know it will come back to me, giving me more to pass on and continue the flow of spiritual energy. I believe, actually I know, that my thoughts originating from my heart center shape the world around me, but I also know that it will take more than just me. If you believe that you are powerless, think again. You have power, divine power, within yourself but it does require action and initiative. Don't be the victim of either illness, political or religious upheavals, or whatever else it may be, but become the light warrior in our spiritual revolution. We all need you, as we need each other to get this job done.

Open yourself up to embrace a new way of thinking, of being. Accept that change comes from within, not without. Healing starts in the soul through awareness and reconnection to its energy Source. We created our Universe through our combined and conjoined thought awareness. We are still creating, daily, minute-by-minute, through our thoughts. Hence, most illness is brought forth as a result of negative thought patterns. What we think, we become. We attract to us the quality of our thought forms, so if we are concerned about our health, we focus on what we fear. Instead, we should release our fears and worries. Focus on wellbeing as a state of normal. Also, another key element in staying healthy is to laugh and play a lot. Add joy to your life, de-stress, and have fun doing the things that you love, and spend time with your loved ones. Don't take life or yourself too seriously. In the end, life is short.

CHAPTER 11

Alternative Energy Centers

Light, Auras, and Chakras

"Travel light, live light, spread the light, be the light."

YOGI BHAJAN

Actually, we are that Light already. We have simply forgotten who we really are and where we come from. We have encapsulated our Divine Light within ourselves and, today, we find it hard to believe that that is our core essence buried inside of us. We are Light and that Light needs to be excavated to balance our energies, to replenish them, and to change their vibrational structure.

Before we plunged ourselves into darkness, we had discovered that by combining and focusing our thoughts, we could achieve anything. We also learned that we could actually manipulate the energy structures and create an entirely different concept in creation—one of solidified matter in physicality. So, in order to get our concept materialized, we collectively focused our thoughts on the energy fields, chose to draw greater quantities from the positive charges, thus deliberately created an imbalance. Additionally, we also used colored light rays that are contained within the atoms of physical matter. As angelic beings are formless and invisible, we needed to use the rays of color to communicate with each other, which is ultimately how we became aware of our potential. As Light Beings, we expressed ourselves through bursts of color that reflected the essence of our messages.[1] To this day, for example, we correlate red as the color of extreme emotion, be it anger or sexually induced feelings, which happens to be also the color of the base root chakra.

We have to understand that human beings are energy centers, invisible to our physical sight, but that doesn't negate their presence. Our sight is limited and only a small number of psychic people can see our auras and their colors. Seeing auras can be learned and improved through practice, but to the untrained eye, our energy fields are hidden underneath the heavy coating of skin and bones. But through awareness and acceptance, we can influence our personal energy, either darken and weigh them down, or lighten them by consciously changing our thoughts. We are not victims of our own emotions and feelings, we are in charge and, in the end, we have to accept responsibility for them. We shape our lives by what we think, thus inducing our auras with correlating energetic responses.

If you are, let's say, constantly angry and hateful, you will transfer those negative charges into the layers of your aura as well as your chakras. And if you do this for an extended period of time, you will

1   Reccia, Michael G. *The Joseph Communications: The Fall.* Burnley, UK: Band of Light Media Limited; 2012, Chapter 4, Loc. 900.

see the effects of your thoughts appear in your physical body. The energies you release have to go somewhere and they do. First, they go into your energy body, either healing or poisoning you, and then they are being emanated outside of your personal energy field into the Universe. Energy flows, as simple as that, and it flows in a circular pattern coming right back to its source: you.

So, the point is, do you feel lucky and think that you can dodge that bullet that you send out minute by minute? Think about it. Is it worth contaminating yourself constantly? Or do you relish being a victim of your own doing? No matter how much love you may receive lying in that hospital bed, you will get far, far more by changing your thoughts and filling yourself with Divine Light and Love. Stop the habitual, unconscious negative mindset by consciously and gently guiding your thoughts toward compassion and love. You will reap the benefits quickly as you feel as if you are walking on cloud nine, even in the midst of turbulence, and observe the atmosphere surrounding you becoming as light as the cloud you're on. This is not to say that you should be an emotionless zombie, but you should grieve or be angry briefly and then move on, let it go and replace it with positive alternate feelings or actions.

In order to get a sense of the visible and invisible human body constituting the whole being, it is important to identify its individual elements. There is conflicting information regarding the auras, their numbers, colors, functions, and sizes, as well as the chakras. Therefore, I will attempt to give a rather general description to highlight the fact that we are all energy, circulating among and interconnected between physical and spirit bodies. On its most basic level, "the human body is a triad composed of spirit, body, and soul. The soul is the astral body. The divine spirit is located within the astral body and is its most important component."[2]

The astral body, which is composed of seven layers, according to most sources, with some reporting of nine, is the spiritual equivalent of the physical body, duplicating its shape. It is like a halo around the shape of the body. It has an etheric substance, operates on higher frequencies, and is composed of astral material. The astral body is attached to the physical at the naval by the astral cord, which acts much like the umbilical cord connecting mother and child. When the astral cord is severed, death of the physical body is imminent. However, during sleep, the astral body is capable of traveling far beyond the limits of the body, which are considered out-of-body experiences. Astral projections can be brought about through trance and hypnosis, and allow you to travel incredible distances. Near-death experiences are also astral projections and here the astral body hovers above the physical body, being completely aware of what is happening at the moment, but incapable of comprehending why nobody sees the spirit or acknowledges its presence. If the cord is overstretched, return to the body may become impossible and will result in death of the physical body.

My late father experienced a near-death experience when he suffered a massive heart attack and went into cardiac arrest. He had been clinically dead for several minutes and he recalled later that he saw the doctors and nurses hovering over his lifeless body trying to resuscitate him. My father, unlike my mother, never fully believed in psychic phenomena but I believe that 30 years of marriage must have

---

2　　Shakour, Cornelia. *The Missing Truth: Angelic Revelations Replace 16 Centuries of Blind Faith*. Pequannock, NJ: Concorde Publishing Inc.; 1997, p. 25.

left their mark on him and allowed him to share his story openly. He told us that he had seen and entered into the white light but he resisted it. He had cried out to the spirits who were awaiting him to let him go, as he had not yet completed his tasks to close his business in Tehran. He pleaded with them that he had to take care of his wife and children and make sure that they were provided for. He was granted one more year to live and finish up his affairs. It was a long year of incredible suffering on account of his failing heart, and he died three days after he had signed the last document needed, on the same date, day of week, time of day, and place as his beloved father. I truly believe that his father came to take him out of his misery. Death came as a friend!

The aura has seven layers, corresponding to the same number of chakras and their colors. The etheric body is the first layer and closest to the body, corresponding to physical life—pleasure and pain or health, well-being, and feelings. It gives vitality to the body as it transmits energy from the higher levels down to the physical. It corresponds to the seventh or root chakra, the color red and the musical note "C." It is the densest layer and belongs to the physical plane.

The second layer, or emotional body, is connected to the sacral or second chakra. It extends between one and four inches from the body, and it resonates to the vibrations of emotions and feelings. It expresses the full range of emotions from fear and hatred to love and joy. It changes colors frequently, based on the particular emotional conditions, and can be all colors of the rainbow depending on the emotional state. However, it will dull and darken as does the mood and will show dark spots where there are emotional blockages. It too belongs to the physical sphere, and corresponds to the color orange and the note "D."

The third layer, corresponding to the solar plexus or third chakra, extends about three to eight inches out, and is considered the mental body. It exhibits people's thoughts, attitudes, and state of mind, while it facilitates cognizance, creativity, and having thoughts and beliefs. Alcohol and drugs influence its level of vibrations, which are higher and finer than those of the emotional body. Also, many perceive it to be the magical layer because this is where you can create everything your soul imagines. It corresponds to the color yellow, the note "E," and is activated by mental stimulation but still belongs to the physical plane.

The fourth layer, or astral body, extends about one foot out and is comprised of colorful clouds. Here the brightness and luster of the colors are reflections of spiritual health, and this layer is the bridge between the spirit and the physical worlds. It both divides and connects them, as does the heart chakra with which it corresponds. The heart chakra also joins the three lower chakras to the three higher chakras. All energy must pass through this layer when moving from one world to another or from one vibrational field to another. This is the seat of love where almost all healing comes from. As we are moving upward and outward, the vibrations increase in frequency and speed. It corresponds to the color green, the note "F," and is activated by meditation.

The fifth layer, or etheric template, extends about two feet from the body and correlates to the throat chakra, which is associated with self-expression, creativity, and the search for truth. This layer reflects, like a blueprint, the physical health of the body through colors—bright or dull—as well as tears, rips, holes, and dark spots.

The dark spots indicate areas of concern that may be disease forming. It is activated by and heals through sound, corresponds to the color blue, and the note "G." This is the first layer that belongs to the spiritual level.

The sixth layer of the aura or celestial body projects about 2.5 feet away from the body. It is able to astral travel, extending out to great distances, as it is linked to the psychic and mind energy centers and therefore it also interacts with the auras of others. It connects us to and reflects any communications we have with the spirit world, but also of our feelings of unconditional love, joy, and ecstasy. The colors here are effervescent and pastel in tone, while its light has a gold-silver shine. This layer correlates to the brow chakra, often referred to as the third eye, which is the gateway to spiritual enlightenment and higher consciousness. It is associated with intuition, psychic powers, and perception. Celestial body awareness can be stimulated through meditation, which raises consciousness and opens to perceiving love and light in all things. It corresponds to the color indigo or violet, the note "A," and belongs to the spiritual level.

The seventh layer, or ketheric template, correlates to the crown chakra, which swirls above the head in a dome, and they both vibrate at the highest frequency of all. This layer is in constant motion and is activated by deeply felt emotions, expressed for example during an impassioned performance or speech. When you are completely engaged and passionate about a particular subject, pouring your heart and soul into it, then "your aura expands and becomes a million scintillating jewels of light. At its smallest, Layer 7 extends about five feet from your body. But when you are in that blissful, natural, euphoric, impassioned state, your aura can expand to fill a room, or a town and even far beyond that." "The jewels of light" are "diamond shaped with sharp edges and three dimensional in shape with eight sides, like two elongated pyramids stuck together at their bases. Rather than being a single color, each jewel" seems "to have a brilliant different colored light shining forth from each individual facet of the gem. All the colors of the rainbow and many more!" These celestial light jewels not only fly around you, but through you and through all other objects and beings, reaching far beyond the area of original emission, and affecting their vibrational state for days, weeks, if not longer.[3]

The seventh level of the aura is associated with the Divine and universal consciousness; from here, we become one with the Universe. It contains the plan of life and reflects all experiences of this current existence, as well as all previous ones. It is the strongest layer and when evolved, it is the most intensive energy. It is stimulated by specific meditation techniques, corresponds to a mix of colors (silver/gold and white/violet), the note "B," and of course belongs to the spiritual plane.

The emission of negative emotions from this layer of the aura will have the same effect in terms of their strength, just of opposite values. I am thinking of such orators as Hitler who gave impassioned speeches rallying up the people in the audience or through the wavelengths of the radio frequencies. They were clearly affected by his hate-filled rhetoric to the point of being brainwashed. It affected every cell of their bodies and infected all those around them who were at risk because of their vulnerability.

Our connections to the Divine and all existence in the cosmos

---

3   Tazkuvel, Embrosewyn. *AURAS: How to See, Feel & Know.* Ashland, CO: Kaleidoscope Productions; 2012, p. 478.

are within us, invisible to the physical eye, capable of taking us into a state of enlightenment and universal consciousness. What is becoming more apparent is that our human bodies are still reflecting thoughts through the medium of color, varying in intensities based on their quality, be they inferior or refined. Thoughts equally affect the matter of the astral layers, and the lower thoughts produce grosser and heavier matter whereas the refined, enlightened thoughts produce their equivalent in matter. You are your thoughts! But, as we can see with the example of the emission of the auric jewels, you can affect the lives of others and even affect the state of inanimate objects. You have the power to bring about positive change through your heart-thought. Just imagine all the good you can do for this Earth! But it is imperative that you sustain balance in your auric field in order to maintain good health and therefore be strong enough to emit radiant light into the atmosphere.

Everything has an aura as everything has the Divine Spark within! This includes both animate and inanimate objects, including the planets, stars, the Sun and the Moon, and of course this very planet Earth. Russian scientists Valentina and Davidovich Kirlian proved the existence of the aura in the 1950s through high frequency photography. They took pictures of humans, animals, and plant life, which clearly showed the presence of a radiant aura around them. They also took pictures of bodies missing a limb and leaves missing parts, but amazingly these parts still showed up as astral bodies with their auras intact. This may explain why so many people still feel their limbs after amputation. But there are more energy centers inside and outside the body. There are hundreds of minor chakras throughout the body, and they are connected to each other through nadis, which are energy channels or conduits. There are thousands of nadis with three major ones: the sushumna, or central channel, which originates at the base of the spine ending in the hindbrain; and the ida and pingala, crisscrossing the sushumna like the caduceus, starting at the base of the spine as well but ending at the left and right nostrils. The kundalini, or universal life force, enters through the crown chakra and flows down to the chakras infusing them with their correlating energy. There are additionally three radiant energy chains that are placed inside the body in a ring-like fashion. They are placed around the temple, neck, and heart areas and contain within them glowing power centers. These too are invisible to the human eye or any medical device yet, but once any one of them is severed, death is imminent and irreversible.

I have become more and more in tune with presence of divine energy within all things. I respect and honor all, be they animate or not. I put light into my laptop daily before I start writing, blessing and thanking it for being there for me. I thank my car for its service and protection, for the joy it gives me when I drive. I talk to my plants now as well and the results are improving, considering I do not possess a green thumb. When we had put our home on the market for sale, I spoke to it, thanking it for the many years of wonderful memories but that it was time for it to have new life again. My children had left for college and it had become an empty nest. I either visualized or had psychic foresight, but I saw a couple with four children moving in—I heard the pitter patter of their little feet, I heard their laughter and their cries, I saw them running in the garden and playing in the pool. New life! And, so it was! A young family with three sons and one daughter became the new residents.

The Earth's Field

*"Sooner or later, we will have to recognize that the Earth
has rights, too, to live without pollution. What mankind
must know is that human beings cannot live without Mother
Earth, but the planet can live without humans."*

EVO MORALES

Everything in God's cosmos operates on the same principle, and as such if the human body has seven major auras and seven major chakras, then the same must apply to the Earth, the entire Universe, and to both organic and inorganic matter. All things have auras, or energy fields, and chakras, or energy centers. The Earth's aura is her atmosphere, which is an energy field that surrounds it, with multiple layers streaming energy from one center or layer to another. It circulates energy between celestial bodies but also transmits it to the Earth's chakras from where it is transported across the planet through its matrix. It nourishes life but is nourished by life as well—it is reciprocal. It stores the frequencies of all thoughts, both positive and negative, emotions, beliefs, ideas, and actions of all of humanity. It was supposed to serve us as our pool of stored energy, somewhat like our present oil storage tanks, refueling us when we were running low. However, as our auras reflect and transmit our thoughts, energy, and health, so does that of the Earth's. We project our energy and thoughts out into the atmosphere, without awareness of their power and potency, and thus unbeknownst to us, we are poisoning all other auras including the Earth's.

In other words, each person's transmission is absorbed by and reflected in the collective whole. Our energy emission is negative and consequently it is being returned in kind. Additionally, the Earth's aura or field has taken on a life of its own, and is perpetuating the spin of negativity. It, like us, needs energy injections of Divine Light, which we can give by channeling Light into ourselves and then project it into the Earth's field.

Our planet Earth is very much alive and conscious. Just like the physical body, it has seven major chakra centers, which are also called vortices, power spots and sacred sites. The aura's energy streams through the chakras into energy circuits called ley lines or meridians that connects them, and weaves its way up from the root to the crown chakra, in a DNA or caduceus fashion. These two interweaving ley lines cross in two places where they create a vortex. They intersect at the Island of the Sun in Bolivia and Mount Kailas in the Himalayas. "According to Robert Cohn, the major chakras are: the Root chakra – Mount Shasta in California; the Sacral chakra – Lake Titicaca in Peru; the Solar Plexus chakra – Uluru and Kata Tjuta, the red rock of Australia; the Heart chakra – Glastonbury, UK; the Throat chakra – the Great Pyramid at Giza in Egypt. The Third Eye chakra is considered to be mobile by Coon, though others say it is Kuh-e-Malek Siah in Iran, and the Crown chakra is Mount Kailas in the Tibet Himalaya Mountain."[4]

The Earth's aura is, like all things, affected by physical and spiritual energies. Physical energies like pollution and greenhouse gases leading to the thinning of the upper atmosphere change the colors of its aura, with "a tan skyline or an ethereally glowing orange and green

4   Andrews, Dr. Synthia. "Mother Earth is Alive and Conscious: Earth Aura, Chakras, Ley Line." *InnerSelf.com*. Available at: http://innerself.com/content/living/science-a-technology/8891-mother-earth-alive-conscious-aura-chakras-ley-lines.html. Accessed September 1, 2017.

sunset"[5] being indicative of sickness. Other signs of poor health and imbalance are holes in the aura, much like the holes in ozone layers, as well as temperature changes and extreme weather patterns. Our planet is in trouble; actually, it is dying. And we are the culprits that brought it to this point. So, it is up to us to do something to save the Earth. If it is easier to do it for selfish reasons, so be it. And, as far as I know, there is no evacuation plan in place yet to another planet. This is the only planet we can inhabit, no matter if there are others out there or not. Due to our particular form of imbalanced creation, we are in quarantine—isolated from all other life forms in the Universe. We really have no choice but to start accepting responsibility for our grievous acts against the Earth and start coming up with a plan to save it. We have to become personally involved in the reversal of our planet's health by doing something from the spiritual level, which is not to imply that we should stop all other policies.

It has been reported by *The New York Times* that large sections of the Great Barrier Reef are now officially dead. There are also reports about the effects of melting ice sheets: "the acceleration is making some scientists fear that Antarctica's ice sheet may have entered the early stages of an unstoppable disintegration. Because the collapse of vulnerable parts of the ice sheet could raise the sea level dramatically, the continued existence of the world's great coastal cities—Miami, New York, Shanghai and many more—is tied to Antarctica's fate."[6] And it was reported by *The Guardian* that the Global Seed Vault, which is buried in a mountain deep inside the Arctic Circle, flooded

5   Taylor, Madisyn. "Earth's Aura." *DailyOM*. Available at: http://www.dailyom.com/cgi-bin/display/printerfriendly.cgi?articleid=380. Accessed September 1, 2017.
6   Gillis, Justin. "Looming Floods, Threatened Cities." *The New York Times*. May 18, 2017. Available at: https://www.nytimes.com/interactive/2017/05/18/climate/antarctica-ive-melt-climate-change-flood.html. Accessed September 13, 2017.

as a result of extraordinarily warm temperatures over the winter. "No seeds were lost but the ability of the rock vault to provide failsafe protection against all disasters is now threatened by climate change … When it was opened in 2008, the deep permafrost through which the vault was sunk was expected to provide 'failsafe' protection against 'the challenge of natural or man-made disasters.'"[7]

These are but a few of the many signs of global warming that are occurring and it may be unstoppable by now. The seriousness and severity of our predicament has not stopped us yet from mistreating and abusing our planet. We are in some places going above and beyond by declaring climate change a hoax, or an alternative fact. President Trump has stated, "The concept of global warming was created by and for the Chinese in order to make U.S. manufacturing non-competitive." Regrettably, some scientists, like Dr. Duane Thresher, PhD Earth & Environmental Sciences, who is "calling belief in global warming a popular delusion," support his views.

"Climate science is one of the most fascinating sciences there is. To turn it into a lie for political purposes is a crime," he stated, before urging the President to stand strong in his convictions.[8] It is only good to know that there are many more who do not close their eyes to climate change because of corporate greed. Tom Steyer, the president of NexGen Climate, states that, "These actions are an assault on American values and they endanger the health, safety

---

7   Carrington, Damian. "Arctic stronghold of world's seeds flooded after permafrost melts." *The Guardian*. Available at: https://www.theguardian.com/environment/2017/may/19/arctic-stronghold-of-worlds-seeds-flooded-after-permafrost-melts?CMP=share_btn_link. Accessed September 1, 2017.

8   Williams, Thomas D. "Climate Scientist Urges President Trump Not to Cave to Ivanka's 'Climate Change Madness.'" *Breitbart News Network*. Available at: http://www.breitbart.com/big-government/2017/04/24/climate-scientist-urges-president-trump-against-ivankas-climate-change-madness/. Accessed September 1, 2017.

and prosperity of every American. Trump is deliberately destroying programs that create jobs and safeguards that protect our air and water, all for the sake of allowing corporate polluters to profit at our expense."

As a matter of fact, President Trump has rolled back 23 environmental rules in his first 100 days.[9] He has chosen to prioritize fossil fuel interests, a giant step back into the past, and has reversed the course of President Obama's policies to protect the environment through rules and regulations reducing America's greenhouse gas emissions. President Obama had pledged in Paris that he would initiate the closure of old coal-fired plants, reduce the methane emissions from oil and gas wells, as well as increase production of fuel-efficient cars. Regrettably, the Trump administration is against the reduction of greenhouse gas emissions and fossil fuel reliance, insisting it would cost jobs when, in reality, every new business venture will open up new possibilities and in this case even reduce the cost of energy, thus the cost of doing business.

Europe has a far better grasp on the severity of our global climate change crisis. They are creating new energy resources, consequently new job opportunities, and moving into the future rather than trying to turn the clock back, which can never work anyway. Germany is getting now 85% of power from renewables, such as wind, solar, and hydroelectric, and plans to phase out nuclear energy and fossil fuels by 2022.[10] Even China and India

9   Popovich, Nadia, and Tatiana Schlossberg. "23 Environmental Rules Rolled Back in Trump's First 100 Days." *The New York Times.* Available at: https://www.nytimes.com/interactive/2017/05/02/climate/environmental-rules-reversed-trump-100-days.html. Accessed September 2, 2017.
10   *Attn: VIDEO.* Available at: https://www.facebook.com/ATTNVideo/videos/1702830436688577/. Accessed September 1, 2017.

are making big strides in reducing their contributions to climate change. Both countries have expedited their investments in renewable energy sources and have already reduced their reliance on fossil fuels. They are well ahead of their targets set in Paris, which is commendable since their living standards are far below those of the industrialized West. As David Leonhardt writes, "China and India are finding that doing right by the planet need not carry a big economic cost and can actually be beneficial . . . their progress also highlights the cowardice and short-sightedness of the Trump administration's climate stance."[11]

Apart from our responsibility to change our ways in how we treat the Earth, by controlling carbon emissions, we need to conserve and increase energy efficiency, re-forest, recycle and renew, and discontinue fracking and other controversial policies. Of course, there is always the threat of a nuclear conflict looming, which of course negates any hopes of having a future. The Earth is responding to our abuse like a patient who is gravely ill. The eruptions, floods and droughts, the intense heat waves, and incredible frosts are comparable to a patient with an extremely high fever accompanied by chills, shivers, and uncontrollable tremors. Our planet is sick and we all have to start healing it. There are many means of healing – decreased usage of pollutants and greenhouse gas emissions for example, and in equal amounts positive energy projections of peace and love through spiritual practices and group meditations. We need to have both in place—spiritual as well as political activism—but the point is that not all of us will be actively working in the alternative

---

11   Leonhardt, David. "Climate Cowards – and Heroes." *The New York Times.* May 22, 2017. Available at https://mobile.nytimes.com/2017/05/22/opinion/china-india-climate-change-paris-agreement.html. Accessed September 1, 2017.

energy industry. However, all of us can contribute by spiritually affecting the condition of the Earth.

We have to send out Light into the Universe and the atmosphere around us to change the vibration and energy of the planet. We have to infuse it again with God Light through the power of our Divine Light within each and every one of us. We have to do so on a daily basis as part of our meditation practice or prayers, and actually also when we are faced with upsetting evidence of our ailing planet as in reports brought to us by the media. There is really no downside in acquiring this habit, no additional costs, or difficult tasks or chores to add on to your busy schedule. Just send out the white Light into Antarctica, the Great Barrier Reef, and the areas where floods have destroyed entire neighborhoods. Do it in complete privacy— nobody needs to know and make you feel uncomfortable. Also, be grateful for all the Earth is providing you with; be appreciative for the beauty and abundance of nature, and learn to treat it the same way you would like to be treated.

Sending Light out will bring about change because we can affect auras, including the Earth's, with our heart-thoughts. Originally, we were not only aware of that but did so by radiating and transmitting light energy. After the fall, though, we disconnected ourselves from God's Energy, which essentially means that no new source of energy is coming through unless we initiate it through actively seeking to reconnect spiritually. Our thoughts, fears, and emotions became negatively charged and we emitted those charges out, affecting the Earth's atmosphere. It therefore became thicker, denser, and heavier and changed its color to shades of dark gray with a slimy, sticky texture. Areas of unrefined and lower, darker energy have dark and slimy auras, too. Due to its density, the Earth's field has closed us off from easy access and communication with the spirit realms and has actually taken on a life of its own.

The field absorbs our negative thoughts and beliefs and, as everything is circular, it returns it right back to us, perpetuating negativity. Hence, we are running on negative energy! We are not receiving any new energy; for one thing, the field is acting as a shield and, secondly, we have deliberately disconnected and distanced ourselves from the energy of God's Light. We are right when we say and believe that we are running out of power and out of energy, because we are. It is just that the origin of our diminishing energy lies in the lack or, rather, our rupture from the Divine energy resources. What happens here is a reflection of what happens in the Earth's field—a lack of positive energy! We are endlessly searching for new power resources, so I believe that it is time that we look in a new direction. Let's harness our Divine Light energy by filling ourselves up with God's Light and broadcasting it. Change your mind, fill it with positive thoughts, and fill yourself with Light and Love! Transmit that energy into the Universe, the souls and hearts of others, and areas where climate control is wreaking havoc or where dangerous, maybe unstable people hold the future of our planet in their hand! We are the authors of our own creation or demise—the choice is ours. We have the power to heal the Earth completely with our thoughts and actions, so let's go!

> *"Humankind has not woven the web of life. We are but
> one thread within it. Whatever we do to the web, we do to
> ourselves. All things are bound together. All things connect. "*

CHIEF SEATTLE

Balance of the Negative and Positive

*"Life is like riding a bicycle. To keep your
balance, you must keep moving."*

ALBERT EINSTEIN

Everything in God's Universe needs both positive and negative charges. That is how movement is created, through friction between two opposite energy fields. If you were to take two magnets and have their opposite poles face each other, then they are pulled into the magnetic field near the pole of the other stronger one. However, if you push the like poles toward each other, they will repel each other, moving in opposite directions. This is how movement and space is created: the opposing energies create friction and that creates movement. If you have ever put an area rug on top of pile carpeting, then you know exactly what I mean. The area rug will move in one specific direction due to the friction between the two materials— the direction of the pile rubbing against the backing of the rug. The pile is moving the area rug forward.

The direction of the movement is a result of the more dominant charge. If they are balanced, then it is a circular movement, as in God's Universe. However, if the negative charge is dominant, then you have a violent environment; if the positive is dominant, then you have stagnation. One cannot be without the other, there must be a positive and negative charge and we can see this in all things in creation. Take a battery, for example: it must have both positive and negative polarities to produce energy. This is not a theosophical principle of good versus evil, but one of positive and negative charges creating energy. Opposite energies highlight each other's unique qualities, such as light shining so much brighter in the dark or your house's warmth after coming in from the cold. Opposites and duality are necessary to create and improve—in other words, to evolve. However, imbalance of any kind will bring with it divergence.

When we are in a state of perfect balance, then it is as if we were set to neutral, like the scales of justice. This does not mean that we have become neutral and stand still; it means that we are in harmony with each other and neutralizing the excessive or dominant charge. Both negative and positive forces flow in their individual direction—upwards, downward, and outward—and then return to their origin to renew their cycle. They need each other to create the energy for their movement, just as we need to have both energies within us to function properly. If we have a dominant energy, let's assume negative, then we are leaning toward violent thoughts and behavior. If our energy is predominantly set to positive, then we have a tendency to be righteous, inflexible, and immovable. Nothing new can come out of just being positive—there would be no new creation as everything would last forever, would never decay or break. People like that can hardly ever think outside the box, or see an issue from a different point of view. They are stuck in their ways. Only through change can we grow; the destruction of one thought form generates the necessity to create a new one.

Often, we are fearful of change, but without it we cannot evolve and grow into greater consciousness. Growth is a result of change, offering new possibilities to experience, which is the purpose of our being. But, what we have always experienced on this planet is negative. Ours is a unique situation in that we have willfully manipulated energies and therefore created a sphere with a predominantly negative field.

As we are both positive and negative, as is God, we cannot deny one for the other. However, we chose to willfully imbalance our energy fields. We chose to manipulate energies by heaping predominantly positive energy into our creation, causing stagnation; therefore, going forward, only predominantly negative energy was left, bringing with it violence. A true lose-lose situation for the Earth and us! We are the reflection of God and what is in macrocosm must be in microcosm. Therefore, it is not good versus bad, it is just energy. It's liberating to understand that we can start looking at it differently. We no longer have to feel guilty when we have negative thoughts, no longer believe that we are sinners or lesser human beings. We all have bad thoughts, let's just admit it. It's human and quite all right. As a matter of fact, it is impossible to have neutral thoughts. They are either charged positively or negatively, they cannot be neutral. What we do with those thoughts is what sets us apart. When we choose to fight them, we create resistance, giving them greater power over us. They need that negative charge to hold onto and to increase their power and efficacy. However, if we learn to acknowledge their presence, notice their appearance as an anecdotal occurrence, and then set them free, we have asserted control over our thoughts, and not the other way around. Embrace your negative thoughts, love them, fill them with white Light from your heart center, and allow them to pass through. Set them free into the ether. No need to worry about contaminating the atmosphere or others, as love and Light are the neutralizing factors preventing this from happening. They are as much a part of us as the color of our skin or the pain in our bodies. Love and release! And no harm done if you put a little laughter in it, too.

*"Holding on to anger is like drinking poison and
expecting the other person to die."*

BUDDHA

We are our thoughts and we are the ones that set the tone—positive or negative. Every day, every hour, and every minute we have a new opportunity to change our thoughts and mind. We can choose to start the day in a dark mood, with only dread and anguish on our mind, and consequently receive same back, fulfilling a self-prophecy. Not only will we ruin our own day, but also wreck others'. We send out negative frequencies, which lowers the vibrations all around us. It really sets in motion a negative chain reaction, poisoning the entire atmosphere. It is also a reflection of self-destructiveness based on the belief of being unworthy of God's love. The belief of being unloved creates not only a feeling of lack but also dark thoughts and bad habits.

Feeling unloved creates a void, and we need to fill that void with more, whatever that may be and wherever it may come from, and that brings with it violence. Usually, we need to take energy from somebody else to make ourselves feel more empowered, to have more and be more. Some people run their whole lives on negative and those are the very people we have to help and heal by sending Light. It may seem a lot to ask for, but the alternative of not helping and healing them is worse. If we send them more negative thoughts, it will only embolden and strengthen their negative charge. Not exactly the way to save our world and us.

Fortunately, there are those of us who start the day with gratitude, meditation, or prayer. We set the tone for the day by making a positive difference in other people's lives, by helping and healing them through our upbeat mood, our positive thoughts and uplifting words, our compassion, kindness, and unselfish love. We alter their vibrational field through ours, no big hoopla required, just thoughts of light and love. In return, we will feel so uplifted ourselves, no matter how badly some things may be. We look at it as an opportunity to grow through being challenged, sometimes to the very core of our existence. We know instinctively to bring laughter and fun back into daily life, giving grieving and hardship respite. We are the creators of how things will turn out and it is up to us to set the tone. We do need both energies, but right now we have too much negative energy in our mix. We have to change that by bringing back balance by increasing Divine Light, positive energy—of which we have too little.

This requires some action on your part! It requires changing your mind, filling yourself with light, and channeling it out. You have to change yourself first before you can attempt to change others, so that you may send out light, not more darkness. You have to start dreaming a better dream for your and everybody else's lives, the world, and our Universe. Start with yourself, one step at a time, with kindness, compassion, and self-love. It's a good beginning and the only place to begin. As you are a creator, you create what you see in your visions, so visualize positive images on a broad spectrum. Believe in yourself, know that God loves you and that you are special, and then flood yourself with His Light and Love. You will feel the difference; it may take a bit to awaken your senses to the new vibration, but they are there.

If we want to end the cycle of violence and terror, then we must change our thoughts of retribution, of hate, and anger. We cannot cure an outbreak of a pandemic disease by being angry about its existence. What good would that do for the patients? No good whatsoever! It would actually be a disfavor for we would add more negative power to the virus. It would infect us all. Terrorism has that same effect. Not only has it poisoned the terrorists' minds, but it poisons us as well. The images of brutality and senselessness are hard to swallow, which is exactly why we have to respond in kindness and compassion. We have to rise up to brutality and violence with Light. If we choose to fight it, it will spread like the plague. I am not the first person, nor the last, who says this. Jesus, for one, has made it one of his cornerstone teachings for us:

> "But I tell you, love your enemies, bless those who curse you, do good to those who hate you, and pray for those who mistreat you and persecute you."
>
> (Matthew 5:44)

If we fail to return balance to our world, we will see an escalation in violence, power struggles, corruption, inequality, and suffering. We are running out of positive energy and out of time. So, the choice is ours if we want to be bystanders, who watch the drama unfold on TV or social media, and perpetrate more negativity through our thoughts of powerlessness, anger, and hatred. Instead, we have to become Light workers and send out Light when we are confronted with the ugly side of our way of life here. Don't whine—just do! Ever since I have learned about the power of our thoughts and their effects, I have started to send out Light to those who hold our future in their hands. In my daily meditations, I send out Light into global warming, to areas in the world that are undergoing horrific crises such as Syria, Iraq, and Afghanistan. I also send out Light to the poor victims who carry heavy burdens not of their own making. I send out

Light to President Trump, Russian President Putin, Bashar al-Assad of Syria, Kim Jong-un of North Korea, and Rodrigo Duterte of the Philippines—they need it most and our fate lies in their hands. I send out Light to the sick in hospitals and to prisoners, and, yes, of course, I send it to the people I love and cherish as well.

We can change people only from within. We cannot force our wishes or visions upon them and tell them to change. We should not hate them either or wish them harm. This will only perpetuate and increase their negativity. It fuels their energy with more negative energy. Instead, "love your enemy"—the dictators, murderers, terrorists—and flood them with Divine Light. Don't seek revenge, don't judge just forgive them. Justice is a consequence of the law of cause and effect. Each soul will get what it needs to advance itself and evolve into greater consciousness—if not in this physical world, then in the spiritual and in the manner and time frame fitting. Each soul though must want to evolve, choose to do so by their own free will because they either have had enough of or learned from their current level, and then reach out for help when ready to move upward. It is our job to send healing, loving Light out to them to bring out their Divine Spark, to change them from within. Change their minds, their thoughts, and beliefs and so you'll save the world.

We are energy, from each layer of our auras to our chakras, and from each and every cell in our bodies, which contain both positive and negative charges just like our thoughts. Therefore, by sending out positive thoughts and Light, we are penetrating the energy fields of others. We are returning balance by not fighting same with same, by not ignoring or denying our thoughts, but by acknowledging and releasing them. Resistance creates persistence. And Light is our tool to bring back a state of contentment. Try to make it a daily habit to send out the Light in your meditations, and apply it whenever the need arises during your day.

> *"Darkness cannot drive out darkness; only light can do that.*
> *Hate cannot drive out hate; only love can do that."*

MARTIN LUTHER KING JR.

CHAPTER 12

Your Spirit Guides

"Everyone who wills can hear the inner voice. It is within everyone."

MAHATMA GANDHI

Spirit guides surround us all from the moment we are born to the moment we die. It is their mission to guide and protect us throughout our lives. Most of us are unaware that we have guardians as we cannot see, hear, smell, or feel them. The more psychic you are, the easier it is for you to know when they are around you. That does not mean that you cannot draw upon their help when needed just because you can't see them. They need you to acknowledge them and ask them for help, giving them permission to work on your behalf. As Jesus said,

"Ask, and you will receive. Search, and you will find. Knock, and the door will be opened for you."

(Matthew 7:7)

Asking your spirit guides to help and guide you is of benefit to them as well. They, like us, have a mission. Theirs is to help us evolve and to go through this life experience safely. They are souls who exist in the spirit world where they are committed to their higher purpose, but they may have lived in the physical for one or multiple lifetimes. We exist and grow in both worlds, physical and spirit, always to elevate our vibrational frequencies. The two worlds are reflections of one another, where the individual souls have opportunities, based on their spiritual level, to advance upward by doing something— learning, teaching, building, or creating. It's not like getting on cloud nine after passing into the spirit world and singing halleluiah while eating manna bread. By protecting and guiding us, they are giving us the support to go the distance and strength to take all the roadblocks in stride, to keep faith and be unwavering, knowing that we are all protected and loved. They help us to attain a greater sense of balance, both individually and collectively, affecting our relationships with one another, as well as with all forms of life on Earth. We have to always remember to thank them and be grateful for all the help they give us. Acknowledge their presence and recognize their efforts and the impact they have had.

If you don't get what you had been asking for, it is because there is a different path for you to take. We may not be able to see the bigger picture when we ask for a particular thing. And maybe, just maybe, what we did receive is better for us in the long run or, maybe, what we asked for is not beneficial for our spiritual evolution. Still thank them and put your needs out to them, state them in an affirmative, specific request and let it go. In other words, don't ask to be free of pain because you have just brought up the image of pain and, therefore, you will receive pain. Ask them for a healthy body instead.

Be specific in what you ask for, ask in the present tense, not future, and let it be a good cause for you personally or even for somebody else. You should never reach out to your spirit guides with unsavory requests, for the higher spirits will immediately vacate you and you will attract lower, darker spirits that match your request and state of mind. Be careful who and what you ask for!

The more positive your thoughts are, the higher and finer your vibrations are, and the more advanced the spirit guides will be that are assigned to you. Consequently, the more negative your thoughts are, the darker and heavier your vibrations will be and thus you will attract low spirits to match the frequencies you're emitting. Like to like, it is just simply the very same principle applied to all things in the Universe. Your thoughts set the tone for the life you live, for the light you give, and for the spirit gifts you receive. Keep your thoughts pure, as pure as it is possible in our negative environment, through daily communication with God and the spirit world, which is your best insurance against invading dark souls who are looking for vulnerable outlets to let their darkness come through.

Spirit guides have their specialties and strengths just as we do—as above, so below. We have strengths and weaknesses as well, creating the great kaleidoscope of Light we are. After extensive research, I have assembled a brief outline introducing the varying kinds of angels and guides to you, combined with their roles and purpose.

There are the *Angels* who are assigned to us from birth and will surround us at all times. We may have one or more, depending on the spiritual level of our mission, and it is their purpose to protect us from any harm that may befall us, physically or spiritually. They are aligned with our second and third chakras. They will protect you from all kinds of negativity, violence, accidents, and self-doubt.

The *Runners* are there to help us find whatever it is we need at the moment. I use them when I need a parking spot and it works most of the time. Sometimes I forget to ask ahead of time, which is unfair to them, as they need to plan ahead, too. They will also assist us to connect with the right people at the right time. You will have the same two or three runners throughout your life.

The *Helpers* are there to assist you with very specific issues. You will attract different ones depending on the nature of the issue you need help with. If a problem is spiritually very complex, then you will receive more helpers, as is necessary to get the job done. The helpers are connected to the third and fourth chakras. They will help you find new solutions, creative new ideas, and find the right people.

The *Teachers* are in charge of your spiritual development. They are there to assist you with remembering who you are on a soul level, and to find the meaning and purpose of your life. They work with you toward greater awareness and stay with you as you grow and evolve. Teachers aim to raise consciousness on a global level by helping the individual find the right information at the right time to stimulate their learning. They are associated with the fourth, fifth, and sixth chakras. Ask them to help you with any emotional issues you may have, to find lessons in the stories of your life, and to improve your spiritual techniques or get answers to your questions. I know that they must have guided me to find, "coincidentally," *The Joseph Communications* when I was checking if my mother's book was still coming up. From then on, I have been given books or had books recommended to me that would broaden my knowledge for the very moment I needed a particular kind of information or message.

The *Masters* are your guides who raise your consciousness to higher levels by helping you discover and remember your true essence and the path you have chosen for this incarnation. They help you to accept and love yourself and others, to learn to forgive and to be nonjudgmental, to let go of that which holds onto you and harms your growth. They help you heal and find peace within. They are connected to your seventh, or crown, chakra. I feel they have lovingly guided me through all my experiences, both good and bad, to understand their educational values and applying the wisdom gained to the greater good of all. I am deeply grateful for their guidance.

There are the *Joy Guides* who will help you see the Light in darkness, bring humor into unchangeable situations like the deaths of loved ones—or in other words, they make you laugh. We all need laughter and, not for nothing, laughter is called the best medicine. They are aligned with your third and fourth chakras. Make it a habit to see humor even in the darkest hours—it helps you get through them with greater ease. Laugh out loud and as often as you can. It will raise your vibrations to higher, finer wavelengths.

And, finally, there are the seven *Archangels*, God's most important and highest-ranking messengers. They can be found in many religions and beliefs. Logically, you would turn to them for the most important and essential spiritual questions and issues. There seem to be some discrepancies between who these archangels are based on the sources, and there are actually more than seven. However, seven constitute the highest-ranking number of archangels, with the top four being the same in all sources. The lower three I have chosen based on the majority of resources who consider them to hold this rank. Their names are Michael, Gabriel, Raphael, Uriel, Raguel, Azrael, and Jophiel. It's no coincidence that all names end in -el, which means "god" or "deity" in many ancient languages like Phoenician, Hebrew, Syriac, and Arabic.

Michael, the highest-ranking archangel, is considered to be a protector, advocate, and healer. Call on him when you need your life to move forward, have more vitality, as well as for guidance and protection. He will assist you when you are confused, afraid, and concerned for your safety, as well as finding your life's purpose, motivation, and self-esteem. His name means "he who is God."

Gabriel, whose name means "God is my strength," is acknowledged to be God's messenger and the patron of communications. She is the second highest archangel, and she helps writers, artists, speakers to find their message and motivation. She can help overcoming fear, anxieties, and procrastination, and in all areas related to children, from conception to rearing.

Raphael, whose name means "God heals," is next in line and he is a physical and emotional healer. He helps individuals to reduce cravings and addictions, overcome illnesses and injuries, but he also protects the healers so they can help those in need. Reach out to him when you need to boost your mental, spiritual, and physical energy levels as well as when you need to restore peace and harmony.

Uriel, whose name means "God is my light," is identified as the archangel of salvation and wisdom, who shines his light into darkness. He is the one to turn to before making major life changing decisions, resolving conflicts and solving problems, but also when needing to let go of destructive behavior and emotions. When feeling stuck and looking for new ideas turn to him for guidance.

Raguel, whose name means "friend of God," is the archangel of justice, fairness, and harmony, and he is considered to be something like a sheriff. He is in charge of overseeing all other archangels to make sure they're working in harmony and orderly manner. Call on him when you need to be empowered and respected, resolve disputes and arguments, and to return discipline and control into your life.

Azrael, whose name means "whom God helps," is often considered "The Angel of Death" as he assists souls with their passing in death while he also aids the loved ones with their loss and grief. You can reach out to him to calm the fears and stress of those who are facing death so they may pass over peacefully. He is the one to approach for all sorts of transitions and endings, such as relationships and jobs, guiding you to manage life's changes smoothly.

Finally, archangel Jophiel, whose name means "beauty of God," is the patron saint of the arts. She helps in creating and manifesting beauty in our environment and in the arts, maintaining a positive outlook through positive thought forms, and thus heals negativity and chaos. Connect to her when you need to change your perspective, be uplifted and seek wisdom.

Then there is archangel Ariel, the spirit of nature, who needs to be included. Her name means "lion or lioness of God" and she is the patron of animals and the environment. Her role is to protect the earth—nature, wildlife, ecosystem, and our natural resources. She also oversees the order of the physical universe and watches over the sun, the moon, the Earth, and all the other planets. When you need guidance protecting and healing the environment, the animals and ensuring sufficiency in food and water supplies, then she is the one to go to.

Archangels are powerful spiritual beings and great forces to draw on. All angels are a fascinating element of our culture and many people have found that they can help them with their personal spiritual progress and interventions as healers and guides. However, there are also dark spirits, Earth-bound ghosts and fallen angels who, according to many religions, were rebellious or even wicked angels and were therefore cast from heaven.

Lucifer, who is also called Satan or the devil, is believed to have been an archangel before his fall. He became the leader of the fallen angels whose evil influence would be felt around the world. He is considered to be a seducer, accuser, and a persecutor with demonic powers. The dark spirits shun the light, so consequently they exist in the darker areas in the spiritual realms where they share the space with their kind. As they cannot absorb the energy from Divine Light, they have to get theirs from others, like energy vampires. They will also gain their energy from you. You will be able to discern between the benevolent and the predatory spirits for it's much the same as on this plane when you encounter a person with higher or lower vibrations and darker thoughts. What is in this world is also in the spirit world.

When the Light in your spiritual field is dark, you will mainly attract dark guides as the higher the guides shun the lower, darker, and heavier frequencies. The higher the angel or guide, the more Light it has and the higher its frequencies are. They cannot tolerate the lack of Light, and the sticky, slimy textures of the dark auras or even the scent they emit. As you raise your consciousness, as you raise the Light and your vibrational levels, you will attract the same in the level of your support team. Like attracts like—the frequencies have to match, to be in harmony, for them to work together optimally. The dark spirits that are attracted and attached to dark souls on Earth incite them to commit evil. They are the voices that rile them up, driving them crazy until the deed is done—unless they fill themselves with Light and learn to let go instead of fighting them.

Protection comes through your daily connection and communication with God and your spirit guides. The more harmonious, loving, kind, and compassionate your thoughts become, the finer your frequencies will be and higher-ranking angels will become your companions and protectors. They will also help you find your path, activate your inner voice, and not only guide you but also warn you of imminent danger or being lured into the wrong direction. You may wonder how you will know when they are around and try to protect you. First you have to become still, silence the thoughts in your brain and stop their chatter. Then you need to tune into your own energy—your body, your mind, and your emotions. In time and with practice, you will become aware of the subtle differences in your body's response system, especially in your second and third chakras, or what is referred to as your gut reactions. This is not so much about doing something but rather about being—be in the moment and allow yourself to register the vibrations you are receiving. They can be very subtle and they can be intense; register them, acknowledge them, and also record them. These are messages and guidance you are receiving from your higher self and your guides. You will sense them though your emotions. Don't wait until you are in a state of crisis— instead, listen to any slight negative feelings and act upon them. Also, we all have the little voice in our head that speaks to us. Learn to listen and decipher the messages given. Sometimes it is the voice of doubt, uncertainty and skepticism, which you have the power to change through your inner dialogue. It is actually your friend and motivator to overcome the obstacles ahead of you, but you will be the one to set the tone of either acceptance or uprising. The voice can also be the one warning you about people or events that may be negative for you. Pay attention to it and to yourself in terms of your emotional responses, and learn to discern their differences without judgment.

I used my inner voice, my gut feelings, and my dreams in helping me to navigate through the mire of spiritual information out there. I believe not all to be of the same truths or high quality, so I protect myself with white Light and listen to what feels right and what doesn't. Unfortunately, there have been times I didn't not heed the warnings and, sure enough, I should have. Listen to your instincts and your intuition from your heart, protect yourself with daily connection to God, and fill yourself and others with the Light.

"Your time is limited, so don't waste it living someone else's life. Don't be trapped by dogma—which is living with the results of other people's thinking. Don't let the noise of others' opinions drown out your own inner voice. And most important, have the courage to follow your heart and intuition."[1]

STEVE JOBS

To connect with God or your spirit guides, you need to become still—shut out all the noise and busyness of your environment and your brain. Choose a quiet place where you won't be disturbed. You can light candles, burn incense, and play soft music to set the tone and elevate your vibrations as those of the room. Sit for a moment and simply relax—nothing to worry about or stress over. Let the day fall off you, let the thoughts stop spinning, relax your muscles and drop your shoulders. Breathe deeply and close your eyes gently. You're safe, you're loved, and now you can open up the channels of

---

1   "Steve Jobs' 2005 Stanford Commencement Address." *Huffington Post*. Available at: http://www.huffingtonpost.com/2011/10/05/steve-jobs-stanford-commencement-address_n_997301.html. Accessed September 29, 2017.

communication. That's how we can break the barrier between this world and the spiritual realms—open your chakras by flooding them with white light, and connect through the heart. Allow your heart space to open up, along with your throat, third eye, and your crown chakra, and feel this unbelievable wave of love pouring in, and let yourself go in the moment. Always remember, God's channels of communication are always open to you but you have to initiate the contact. He has never left us—we have left Him! That is why we exist in isolation, in a bubble if you will, separated from the other parts of God's Universe, but through our real connection we can poke holes into the glass ceiling and start shattering it. If you don't believe in God, you can still connect to the vast energy of the Universe and change or even elevate yours through meditation. There is no prerequisite of any belief in order to meditate effectively.

Before you start to either meditate or pray, ground yourself by planting both feet on the ground, either sitting or standing. Then, start breathing in deeply to your stomach, hold your breath, and then exhale and hold your breath again. You can do this to a count of eight in, hold for a count of four, and then count eight to exhale, and another four to hold. Repeat this a few times, maybe six or seven. While you inhale, imagine a large white ball of Light entering you through your crown chakra at the top of your head and going through you into the ground. As you exhale, bring up that White Light ball back to your crown and repeat maybe a few times until you feel "lighter."

As you start your meditation, calm your thoughts and begin to bring body, energy, mind, and emotions into the present moment. Consciously release all that has happened before, such as events, attachments, people, or distractions, and all that has not yet transpired, like fears, worries, imaginary events, and projections. Do not rush through this and if your mind starts wandering, gently push it back on track. Do not get angry or frustrated at any time during your meditation; just continue your practice with patience and loving-kindness. Meditation is not about forcing your mind to be quiet, but rather to find the inner stillness that is already there. Behind all that internal dialogue and chatter is the silence of true awareness. From here you gain access to creativity, healing, and transformation, enabling you to make life-affirming choices.

If you choose to meditate using a mantra, which is a sacred syllable or formula, then start by either reciting it to yourself or chanting it. The most powerful and well known is OM. It is called the mother of all mantras and will activate and accelerate your creative spiritual forces within and endow you with a deep sense of harmony. You need not use the mantra for the entire duration but it will help you stay focused. Usually, it is recommended to meditate twice daily for about 30 minutes, once in the morning and once at night. I personally believe you should meditate whenever you feel at your most relaxed state. Also, I think it will be easier to start with shorter sessions and work your way up. At the end of your meditation, stop thinking the mantra, but remain seated with your eyes closed for another two or three minutes. I personally use that time for my gratitude practice; I thank God and my spirit guides for all their love and assistance making my life better. Then I rise slowly, filled with new vigor and strength.

Also at the start of your practice, imagine all negative attachments falling off you so you can release their grip and feel them dissolve into the ether. At the end, fill yourself with bright white Light from top to bottom and outward, to cover your auras. It could be like standing in a cone of Light—radiant, bright, and protected. You can also add three rings of Light around yourself: one around the forehead, one around the throat, and the third around your chest at heart level. This will add another layer of positive energy. Finally, starting with the base and ending with the crown chakra, I infuse each chakra with Divine Light. Visualize the Light penetrating each chakra and both energizing and illuminating it, giving it greater radiance and brilliance.

When you are done, you must close your chakras, starting at the base and ending at the crown. You can do this by imagining zipping yourself up or, alternatively, like closing doors. If you forget to do this, you will leave yourself open and vulnerable to psychic attacks. Again, fill yourself with Light and thank all your spirit guides, your family and your friends, and, of course, God for being there for you. Consider yourself lucky that you are the one who has found the connection back to your Heavenly Father and His spirit realms; that you are the one who can draw on His Strength and Support throughout your day; that you are the one who will always be safe. That is not to say that your journey will be on calm waters, but it will be a safe one despite the rough seas. Actually, the rougher the seas, the greater is the opportunity to learn.

That sounds well and good, but it is a tough one to go through when it happens to you. I have been there, and I do not believe that I could have made it without the knowledge that I was loved and protected, that God had sent me the support I needed to get me through the rough patches—and there were many. He sent me miracles disguised in the form of people appearing out of nowhere to help, and venues opening that would seem impossible even under the best of circumstances. The days of extremely rough seas are the days when I remember my relationship with God and reconnect. Whatever situations I have had to go through were a learning experience created by my soul to lead me to my destiny—the path I myself chose before entering this incarnation. I absolutely believe that I chose to devote myself to be of service to others, to help and heal them as best I can. I must have chosen to have a voice and have a say in the direction we are taking as a society. I am convinced that I decided to become a messenger of the truth.

There is a message that needs to be spread by as many souls as possible. The message is of hope that one day we will return to our promised land, our promised state of being—but it requires action and knowledge. So, we have to share and spread this message of bringing back God energy and Light to ourselves, to those we touch and affect with our raised frequencies, and thus elevate us to higher vibrational states more in tune with those of God's Universe.

CHAPTER 13

All You Need is Love and Light

"Cowardice asks the question: is it safe? Expediency asks the question: is it politic? Vanity asks the question: is it popular? But conscience asks the question: is it right? And there comes a time when one must take a position that is neither safe, nor politic, nor popular–but one must take it simply because it is right."

MARTIN LUTHER KING JR.

Hatred is a powerful energy—it blinds those that are held in its throws and destroys everything that crosses its path. Its antidote is love and compassion, not more hate. Love, by the way, is thousands of times more powerful than hate will ever be as, "Love is the food of the Universe." In hatred, we cut ourselves off from positive energy and benevolent influences, throwing us into ever-greater isolation and distance from healing and uplifting vibrations. At all times, however, we have free will and it is up to each and every one of us to choose our own path. Granted, for those who live in so much darkness, it is far more difficult to see the Light, but there are always rays that break through to help us change our ways. That is why we, who have more knowledge and more awareness, have to send Divine Light into their darkness. Light is our tool to return love and hope back to Earth. We help ourselves by helping them.

Our life on Earth was meant to be a dream, not a nightmare. However, we are responsible for the mess we are in, not God. There is no point in being angry with Him or blaming Him for our troubles. In effect, we are all brainwashed, to some extent. We believe that there is nothing that we can do to bring about change and to stop the violent ways of this planet. We act as if we were bystanders, passively watching in horror as the train wreck is unfolding. Some look upward to the heavens, shaking their heads and clenching their fists at the presumed injustice of an angry, vengeful God. Others simply can't understand why God would allow such atrocities against humanity to happen. Surely, He has the power to stop them from occurring, over and over again?

We are brainwashed by the negative energy of this Universe. We have been conditioned to believe that this negative way of life is all that there is. Violence, pain, and suffering are part of the human condition and, at best, we can try to fight them but we know that we will never win. History would most certainly bear witness to that being truthful. From the very beginning of our civilization, we have been a violent society, driven by fear, lack, and greed. Fundamentally, nothing has changed since but the level of sophistication of our weapons, killing more people in less time. Millions of people can be killed with the push of a button. All very anonymous, clean, and efficient from the perspective of the deliverer! Not so much, of course, on the other end—mass killings, maiming and traumatizing entire countries. We believe that wars are normal and a justified means of settling conflicts, trusting that here the sixth commandment, Thou shalt not kill, does not apply. If nations kill, then it is justified, and not a criminal act. Equally, death penalties are justified, as it is the law of that country or state within a country. However, as long as we support those beliefs, we will not end violence.

If one country has the right to be armed to their teeth, another must follow suit for reasons of self-protection, as simple as that. Once there is a war machine, it will be built up and eventually used, guaranteed. The only way to end that is to change our thinking. We have to stop the hyped-up feelings of nationalism, of defending what is presumed to be ours. In effect, in the end, nothing belongs to us. We are simply temporary custodians and caregivers, but nothing really belongs to us in the end. It belongs to none and to all. We also must stop believing the notion that it is 'us against them', whoever *they* may be. There is no such thing as "them." They are 'us' and we are 'them'.

Just for a minute, imagine that it were you on the other side of the border, the side where poverty is rampant and simply staying alive is treacherous. How would you feel? How would you feel if you couldn't earn a living to provide for your family? Or if you couldn't even be sure that your home would still be standing at the end of the day? Maybe it would be bombed, or robbed, or your children would be abducted? I know these are awful images but they are the reality for many people, our brothers and sisters who are living under terrible, inhumane conditions. How can we say that we will not help them, even worse, that we will build a wall to keep them out, and have travel restrictions for those that need refuge the most? What if this were you? And, actually, it is you, for we are all One. We are all children of God and we have to treat each other with love, compassion, and respect if we want to turn this nightmare into a dream.

I realize that this is a tall order. It is hard to change our thinking and our minds—hard to change how we deal with crises at home and around the world. I am simply asking you to consider the possibility of looking at it from a new perspective. We have tried the same approaches over the millennia and have gotten the same results. We have not been able to change or improve the human condition. At some point, we have to stop using the same tried-and-not-so-true methods, as we know they cannot bring any different results. If we were to input poor or wrong information into a computer, it would have to calculate incorrect results every single time. Garbage in, garbage out! It is scary to try a different method. Change is often uncomfortable but change is part of life. God Is Change and change is an opportunity to create anew, to experience a new vision, and, in our case, to correct what we gotten wrong so long ago. Of course, it is possible that we could go wrong, but it's highly unlikely as God Is Love and Light. We would be using divine, not physical, methods to change our world. I imagine the entire Universe functions quite well with God's Laws of Love, so why would it not work here?

The Dalai Lama stated that, "praying to God to save us was ridiculous and didn't make sense since those events were started by humans only. People are responsible for the bleeding that terrorism brought—not God. . . War is neither glamorous nor attractive. It is monstrous. Its very nature is one of tragedy and suffering...change has to come from within. We are the sole reason why war exists in the first place. We start it, we participate in it, and we prolong it. Of course, war and the large military establishments are the greatest sources of violence in the world. . . . We should feel fed up with the violence and the killing going on around us. If a human being is killed by an animal, it's sad, but if a human being is killed by another human being, it's unthinkable. We have to make a special effort to think of each other as fellow human beings, as our brothers and sisters."

It is an injustice and a travesty to claim that there is a god who would want his followers to go out and kill "infidels." That is human-made and self-serving for the good of the few power hungry, dark souls. We must start thinking from the heart, open our arms and include all, tearing down the walls that separate and divide us. We have to be the ones to let other people in first, and then in time they will let us in as well. "United we stand, divided we fall."

We have so many walls built up between us: social, political, and intellectual status; race and religion; and emotional and mental barriers. The intent of walls is to separate you from others, that which defines you and identifies you through your beliefs and your form. It is designed to create another perspective apart from God to experience in. In other words, to experience from a different point of view by having a separate identity from God. Through greater physicality, the barriers became more pronounced, though, and more difficult to penetrate, creating our state of division found on the basis of singularity.

We are closing ourselves off from others, shutting them and the world out, as we have done with God and the spirit realms. Unfortunately, today's greater connectivity through social media and the Internet have actually isolated us further from one another. It is now absolutely common for people to sit together and share a meal while using their cell phones—checking out their emails, feeds, and news—rather than being in the moment and being together.

The shift toward division is on the rise in global affairs as well—many countries exhibit strong nationalistic tendencies where they put their own interests above all others, declaring that they are first and have no intentions of being a member of a unified group of nations protecting and supporting one another. In the end, division and separation will only foster greater physicality and darkness. We have to move toward the Light; each one of us individually has to come to the conclusion that Light and Love are the way, and that we have to do this together, in unity and harmony.

We must seek stillness, away from all the confusing noise and buzz, to find inner peace and clarity. In clarity, we find the Light, the truth, and our essence. It is from this point, within us, that we will start dreaming a better dream. Only from within can we make changes and bring them about. Only from here will we find the comfort of love and acceptance, of being Whole. Within our innermost being we will become one with the One. We feel the overflowing and abundance of Love, which is to be shared and spread amongst all. It is from within that we *know* what we really want and that is Love—to love and to be loved, to give and to receive God's Love abundantly. No need for complexities, dogmas, and doctrines, just simply Love. All you need is Love.

You will probably think that that is too simplistic and too naïve. Yes, it is, and that's why it is good. God's messages are simple; just take the 10 commandments as an example. They are short and to the point. Everybody understands their meaning, and understands that they tell you to respect, honor, and treat others as you would like to be treated yourself. They are the basis of our human rights, of civility and equality. Fundamentally, they tell us to love one another.

We cannot go wrong in believing that Love heals and protects us. It is just that we have forgotten God's Love and we have also forgotten that we are Love. As we are His children, an aspect of Him, we are Love and Light as is He. If it works for Him, then it must work for us as well. As above, so below! We are being intentionally confused by the negativity of our physical circumstances, the chaos and noise we live in, and we are blinded by the darkness of our planet.

If we were to learn to love again, especially those we dislike or even hate, then we would start our healing process. There is the old saying that, "You catch more flies with honey than you do with vinegar." You catch more souls with Love than you do with hate. Love is eternal and divine whereas hate is temporary and human-made. It will always lose its energy and burn itself out. By giving out loving thoughts, being kind and compassionate, and respecting those you disagree with, you will help them heal through love. They may never know it but that's irrelevant. The fact is that whatever little change we can bring about is another milestone in our spiritual evolution and revolution.

You must give up the notion that the love and the light you are sending out cannot change anything. Do not fall victim to that falsehood! You can have a huge impact on your world—your neighborhood, your family, friends, and coworkers. And they in return, having been affected by your elevated loving frequencies, will radiate and reflect the Light and Love they have received. That's how it will be done. One by one, we become One again. Don't sit on the sidelines, passive and immobilized, but rise up, in heart-thought, and send out God's Love and Light.

Remember who you are, at your soul level, and what you believe in. Don't let chaos and confusion intimidate you. Don't be shut down by threats and fear. Don't fall victim to falsehoods and peer pressure. Let your heart-mind guide you to rise up against injustice, inequality, discrimination and hatred. Don't forget that you have the greatest instruments of all—Light and Love. Become a Light worker and change the reality we are presently living in. You have the power to bring about change. Remember we have created these conditions in the first place and thus we will have to be the ones to change them. It will have to start with You and me–every single step is a victory dance. Every single Light worker will help return balance to a world weighed down by its own false beliefs. As it stands now, positive energy levels are being depleted rapidly, and the more negative energy we are creating through perpetuating negativity, the more difficult it will be to turn things around. It is now, when we have not yet passed the point of no return, to flood this world with Light–God's Energy. If we wait and pretend to be spectators, it may be the beginning of the end. But that is not who we are. We will rise up to the occasion, face our challenges, unite and know that we are powerful. We have the awareness that God is with us; we know that we will bring about change through Love and Light. We need not fear for we are protected and loved. We have the power to change our World. It will take action and yes, it will take a village. We must come together in unity and love and we will succeed. Always remember, the greatest power in the Universe is the Power of Love!

Purpose of Life

"It does not matter how long you are spending on the earth, how much money you have gathered or how much attention you have received. It is the amount of positive vibration you have radiated in life that matters."

AMIT RAY, Meditation: Insights and Inspirations[1]

What is the meaning of life and what is it all about? Why are we here? What are we supposed to accomplish after all? Everybody asks themselves these questions, throughout their lives. Whenever we come to crossroads or endure crises, we come face to face with figuring out the purpose of our life and what meaning it has. Those are the moments that gently push us to dig a bit deeper, beneath our surface, to find what it is that we, at our core level, are looking for in our lives. What legacy would we like to leave behind? What do we want to have accomplished at the end of our lives? Are we only looking to fulfill our material dreams and expectations placed on us? Or, are we going to pursue what we need to do from the heart level? Can we combine the two?

Everybody has a different, unique purpose in every lifetime. Each incarnation will bring with it a new set of values that need to be explored and accomplished, aiming to reach higher every time. Higher purpose is when you find what will help you to evolve spiritually, to grow and expand, while reaching upward and outward. Higher purpose is also when you create something that will benefit humanity through healing and helping others' spiritual evolution.

---

1   Ray, Amit, PhD. *Meditation: Insights and Inspirations*. Atlanta, GA: Inner Light Publishers; 2015, p. 109.

To find your higher purpose, you have to be honest with yourself in answering what it is that you, at your soul level, want to achieve. Deep down, you know what you want to create in this life, but often feel pressured by expectations, self-doubt, and financial pressure to simply follow the money. However, when you are not aligned with your soul's purpose, you will face many struggles and crises. The reason is that you are going against your purpose, which you chose before birth. You need to bring your higher, or soul, purpose into harmony with your physical being to create a sense of balance between the two polarities.

When you know what your purpose is, you will create it through your thoughts. Your thoughts have the power to bring your visions and dreams into reality, but it will take some time to materialize. There is a time delay to bring your ethereal thoughts into form as here on Earth we are living in a physical, dense matter. When you know what you want, though, you will bring forth results much faster than those who are still aimlessly searching to find their purpose. When you go to a store and you know exactly what you need and where to find it, you'll be out in no time. But those of you, who are not quite clear what you want, will spend a lot more time looking around in the store.

The higher your soul purpose, the finer your vibrations and the greater your spiritual evolution will become. This too will speed up the process of spiritual growth, but there are really no time limits or restraints set on how long it should take you or by what age you should have found your higher purpose. This is your journey and your path—you should grow at your own rate, reaching the highest possible stage from your current level. Everybody is at a different level on his or her evolutionary path and everybody has his or her own journey. Therefore, you should never compare yourself to somebody else. That person may have chosen a completely different purpose and be at a different evolutionary level wherefore their experience varies from yours. All you will create in comparing is self-doubt, judgment, and envy or pity. You are responsible for your spiritual growth and achievements; therefore, focus on your own.

If you believe your purpose is to be financially successful, own a business, be famous or pursue a public career, make sure that you do not confuse the *want to's* and *have to's* with your soul's needs. At your soul level, the purpose is not the object you create but the essence behind it. In other words, the emotions and feelings created in achieving your purpose are what will always be with you and part of you. The object itself is of temporary value and a means to an end.

So, ask yourself what the motives are behind your purpose. If your motives are for the greater good of all, then not only will you receive the Universe's outpouring of help but also merge your higher self with your physical needs and being. However, if your intentions are only of a material value, it will take you much longer to find your purpose. What that means is that you are still at a level of greater attachment to form, the object itself, not its essence, and to possessing it. Therefore, you will want to hold on to it, even when it no longer serves you. Your growing process is hindered through attachment as you are limiting yourself—in holding on, you have little capacity left to be open for new creation. In other words, you are holding on to things that belong to your past, whether they are objects or relationships; you have lived those dreams already and there is no energy left in them anymore. You have experienced them, but you fear that you may not be able to replenish them due to scarcity will keep you stuck or, at the very least, slow you down. If there is nothing left to give or to receive, you need to let go and be open to new possibilities. Change is an opportunity to experience, grow, and evolve into higher spiritual levels. There is no such thing as scarcity either—the Universe is abundant with all the love you need and all the money you need to do good for others, and yourself.

You will find your purpose by going within and asking yourself, at your soul level, what it is that you want to create and accomplish in this life. If you choose not to listen to your voice but to please others, be they your parents or spouse, or succumb to what is expected of you as a successful member of society, then you are living a lie and will fall short in the end. For some of you, you will figure this out through hardships, failures, and conflict. When you are swimming against the currents of your life's waves, you will pretty much stay where you are. It causes stagnation and utter exhaustion, leaving you seemingly helpless and defeated, while swimming with the flow of your higher purpose you are streaming energy into what you create.

Your true purpose is to elevate your higher self and to join it with your inner essence for the combined goal of serving humanity. You decided before you were born what areas you wanted to focus on for your personal, spiritual growth and they didn't have anything to do with what car you wanted to drive or what house you wanted to own. The objects are the materializations of your thought forms, but it is the thought that created them. The thought, and the experience that comes along with it, remains with you and brings joy into your life. You will be able to fulfill your purpose and reach your goals with ease and harmony.

You have to believe in yourself and love yourself if you want to create your dreams. Do not look around and watch what others are doing, but look within and find what you want to be doing. Do not doubt yourself or the Universe for providing what you need to fulfill your purpose. It is there, waiting for you once you have decided to fulfill your destiny. Time is not of essence, but what is of essence is that you decide at the right time to follow your true purpose. Also, keep in mind, what you create today through your thoughts and manifestations will materialize tomorrow, or rather in the future. Don't become impatient and allow doubt to enter your dream and destroy it. You are the maker of your dreams, so believe in their validity and benefits for all. Set yourself the highest possible goals, reach for the stars and the moon without second thought or doubt, and believe from the bottom of your heart. If your higher purpose is in alignment with those of the Universe, you will be showered with abundance and success. Trust the Universe, believe in its goodness, and trust and believe in yourself. There may be times when you are tempted to just forget about it as negative voices are putting doubt into your thoughts. Be kind to those voices, lovingly set them free and instead, consider them to be your motivators. You know there are plenty of good reasons to move forward, more than letting go.

That is how you let the Universe know that you are ready to grow. Suddenly, you will notice new opportunities that were unimaginable beforehand, and doors will open that you thought were impenetrable, all to assist you in evolving spiritually. Most likely, there will be some challenges but none that you are not capable of overcoming, but they may be there to keep you on course. The higher your purpose, the more help you will receive from your spirit guides as you are creating higher vibrations thus finer frequencies. The lower your purpose, the greater the hardship, as the energy is harder, denser, and heavier. Aim high—it's actually easier, more fun, and so much more rewarding.

Before you set out on your purpose-driven path, you may be concerned that you do not have enough time to create what you had in mind. Yet again, you will notice how, magically, you will find the time to pursue your vision. It is as if all else disappears from your plate, and you have all the time necessary. To get started, you have to make a personal commitment to keep your purpose pure and to stick with it. Then, you have to manifest your dream into reality by seeing yourself in it as if it were already real. Visualize yourself as the person you will be when your higher purpose is materialized.

In other words, look ahead to see yourself in your future reality. Hold on to that vision, believe in it from your heart, and make sure that its purpose is to help and heal, serving the greater good of all. One of the basic laws of achieving anything is honesty, which applies to you personally as well. Be honest with yourself and your feelings. Don't do anything because you feel you have to or because it would look good in the eyes of others. Be honest with your feelings and emotions, for if you are not happy and balanced, neither will be your dreams, or your higher purpose. You are as important as the next person, but you are the most important one in achieving your higher purpose successfully. You have to make your own life's work before you can heal and help others effectively.

You decide what kind of a world you would like to create. You decide on dreaming a better dream for yourself and the world. You will find all the strength necessary within as without through the support of your guides and God. Find strength in your challenges; embrace them and love them for they will firm your resolve. You are the creator of your dreams. Align yourself with your soul's highest purpose and change the world from within.

The Future You

*"Power is of two kinds. One is obtained by the fear of
punishment and the other by acts of love. Power based
on love is a thousand times more effective and permanent
then the one derived from fear of punishment."*

MAHATMA GANDHI

Pope Francis gave a TEDx talk on April 25, 2017, with the title "The Future You."[2] It is most appropriate in defining our role and our responsibility in changing our way of thinking and our behavior. Here are some excerpts of what His Holiness had to say on that subject:

"I would love it if this meeting could help to remind us that we all need each other, none of us is an island, an autonomous and independent "I," separated from the other, and we can only build the future by standing together, including everyone. We don't think about it often, but everything is connected, and we need to restore our connections to a healthy state... Through the darkness of today's conflicts, each and every one of us can become a bright candle; a reminder that light will overcome darkness, and never the other way around...Hope is the virtue of a heart that doesn't lock itself into darkness, that doesn't dwell on the past, does not simply get by in the present, but is able to see a tomorrow. Hope is the door that opens onto the future... And it can do so much, because a tiny flicker of light that feeds on hope is enough to shatter the shield of darkness. A single individual is enough for hope to exist, and that individual can be you. And then there will be another "you," and another "you,"

2   His Holiness Pope Francis. *Why the only future worth building includes everyone.* Available
     at: https://youtu.be/36zrJfAFcuc. Accessed September 14, 2017.

and it turns into an "us." And so, does hope begin when we have an "us?" No. Hope began with one "you." When there is an "us," there begins a revolution...The message I would like to share today is, indeed, about revolution: the revolution of tenderness... Tenderness means to use our eyes to see the other, our ears to hear the other, to listen to the children, the poor, those who are afraid of the future. To listen also to the silent cry of our common home, of our sick and polluted earth...Yes, tenderness is the path of choice for the strongest, most courageous men and women. Tenderness is not weakness; it is fortitude. Please, allow me to say it loud and clear: the more powerful you are, the more your actions will have an impact on people, the more responsible you are to act humbly... The future of humankind isn't exclusively in the hands of politicians, of great leaders, of big companies. Yes, they do hold an enormous responsibility. But the future is, most of all, in the hands of those people who recognize the other as a "you" and themselves as part of an "us." We all need each other."

Any successful revolution or uprising needs people, as does this one. We need you. The more of you, the better! To bring about change, we need to tilt the scales back to a balanced state. We can only do that if we get more people on the spiritual side of the scales, thus decreasing the amount of people on the physical side. It is all about balances, or the lack thereof. But it all starts with you, and me of course. It is like an avalanche that is set in motion by a tiny snowball rolling down the hill. The mountain snow gets attached to the snowball and it grows and grows as it gains more and more momentum, which is precisely what we need so that change can come about. Our snowball is thought. It is the thought that believes in a better way—believes in harmony, love, and equality. The thought has to be originating from the heart center so that it is as pure as it can possibly be under our current negative and tainted conditions. In meditation, this thought is filled with God Light and Love, elevating its frequency and increasing its radius as it is being channeled out. Every Light-filled thought will affect our current state positively and bring another ray of Light into the darkness, piercing through it and slowly breaking night. It is the "drip-drip" effect and, in this case, it's the positive drip.

As it stands right now, we are in need of an enormous amount of Light. We are witnessing an ever-increasing state of chaos, war mongering, hate, violence, and intolerance. On the political front, we are witnessing the disintegration of unions between nations that have stabilized peace and encouraged cooperation for decades, while tensions are rising between more hostile ones. Global balances of power are shifting, as we are entering a new era of instability and insecurity. Economically, we are witnessing the rise of great imbalances of wealth, with the very few owning the greatest percentage of wealth. Our youth around the world are struggling to make ends meet, pay the rent or mortgage, and/or pay off their student loans while considering starting a family of their own. The cost of living is going up whereas, at best, wages are stagnant—at worst, wages have come down.

Socially we are witnessing more forms of discrimination against races and religions, which really means we have never learned from any of our historical upheavals and tragedies. Frankly, we seem to be rotating rather than evolving. In addition to all the havoc we are finding ourselves in, we are now also in an age of greater mass communication. Negative news and media do not only inundate us, we ourselves perpetrate that negative energy by absorbing it into our thoughts and passing it on. I realize how difficult it is to stop that constant flow of negative energy in the form of "breaking news" and more news being piped through the media outlets. Nobody is immune to the barrage of information!

News per se, is a reporting of negative events, because that's how the money is made, as people won't watch a whole lot of "feel good" coverage. That's what we are used to watching but, frankly, it's also what we want to see, otherwise it wouldn't be selling and therefore not get the all-important high ratings. It's in our DNA— we are heavy on the negative, light on the positive. In other words, too much physicality and not enough spirituality! But, we are in charge of our thoughts and we can turn off the constant chatter, the negative repetition of events, be they from personal experiences or public events. We have a choice in how we think or how we are influenced by the thoughts spewed into any given sphere.

The Field, having a mind of its own, is creating confusion and chaos by design. Why, you should ask? As it is to the Earth what the aura is to the human body, it equally has a consciousness charged by the energy of the thoughts and beliefs of humankind, which is set to predominantly negative. When we are in a dark mood or physically ill, then our aura not only reflects and absorbs that state of being but also transmits that energy right back into us. But in moments of heightened states of negative emotions, such as rage for example, it seems as if they were in control of mind and body determining the actions taken. So, it is with the Field. Our source of energy is physical and negative, as it is for the Field, due to our mutual disconnect from Divine energy, unless we consciously re-energize ourselves with God Light. We can affect change by transmitting positive Light energy into the Field, which will transform it for the advancement of humankind and the planet. In chaos though, you can't focus, you can't think clearly, and consequently you can't find the underlying causes creating the existing conditions. Aristotle already stated that, "the least initial deviation from the truth is multiplied later a thousandfold," which really means that a small effect, such as a lie, will have an explosive growth causing chaotic conditions that are difficult to scrutinize. The intent of the Field's consciousness is that we should not discover the power our thoughts have, thus keeping its position as the perpetuator of negative thoughts and beliefs causing havoc and great damage to the planet and us.

Chaotic and disorderly circumstances are sought for by anybody who has an agenda to confuse and therefore mislead others. If you were to set a fire in your neighbor's house, the neighborhood would cease focusing on rumors about any of your possible misconduct. Confusion, distraction, and sheer havoc have caused many great wars just as a means to hide internal problems from the public. That's how it's done. This is precisely what is occurring now.

The speed of our planet is increasing—we are burning up. There seems to be less time in a day. It sounds ridiculous as there are still 24 hours in a day, but what has decreased is the time set aside to be quiet and relax. We are so addicted to technology right now that we have to check our cell phones constantly, even before turning the lights off at night. We are held hostage by a negative flow of energy residing all around us, which is systematically leading us away from what truly matters most at the end of our lives. The negative energies present, and ruling our environment, have discreetly taken control over our brains and really brainwashed us. We have become immune to all the terror occurring all around us. We barely flinch when yet another story of a terror attack hits the screen, or a news story covering the opioid addiction, with its heart-breaking consequences for those who watch, unable to help.

But, we are rather suspicious when somebody comes along and claims to have messages from the spirit world. No can do! That's got to be fake and we must be cautious. Unfortunately, there are fakes and frauds, but we should not dismiss the urgent messages coming from the other side. The way to protect yourself from scoundrels and charlatans is to go with your gut. All legitimate spiritual messages will resonate with your heart. Let your instincts guide you to discern between the fake and real. If they don't feel right, let them go. Your heart will know. Whatever you do, don't decide with your brain— it is ego driven and influenced by the negativity of our planet, just like the Field. There should be logic and simplicity in true spiritual messages, versus the complexities fed to us by the propaganda of the Field.

The antidote to all that noise is meditation. Indulge and pamper yourself with time taken for calming your mind. Positivity begins within. In order to survive—no, actually, to improve our lives—we have to find our personal time-out zone. Recently, I spoke to a young man who was working in a restaurant at the sushi bar. He told me that he had just taken his first day off in four months. That one-day off had felt like an extravagancy! That is the perfect prescription for burning out physically and, of course, mentally.

We need time to reflect and connect if we want to protect ourselves from all the negative and hostile forces invading and attaching themselves to us. We can't walk it alone. We need to activate our support team to give us strength and guidance. Most of us can't see, hear, or feel our spirit guides but that doesn't mean that they're not there. This is where we have to rely on faith and trust—we cannot measure or prove spiritual phenomena but we can see the results. Through the regular practice of meditation, you will notice a renewed and growing sense of hope, love, and inspiration, as you leave behind doubt, worries, and anxieties. You will notice the benefits of your calmed state of mind in your work, relationships, and your health.

By tuning out of the negative airwaves, and tuning into the higher spiritual frequencies, you are creating a shift in consciousness. Less attention is given to the anxiety-driven emotions, thus decreasing their power over you, while more attention is given to a deep knowledge, to faith, that you are loved and protected. You are expanding your awareness, which assists you in halting the endless cycle of negativity. You become aware of your negative thoughts, learn not to judge them and instead release them into the ether. Once you are able to recognize the nature of your thoughts, you can discard the ones that will only harm and harness the ones that will be beneficial. You have taken control over your thoughts and the direction of your life, which will affect other lives. As we well know, we are part of the Whole, and if one gets illuminated, the effects will be felt elsewhere. When you turn on the light in a dark room, even if it's only one single bulb, it will light up a large area. The darker the room, the greater is the impact of even one single light bulb. That is the power of Light.

We have to come to a point where we start understanding and, most importantly, believing that true change comes from within, not without. History bears witness that there have been no real fundamental changes in who we are as a people, over the millennia. We are still and have always been a violent society. From the moment we became humanized, we felt fear and lack, doubt, and insecurity.

Our intentional separation and distance from God and the spirit realms left us weak and vulnerable, while our physicality buried all memories of our true origin and essence. Thus, a society based on flight and fight, on survival of the fittest was born. However, we still have and always had the divine spark within us, which is why we are aiming to improve our humanity.

We have approached change through the physical means at hand, meaning through political, social, economic, and religious means, but in the end, all failed. They are a bit like a bandage on a deep, stenchy wound. The reason being that all things physical are contaminated by negative energy, thus have no lasting effects on the changes brought forth. We have to change the entire structure on which this world was created, from the foundation up. In other words, we have to change the condition if we want to have a successful outcome. Just like diagnosing and treating an illness. We can opt for handing out aspirins when the patient has meningitis, or choose to treat the root cause of the illness and eliminate it.

In our case, we have to approach change from a spiritual aspect, not from a physical one. This is where trust has to come in, for we have never tried it therefore have no clue if it's going to work or not. But one thing we do know: what we are doing now is totally ineffective. As all things in creation are both cyclical and circular, life follows along the curvature of a half-circle, or an arc—one half in physicality and one in spirituality, completing the circle and the cycle. It is like the sun and the moon—as one rises, the other one declines. All animate and inanimate matter, as well as all thoughts and beliefs, civilizations, cultures, and even fashion trends follow the arc shape. They rise like the sun with its golden pink rays breaking night, filled with all its future potential, climbing along its curved path to reach its zenith at mid-point, from where it exerts great levels of energy and power. Although the energy is still felt for some time, the descent has begun, ending with the sun setting in a warm orange-golden glow. So, the question is, what point of the arc are we on now?

We are certainly observing the heightened tensions politically, economically, socially, and religiously on a global level. There is an almost hostile atmosphere in the air. Divisions between people are growing deeper and wider. It has become difficult to have civil arguments about issues concerning our policies and the direction they are taking.

Globally, there were 156 terrorist incidents in January 2017 alone. There is cause for concern. We are losing our war against terror because we are fighting terror with terror. We believe that our might will win in the end but it is undermined by the increased flurry of global negativity. It is yet another example of the law of attraction: we attract more of what we are so preoccupied with. We have to put an end to the hate and the philosophies that we are applying to heal a serious condition. We have to consciously, through our awareness, stop this cycle of negativity. Do not participate in it and do not perpetuate it. Instead send Light and Love into these situations. Send it to the politicians and the religious leaders who stoke hatred and fear through the misuse of God's will and His name. Let us stop the cycle of hate and violence now. Let us be the founders of a new way to heal and save us all. If we don't change soon, there may be nothing left to worry about or to change. Time is running out, tensions are heightening and the Earth is heating up. What are we waiting for? Until it's too late and we have to start all over again?

We have to go within to see things differently again. There is no other way. God Light has never been taken away from us; it's just buried beneath layers of construct. So, it's time to peel away and uncover the power we hold within. Only God Light can reverse the effects of the fall and save us from yet another destructive end of a cycle. It is therefore an absolute priority to step aside from what's happening and visualize what we would like to see happening. Change your vision and change the world.

Change what you wish for. Let it be peace and harmony, and a better way of life for all, instead of attracting more personal wealth to you. Presently, we are very much invested in the physical and material elements of this world. We are preoccupied and enamored with wealth and power, social status, and fame. Money and material values are idolized in today's society, which makes our quest and an often insatiable greed the driving force of our waking hours. I am not referring to earning a living—we all obviously have to do that—but to the element of greed and the gratification of our senses through materialism. It leads us away from spiritual values and gains, which we can actually take with us when we leave this world. Money is, like everything else, a form of energy, but it attracts a lot of negativity to itself. Infuse Light and use it to do good things to those who need help. For those who cannot help with money, channel Light instead and it will have a huge impact for a long time. We all have to give to receive ourselves. We need better lives, but we cannot get them through the power of wealth. That is always empty and hollow. We can get better lives through the use of Light—what we send out in love and compassion, will come back to us multiplied. A fabulous return on investment!

It is a rather simple approach and an inexpensive investment in our future. Illuminate yourself and others with God's Light and Love. In simplicity, we will find our solution; in complexity, we will find our demise. All it will ask for you is to have faith, to truly believe with all your heart that you too can and will make a difference by sending out Divine Light. Believe it and just do it. Become a Light worker and be part of the revolution. Become the Light that shattered the darkness. Start the Light revolution from within. May the Light be with you!

"That's been one of my mantras—focus and simplicity. Simple can be harder than complex: You have to work hard to get your thinking clean to make it simple. But it's worth it in the end because once you get there, you can move mountains."[3]

STEVE JOBS

---

3   Burrows, Peter. "Back to the Future at Apple." *Bloomberg News.* Available at: https://www. bloomberg.com/news/articles/1998-05-24/back-to-the-future-at-apple. Accessed September 29, 2017.

CHAPTER 14

Meditations
and Visualizations

*"The intuitive mind is a sacred gift and the rational mind
is a faithful servant. We have created a society that
honors the servant and has forgotten the gift."*

ALBERT EINSTEIN

Our society certainly has become enamored with materialism and forgotten the true values of a life well lived. It is no wonder when we are inundated with images of happy, smiling people surrounded by their wealth. Those images become motivators to pursue that very ideal which hopefully will be accompanied by happiness. The Pursuit of Happiness is about chasing the dream of making money and, in all fairness, money is what is needed in our society to make ends meet. How else would we be able to provide for our children's future and our own? Per se, money is energy like anything else—it is how we regard it—and what emphasis we put on it that makes the difference. The question is whether it controls us or whether we are in control of it. If our every waking moment is consumed with thoughts of making more, needing more, and taking more, then we are in its grip. Then it has become a negative force. The simple reason is that money can have attachments of fear, greed, eternal lack, and need, but also of empowerment and broad spheres of influence. When you have those attachments, you become a servant to the negative energies of money. However, if money is serving us to make ends meet and to give to others, then it has a very different vibration. The reason is that you will affect the frequencies of that money depending on the role it plays in your life. Take a knife, for example—it can be used to butter your bread or, sadly, to kill. It's what we do with it that makes the difference.

If the materialistic side of money wins, the pursuit of happiness will be based on the amount of money needed to buy joy, security, and the prized possessions of our dreams. Yet, there is still that nagging lack within, for money is shallow, in and of itself. Money does not buy happiness. It doesn't buy security either or, put differently, it doesn't buy safety and security. In the blink of an eye, money can and has been lost, and lost with it are the walls that were there to be protective of such loss. Protection, security, and safety throughout the ups and downs of life can only be found within. That is why it is so important to learn to connect. Everybody here has to fall into the Earth's rhythm—but choose to make it your tool, not be its tool. For that, we must learn to appreciate the intuitive mind and give it a priority status over the rational mind. Meditation is the way to achieve that goal.

"The worship of the golden calf of old has found a new and heartless image in the cult of money and the dictatorship of an economy which is faceless and lacking any truly human goal."

POPE FRANCIS

Life is a journey leading us from darkness into the light, finding our deepest truth. And meditation is our tool to help us navigate the waters of our life's events—guide us through the storms with its high waves as well as the stillness with its flat waves. It is through meditation that we find our balance, steadying our vessel. It is not easy for anybody to get through life's challenges, to overcome all the doubt and daily worries that our survival instinct throws at us. Without it we may fall prey to being misguided into the depth of anxiety, of not *knowing* that we are safe, somehow or other. There is a *knowing* found in meditation that is like the light shining from the light tower in the dark of night on high seas—a true *knowing* that we are safe. All we have to do is reach out. It cannot come to us, but we can go to it. We have been endowed with a great gift that keeps on giving. The peace and certainty we find reaches far beyond our circumference. It touches all those we are surrounded by.

Let's assume you have a crisis in your life. There are two ways to handle it: lose yourself in the overwhelming onslaught of problems, or remain calm and assured that a way will be found to solve the problem, one way or another. That is the difference meditation will bring to your life. You are able to become still and focused. You will have clarity to navigate safely out of this situation. My Dutch grandmother used to say that God has not promised us calm seas but that He would guide us through the high seas to safe harbor. And meditation is your best tool to get His guidance directly from Him.

If you care enough about yourself and love yourself enough, you will give yourself the gift of time. Take time out of your busy day and use it wisely in meditation. You are worth it. It will be the greatest gift you have ever received. Not to mention that it is easy, always at hand, and cheap. All it takes is time and a bit of effort to get used to being still.

When we step aside for a moment and look at daily life as if watching a movie, we realize just how chaotic it really is. There is so much noise from our government; it is actually in a total state of chaos, which affects not only all branches but also all government agencies and aspects. Undoubtedly, this chaos will affect everyone's equilibrium—a trickle-down imbalance. It will affect the sense of stability in our personal lives and bring with it concerns about our income, access to healthcare, global policies, and the effects of climate change. The chaos and noise clutters our brains with so much baggage and overburdens us to the point of collapse and utter exhaustion. It is a tool to distract us from finding the truth, be that from the current White House administration under President Trump, from life in general, or from within. Typically, smoke screens are used to conceal something of great importance or value from those who are seeking to discover the truth behind them. Our smoke screens are chaos, the ego, and the Field who keep us distracted so we remain ignorant about our power and the fact that our thoughts activate and motivate our energy, creating our reality. Subsequently, we are unaware that our negative thoughts fuel more negativity throughout.

> *"All that we are is the result of what we have thought. The mind is everything. What we think we become."*
>
> Attributed to **GAUTAMA SIDDHARTHA, THE BUDDHA**[1]

1　　Vintini, Leonardo. *Do Our Thoughts Have the Power to Affect Reality?* Available at: http://www.theepochtimes.com/n3/67071-can-the-mind-affect-reality/. Accessed September 14, 2017.

By seeking stillness though, and by choosing to go within, we have the ability to expand our awareness of our core self, and bring the unconscious into consciousness. From here, we can re-charge our positive energy and re-create our reality into one of positivity—transmitting it out into every cell of our body as that of the Universe. Thus, we take back control of our thoughts, the ego, and the Field and reverse the negative state of affairs to a positive one.

It is imperative for the pursuit of true happiness as well as for our survival that we find that calm place within. When all the constructs of confusion and distractions fall away, we can hear our inner voice guiding us and actually see our own visions turn into reality. Decide what you want to create, who you want to be, visualize it, and, then, with the power of your thought-energy, take action and make it come true. Visualizations are one step toward your goal, but without action/energy they won't go anywhere. As with all things in creation, movement requires the polar energy charges of both negative and positive, or physical and spiritual. One drives the other forward, as one without the other goes nowhere.

By allowing yourself some reflective time, you are giving yourself the ability to look inward, to find answers and to know who you truly are at your soul level—your highest self. You should also establish what it is that you want in life. What is your highest purpose? A quiet mind will allow you to get to know yourself, to accept yourself for who you are—not who you should be according to other people, or may have been—and to love yourself. As you get in touch with your essence, and shut out all the noise, you can actually hear the voice of your soul and see the images you are creating in your mind. Open up to the Universe and allow your intuitive mind to roam free, creating everything that you desire. If you are looking for guidance, have faith in the messages that come into your mind. If you are looking for specific things, then focus and visualize on them. But you should ask yourself, if you really want those exact items or do you want their essence, or rather is it the new house you want or the security and safety behind owning it. As you connect with your higher self and understand the essence behind your needs and desires, you can receive them in many ways. This is being nonspecific and open to the enormous potential the Universe has in store for you. Either way, once you have established your true motivation, put it into action by asking for it.

Many people avoid stillness—they choose not to sit still and to reflect on what really matters and what would bring real change to their lives. They will always find an excuse to do a hundred other things, like mundane chores just so to be physically busy and mentally unavailable. Generally, there is the flawed perception that productivity is the only means to attaining your goals and creating your future. Alternatively, multitasking is another misconception because, in reality, very little will be accomplished as you are stretched out too far and too thin while being unfocused to have an impact on any one task. Instead, if you want to move to higher levels of consciousness, you must focus. Respect and honor the time you have gifted yourself by being quiet mentally, emotionally, and physically. In these reflective times you re-vitalize your energy, get a clearer sense of self and connect to the seat of your intuition and inspiration creating your new ideas. When you clear your head of all that clutter and think of nothing, you open up more space in your mind to bring life to new creation.

Meditation will give you clarity of thought and the capacity to focus that thought. Just imagine thought being a light bulb. You can either illuminate an entire room depending on the strength of the bulb or instead, when putting it into a flashlight, you can focus and enlighten one spot at a time. There is clarity, focus, calmness, and utter strength found through the support of the spiritual energy source—all by going within.

The advantage meditation has over prayer is that it is nondenominational. There is no danger in being misled by falsehoods of any organized religion, trying to lead us in what to believe or not. Some religions are nothing but propaganda machines for a certain cause and deceive people into doing unthinkable things, committing crimes of unimaginable violence, lured in by falsehoods and empty promises. Be your own guide instead, in purity and without any religious propaganda. It's your one on one with God. Actually, there is a whole light force behind you once you start the practice of daily meditation. And sometimes the greatest sense of joy is in realizing that you are not alone. Just know that if you ask for guidance or help, it will be there for you. When you connect to the Universe, you can have anything you want. As you focus on your highest purpose, you will find that "miraculously" every door opens for you. When your motivation is in alignment with that of the Universe, you will receive new creative ideas abundantly as well as support through people who will reach out to you to help you with money, advice and/or connections. Keep that vision and be open for surprises!

Another difference between meditation and prayer is that in meditation you listen, you open your heart to hear and listen to the messages brought forth. In prayer, you talk to God. Personally, I use a combination of both, but always from the heart. It has to be heartfelt in order to go anywhere. As we now know, the heart center is the original thought center—not the head, which is ego driven, and like the Field, negative. So, through the heart, connect in mediation or prayer to the greatest strength found in the Universe and it's right within you. How convenient! If you choose to recite memorized prayers, like a ritual, frankly, they won't even reach the ceiling of the room. They have no strength, as they do not come from the heart. They are simply recitations without any genuine feelings. Take communal prayers during a sermon—everybody repeats the prayer but how deeply felt are they really?

In recent years, there have been many scientific studies evaluating the benefits of meditation and the results are more than impressive. This, needless to say, does not come as a surprise to the Eastern cultures that have practiced meditation for centuries. They know the benefits, no studies needed. The West only believes its benefits with scientific proof in hand, at least as a society. Many have embraced it without research or proof and are aware of the benefits it brings into every life. It starts by taking away the agitation of the mind. Daily stress brings with it agitation, and agitation is the chaos of the mind. Everybody deals with stress daily. There is simply no way to avoid having stress in our lives. Stress drives anxiety and most people don't know how to cope with anxiety, which explains the increase in prescription antianxiety medications. We need to regulate and balance our emotions by changing our thoughts from negative to positive, from dark to light, from anger and despair to love and hope, through the power of a focused mind. Therefore, meditation is the best prescription to calm the mind.

"If every 8-year old in the world is taught meditation, we will eliminate violence from the world within one generation."

DALAI LAMA

Meditation has many benefits, including improving concentration and focus, learning and memory, mood and well-being, the ability to work under stress, information processing and decision making, empathy and positive relationships, optimism and positive emotions, mental strength, resilience, emotional intelligence, academic performance and cognitive retention, self-esteem and self-care, happiness, social skills, job performance, immunity, and overall health.

Meditation reduces mind-wandering, worries, anxiety, fear, physical and mental stress, depression, feelings of hostility, emotional eating, feelings of isolation and loneliness, compulsion, pain symptoms, social anxiety, symptoms of panic disorder and ADHD, alcohol and substance abuse, symptoms of asthma and rheumatoid arthritis, inflammatory diseases, inflammatory bowel disease, cellular inflammation, fibromyalgia, premenstrual and menopausal symptoms, signs and symptoms of aging of the brain, Alzheimer's, high cholesterol, high blood pressure, risk of heart disease, and stroke.

Meditation helps to quiet the mind. Especially when we are in a not-so-perfect state. When we are not happy, then our mind wanders and reviews and highlights all those details ad nauseam. That's when our head thoughts become our greatest enemies that won't stop until they have destroyed us, totally overwhelming us. It's like a wave taking us right down with it. Meditation helps you swim with the flow, not against the wave. We learn to dial it down and not kick it up a notch. In calmness, we can collect our thoughts and cool things down. Calmness brings the ability to see through a problem clearly, while letting go of anger and hostility even in the most heated situation. We have the tools and knowledge to take ourselves out of the moment, taking the power away from the ego and giving it to the heart. We become more compassionate and develop empathy for the other person with whom we have conflict. It takes the sting out of our anger and even hatred by turning it around into love and compassion. Meditation helps us find self-awareness through introspection. It is not a method to avoid or flee our thoughts but to learn to accept them, not judge them, and to let go of them.

There is no question that there is a mind–body connection. Your mental attitude and state of mind can and will influence your health. If you allow your emotions to run you, then you will become their victim. If you allow arguments and hateful rhetoric to poison every cell in your body, then you will not only shorten your life span but also ruin the quality of your life in the meantime. A life lived in a negative state of mind not only ruins that life but also ruins all the ones it affects. It's a pesticide. When you spray pesticides, you will clear the field of weeds and insects temporarily, but you will also poison yourself through the ingestion of food produced from those sprayed crops—along with all those beneficial insects. Through meditation, we can control our mental state and choose an optimistic and positive outlook no matter how tough life may be at the moment.

When I started meditation, my mind really played tricks on me. I was flooded with unimportant thoughts about what to make for dinner, what I needed to buy at the grocery store, my daily activities and schedule, and what somebody said to me and how I responded. I learned to let it go, and not try to suppress them. I learned to become more comfortable with me, my thoughts, and not to fight them. For in fighting, we create negative energy, which is exactly what we don't want. Once I did that, their meaninglessness and distractive nature became quite clear to me—and it became apparent how I had been a servant to my thoughts. Once you get over that point, there is no greater freedom and a little heaven on earth while meditating. It is from here where we connect to the real source of energy: God.

"If I had no sense of humor, I would long ago have committed suicide."

MAHATMA GANDHI

With all the seriousness of our lives, we can and should never, never forget the power of laughter. Learn to laugh again at yourself and also at the humor in others or other situations. If we want to survive and survive it well, we better learn to laugh and not take ourselves so seriously all the time.

Meditation Practice

As defined by Giovanni Dienstmann, there are three types of meditation:

- Focused attention
- Open monitoring
- Effortless presence

In focused attention, the meditator is focusing on a single object, be it the breath, a mantra, or visualization, during the entire course of the meditation. The chosen object can be anything—a flower, the sound of waves, or a body part. With practice, the meditator will be able to extend the time to hold that attention on the object longer and longer, and thus to withdraw from all outside stimuli and distractions. This helps to steady the mind and deepen the experience. In open monitoring meditation, the meditator does not focus on any object but, rather, allows the mind to flow freely. It monitors those thoughts; in other words, perceives them without judgment or resistance or attachment to their experience. It guides into a state of being detached from experiences and simply viewing them without dwelling on them. There are no restrictions as to what our attention is given to—be it external or internal stimuli. Effortless meditation, as Giovanni Dienstmann explains, is where—in the final analysis—all meditation will end up. Whether the meditator chooses to focus on an object or to freely roam, the process trains the mind to keep the thoughts still. It's no different from going to the gym and training the muscles in your body to keep it strong. Meditation is a mind trainer. This is the ultimate purpose of meditation: by training the mind to be empty, steady, and still, we can attain greater awareness and deeper states of consciousness. With practice, we can reach these states of heightened awareness effortlessly.

It is a personal choice as to which one of these techniques works best for you. Obviously, you are free to create one that works best for you. The best meditation is the one that gets the best results at your stage of development, and sometimes for a particular day. There are days that I find it difficult to concentrate, and so I choose open monitoring meditation. Other days, it is best to focus. I also always include prayers at the end of my meditation. I visualize bright white light entering me, enveloping me, and bathing me. Then I channel that light out into the Universe—be it a friend or stranger in need of help, be it a humanitarian crisis that needs light, or to reverse the effects of global warming on our planet. It is important that we give out the light that we have received. It is through this light that we can bring about change.

"You must be the change you wish to see in the world."

MAHATMA GANDHI

How to Meditate

First, you must find a quiet place in your home, a designated room for example, or outside in nature. You certainly can create a little shrine with your dedicated cushion or chair, your incense or candles. Sit straight on the cushion on the floor with your legs crossed, and your feet should touch the ground. You can also sit straight on a chair with your feet planted on the ground. Place your hands in your lap and relax. You can either fully close your eyes or keep them in a soft gaze on the ground. Keep your mouth closed, as you will be breathing in and out of your nose, sinuses permitting. I have also found a practice where you breathe in through the nose and then breathe out through the mouth. Relax, drop your shoulders, pay attention to the parts in your body where you feel the tension, and let go. You can say to yourself: relax, relax, relax, and send light into those body areas.

Then, start concentrating on your breath. Calm it and breathe deeply into the stomach, hold to a count of 5 to 10, then exhale and hold the breath for a count of 5 to 10. Repeat this 10 times, as deeply as you can and as focused on the breath. If you lose your concentration, no worries, start again. I then visualize that large white ball of light flowing through me, from the top down into the ground, and then back up again. I clear all negative attachments from me, both external and internal, and replace the void with more white light. Then I thank God and all my spirit guides for all their help and support, after which I go into stillness. That is where I connect to my true self, my real source of energy. Upon completion, I close my chakras, thank God again, and open my eyes.

Visualizations and Affirmations

The Universe is yours for the asking, but you have to know how to ask and what you should ask for. Under no circumstances should you ever ask for anything that may harm somebody else. It is against any and all laws of the Universe, specifically God's Laws. And, never forget, what you ask for will come back to you as well. That goes for positive and negative thoughts and wishes. So, do yourself a favor and send out loving thoughts and have wishes that will only benefit you and others. Do no harm—not in deed nor in thought. Do not wish anybody ill, even under the most extreme of all cases. It is not for us to be judge or jury, but to be healers and helpers for only in that spirit will we bring about lasting change and ultimate justice to all.

It is equally important to understand that you must be able to give as much as you wish to receive. Giving and receiving are part of the same flow of energy—in and out, up and down. If you only take, you will successfully block the flow of energy. This is the balance system the Universe is based upon–positive and negative energies or, if you prefer, plus and minus in a state of equilibrium.

> *"That we spent we had:*
> *That we gave we have:*
> *That we left we lost."*

EDWARD COURTENAY,
3rd/11th Earl of Devon (c.1357 – 5 December 1419)

Whatever we give to others, will forever be ours. We cannot lose what we have given to others. My mother used to tell us that, "You will never become poorer from giving."

Give generously, love deeply, and dream without fear or worry. Send your thoughts into the Universe, with love and light, and you will get a return. There is no other way. There is perfect balance in the Universe. If you want love, give love to others first. If you want to feel happy, then make somebody happy first. If you feel down, boost somebody else up first. If you want peace in the world, then give peace first and start in your own home or work. If you want a better job, make your current one better first by changing your negative attitude. If you want more respect, then respect others first. Whatever you want, learn to give it first. This will work for anything you wish for.

Never wish to get more at the expense of somebody else. Do not take from others—on the contrary, give more to others instead. There is enough to go around in the end. What you take, will be taken from you in due time. Learn to be patient; all will come to you when it is meant to be and at the best possible time.

If you want or need specific things, learn to be specific about your wishes. Do not be vague about them and leave it to the Universe to decide for you what kind of car or new house you would like to have. You have to tell the Universe exactly what you want, write it down, put it out, and be patient. Make a wish list and write it down in a special notebook, on your computer, pad, or phone. Start each wish with "I want . . ." or, alternatively, I have also started with "I am . . ." and keep on going until you're done. Don't be shy—it's only for your eyes and the Universe anyway—and be specific and detailed, but keep it real. Ask for things that are actually attainable rather those that are impossible and would violate Universal Laws. Keep it positive. Don't write, for example, "I want no pain," which brings up the image of pain. Instead, affirmatively state, "I am in perfect health and enjoying every moment of my life."

After you have completed your list, you have to truly believe in its validity. Don't let doubt cloud your visions and your dreams, but believe in them with absolute conviction. Sometimes you may not get exactly what you asked for, but an alternative version of it, which will most likely turn out to be better for you in the long run. Never give up hope or become impatient. Let the Universe take care of it while you do the best you can to be positive, optimistic, and at the top of your game. Also, don't forget to help those who cross your path and may need your help. If you are stingy when it comes to giving, trust me, the Universe will be stingy with you as well.

You need to understand that only you can create for yourself what you want and, frankly, that is your greatest gift and one that is the least understood. If you want a better future, picture it in your mind and talk about it to yourself and others. Every statement you make about your beliefs will become a truth. Thus, beware of the thoughts and images you project about yourself. Be careful with the words you utter throughout the day, even if they are to yourself; so, don't undermine your positive vision by thoughtless phrases that enter doubt into your consciousness. I am referring to sayings such as, "I can't ever achieve that" or "I'm not good enough." Whenever you think of the future you project your energy into it, and if you project doubt, you will direct your energy toward that. What you need to do is to stop yourself when you notice doubt creeping into your mind and notice your energy dropping. Take a deep breath, revisit your vision and turn your energy around, and then transmit those images out. Change those negative or uncertain images in your mind and replace them with visions of determination and tenacity, and mumble to yourself, "I got this," "I am powerful," or any variety of "I am loved, rich, successful" etc. This will change the energy around you and influence others as well. Be confident that you have all it takes to become what you want to be. We have so much untouched potential within us, that if we were to use only a small portion of it, we could create miracles. And miracles we need to create a better world and a better future for all of us. Go for your highest good!

One of the most important elements of life is to be grateful at all times. Thank God and your spirit guides for all they do for you daily. Thank them for what they have done for you all your life. Be grateful for all your life's experiences—good and bad! Be grateful for the food you eat, the smile on somebody's face, the summer breeze, and the flowers blooming in the garden. Gratitude is an attitude. Learn to expand your gratitude daily, for it will change your vibrations and attract more of what you want.

Think and actually visualize having all those things you have put on your list. After your meditative state, add a few minutes and visualize those things on your wish list as if you had them already. That is why you should use the affirmative "I am . . ." If you have asked for something for a loved one, do the same and visualize them having that which you had asked for. If it is health, see them as being perfectly healthy. If it is success, see them in the position you had in mind. If it is a personal relationship, see them with that person in blissful joy and happiness. And you have to keep repeating your affirmations. That is how you keep feeding the seeds for them to grow.

In all things remember that it is not all about you but about all of us. In all things, remain humble and grateful. And always give to others. Giving is not about money alone, it is about giving love and your time, your attention, compassion, a helping hand, and respect. Just a simple heartfelt smile can change a person's day! Use your positive power to make this world a better place, day-by-day, minute-by-minute. As John F. Kennedy said in his inaugural speech on January 20, 1961, "My fellow citizens of the world: ask not what America will do for you, but what together we can do for the freedom of man." We all must work on our ultimate destiny together—in peace, joy, and with love for all.

Ask not what God can do for you,
Ask what you can do for God.

Based on JOHN F. KENNEDY'S INAUGURAL SPEECH

Bibliography

Atlantis. *Rosicrucian Digest* 2006; 84(2).

Atkinson, William Walker, and Swami Panchadasi. *The Human Aura. Astral Colors and Thought Forms*. Charleston, SC: Create Space; 2015.

Byrne, Rhonda. *The Secret*. New York: Simon & Schuster, Inc.; 2006.

Canfield, Jack, Mark Victor Hanson, and Amy Newmark. *Chicken Soup for the Soul: 20th Anniversary Edition*. New York: Atria Books; 2006.

Canfield, Jack, and Janet Switzer. *The Success Principles*. New York: HarperCollins Publishers Inc.; 2006.

Canfield, Jack, and D.D. Watkins. *Jack Canfield's Key to Living the Law of Attraction*. Deerfield Beach, FL: Health Communications, Inc.; 2007.

Cayce, Edgar. *Earth Changes. Historical, Economical, Political, and Global*. Virginia Beach, VA: A.R.E. Press; 2013.

Cayce, Edgar. *A Search for God. Books I & II*. Virginia Beach, VA: Edgar Cayce Foundation; 2012.

Chopra, Deepak. *The Seven Spiritual Laws of Success: A Practical to the Fulfillment Your Dreams*. San Rafael, CA: Amber-Allen Publishing & New World Library; 1994.

Choquette, Sonia. *Ask Your Guides. Connecting to Your Divine Support System*. Carlsbad, CA: Hay House; 2010.

273

Choquette, Sonia. *The Psychic Pathway–A Workbook for Reawakening the Voice of Your Soul*. New York: Harmony Books; 1994.

Choquette, Sonia. *Your 3 Best Super Powers. Meditation, Imagination & Intuition*. Carlsbad, CA: Hay House; 2016.

davidji. *Secrets of Meditation. A Practical Guide to Inner Peace and Personal Transformation*. Carlsbad, CA: Hay House; 2012.

Elrod, Hal. *The Miracle Morning: The Not-So-Obvious Secret Guaranteed to Transform Your Life (Before 8 AM)*. Camarillo, CA: Hal Elrod; 2012.

Goldsmith, Joel S. *The Art of Meditation*. New York: Acropolis Books; 2012.

Greaves, Helen. *Testimony of Light: An Extraordinary Message of Life after Death*. New York: Tarcher Perigee; 2009.

Kornfield, Jack. *The Wise Heart: A Guide to the Universal Teachings of Buddhist Psychology*. New York: Bantam Books; 2008.

Maxwell, William. *The Secret: Law of Attraction Revealed—A Practical Guide to Manifesting Your Desires*. William Maxwell; 2014.

Milanovich, Dr. Norma J., and Dr. Shirley McCune. *The Light Shall Set You Free*. New Braunfels, TX: Athena Publishing; 1996.

Moore, Tom T. *Atlantis & Lemuria: The Lost Continents Revealed*. Flagstaff, AZ: Light Technology Publishing; 2015.

Murphy, Joseph. *The Power of the Subconscious Mind*. Radford, VA: Wilder Publications; 2007.

Pearl, Dr. Eric. *The Reconnection: Heal Others, Heal Yourself*. Carlsbad, CA: Hay House; 2001.

Peniel, Jon. *The Children of The Law of One & The Lost Teachings of Atlantis*. Walnut Creek, CA: Windsor Hill Publishing; 1997.

Ray, Amit, PhD. *Meditation: Insights and Inspirations*. Inner Light Publishers; 2015.

Reccia, Michael. *The Joseph Communications: The Fall. You Were There, It's Why You're Here*. Burnley, UK: Band of Light Media Limited; 2012.

Reccia, Michael. *The Joseph Communications: From Here to Infinity*. Burnley, UK: Band of Light Media Limited; 2015.

Reccia, Michael. *The Joseph Communications: Illumination. Change Yourself; Change the World*. Burnley, UK: Band of Light Media Limited; 2012.

Reccia, Michael. *The Joseph Communications: Revelation. Who You Are; Why You're Here*. Burnley, UK: Band of Light Media Limited; 2012.

Reccia, Michael. *The Joseph Communications: Trance Mission. Enlightening. Informing. A record of Joseph in Public*. Burnley, UK: Band of Light Media Limited; 2013.

Reccia, Michael. *The Joseph Communications: Your Life after Death*. Burnley, UK: Band of Light Media Limited; 2011.

Roman, Sanaya, and Duane Packer. *Creating Money. Attracting Abundance*. Bend, OR: LuminEssence Productions; 2008.

Roman, Sanaya. *Living with Joy: Keys to Personal Power & Spiritual Transformation*. Bend, OR: LuminEssence Productions; 2011.

Roman, Sanaya. *Personal Power through Awareness: A Guidebook for Sensitive People*. Bend, OR: LuminEssence Productions; 2011.

Roman, Sanaya. *Soul Love. Awakening Your Heart Centers.* Bend, OR: LuminEssence Productions; 2011.

Roman, Sanaya, and Duane Packer. *Spiritual Growth: How to Channel with Your Guide.* Bend, OR: LuminEssence Productions; 2011.

Schwimmer, George Ph.D. *How to Regress Yourself to Your Past Lives and Heal Yourself.* Santa Fe, NM: Phoenix Production; 2013.

Shakour, Cornelia. *The Missing Truth. Angelic Revelations Replace 16 centuries of Blind Faith.* Pequannock, NJ: Concorde Publishing; 1997.

Sharma, Robin. *The Monk Who Sold his Ferrari: A Remarkable Story about Living Your Dreams.* New York: HarperCollins E-Books; 2012.

Tazkuvel, Embrosewyn. *Auras. How to See, Feel and Know.* Lincolnshire, UK: Kaleidoscope Publications; 2012.

Tolle, Eckhart. *A New Earth. Awakening to Your Life's Purpose.* New York: Penguin Group; 2005.

Tolle, Eckhart. *The Power of Now: A Guide to Spiritual Enlightenment.* Novato, CA: Namaste Publishing & New World Library; 2004.

Virtue, Doreen Ph.D. *Divine Guidance. How to Have a Dialogue with God and Your Guardian Angels.* New York: St. Martin's Griffin; 1998.

Walsh, Neale Donald. *The Complete Conversations with God. An Uncommon Dialogue.* Newburyport, MA: Hampton Roads Publishing Company; 2005.

Weiss, Brian. *Messages from the Masters: Tapping into the Power of Love.* New York: Grand Central Publishing; 2001.

Weiss, Brian. *Many Lives, Many Masters. The True Story of a Prominent Psychiatrist, His Young Patient, and the Past-Life Therapy that Changed Both Their Lives.* New York: Simon Schuster; 1988.

Weiss, Brian. *Through Time into Healing: Discovering the Power of Regression Therapy to Erase Trauma and Transform Mind, Body, and Relationships.* New York: Simon Schuster; 1992.

About the Author

MARINA SHAKOUR HABER was born in Tehran, Iran, in 1955. She lived there until she was eight years old when her parents decided to relocate the family to Munich, Germany, where she spent her youth. Then she studied for two years in Paris at the American University. The Shakour family immigrated to Vancouver, Canada in 1978 where she continued her studies at the University of British Columbia, graduating with a Bachelor's degree in Fine Arts. When she was offered a position in Manhattan, she moved yet again, this time by herself. She married in 1987 and moved to New Jersey where she raised her two children. In 1999, she started her own nurse staffing agency and within two years, she was a leader in the industry. After 15 years, Marina decided to pursue other interests and moved to West Palm Beach, Florida.

Marina was born into a line of highly psychic women—from her mother, maternal grandmother to her great grandmother—where the paranormal was normal. It comes as no surprise that she was always interested in psychic phenomena and spirit teachings, beginning her lifelong journey to find answers to the underlying reasons causing the hardships and burdens endured by humankind.

For centuries people from around the world have come to this nation to pursue the American Dream. Yet, is it still viable or has it been snuffed out by a collective nightmare? Marina has been observing the increasing levels of divisiness, racism, bigotry, misogyny and isolationism, which led her to find her voice. Therefore, she wrote her book to help people rise up peacefully and transform the negativity of our society into one of hope and great new potential.

CPSIA information can be obtained
at www.ICGtesting.com
Printed in the USA
LVHW081348030720
659680LV00015B/1019